For those who see past punching, kicking & styles …

拳聖
喜屋武朝徳
その男と武芸

Kensei
Kyan Chōtoku
The Man & His Art

This work is a collection of various materials on Kyan Chōtoku, including previously published articles in English and Japanese, as well as a newly discovered, and previously unpublished work. It also includes personal accounts by respected and well-known experts, selected texts, periodicals, and vintage photographs.

IRKRS © 2023 All Rights Reserved

Author's note
Throughout this work, I write Japanese names according to local custom; that is, surnames first, followed by given names. It should be noted that some of my colleagues have followed Western custom in writing Japanese names; first name first, followed by surname. I wanted to have uniformity throughout this work and didn't think that changing this format would cause confusion; therefore, all Japanese names appearing in this work are rendered according to Japanese custom, that is, surname first, followed by given name. There's also another issue regarding the spelling of Japanese names in general; the English spelling of Japanese names is called *Romaji*, which can and does lead to variations; the most common is Jujutsu, which is rendered as "*Jiu-jitsu.*" Although this is incorrect, it is, nonetheless, widely accepted, even within the *Jujutsu* community. In the case of Kyan's last name, it should be noted that there are two perfectly acceptable ways to render his family name; *Kyan* and *Kiyan*. Again, for the sake of simplicity, I will use the more commonly used version, *Kyan*. Throughout this work, wherever the spelling "Kiyan" is used, I have changed it to "*Kyan*" without citing the change.

Photographic credits
All photographs and images contained within this work are either from my personal collection, public domain content and/or used with permission of the copyright holder. No photos may be reproduced, imprinted, or electronic form without the written permission of the author. If there are any photos, illustrations, and/or diagrams, which appear in this work, that have not been properly cited, I would ask that the concern party reach out to me, privately, with proof of ownership, and I will correct the oversight.

Disclaimer
The author/translator[s] of this work will not be responsible, in any manner whatsoever, for any injury that may result from practicing the techniques and/or instructions given herein. Since physical activities described may be too strenuous in nature for some readers to engage in safely, it is essential that a physician be consulted prior to training.

Contents

Acknowledgments by Patrick McCarthy — 9
Preface by Konno Bin — 11
Exordium by Irei Hiroshi — 13
Congratulations by Hokama Tetsuhiro — 15
Preamble by Joe Swift — 17
Prologue by Patrick McCarthy — 21
A Moment with a Student of Kyan Chōtoku by Patrick McCarthy — 26

Chapter 1
Unveiling the Enigma: Exploring the Life of Kyan Chōtoku
Kyan Chōtoku by Nagamine Shōshin — 30
Busaganashi by Tokuda Anshu — 40
Deeds of Valour by Shimabukuro Eizō — 43
Kyan Folktales ~ Youtube Translation by Patrick McCarthy — 46
Okinawan Karate … A Man Called Chanmie by Irei Hiroshi — 50
Masters of Shōrin Ryu ~ Kyan Chōtoku by Graham Noble — 95
Chanmī ~ Kyan Chōtoku by Graham Noble — 105
Sunabe Shozen by Charles Goodin — 136

Chapter 2
Through the Lens of Time: Vintage Treasures — 175

Chapter 3
In the Words of Kyan Chōtoku: Insights and Teachings
Karate Training & Fighting by Kyan Chōtoku [1929] — 189
Okinawa Kenpō Karate-dō Kihon Zukai Kumite by Kyan Chōtoku [1932] — 195
1936 Round Table Discussion [1936] — 217
Memories of Karate by Kyan Chōtoku [1942] — 234

Chapter 4
Beyond Boundaries
Challenging the Legacy of Kyan Chotoku — 243

Part 1
Rising from The Ashes by Charles Joseph Swift — 244

The Fall of a Kingdom 246
The Decline of the Class System 249
The Practice of *Yaadui* 252

Part 2
A Scandal! 255
The Downfall of a Privileged Man 258
The Downfall of a Privileged Man 2 259
The Prostitution Broker 260
The Prefectural Governor Saves the Prostitutes 261
The Evil Actions of Kyan & the Kagoshima Newspaper 262

Part 3
Analysis 264
About the *Ryūkyū Shimpo* 265
Indentured Prostitution during the Meiji Era 266
Fake News! So Sad! Unbelievable! 268

Appendix
Haiban nu Bushi [Samuree] 270
The Background 271
The Song 272

Chapter 5
Unraveling the Legacy
Delving Deeper into the World of Kyan Chotoku 275

Kyan's 1932 Book Lecture by Sonohara Ken 276

Chapter 6
Tradition Continues
Lighting the Pathway for Future Generations 293
Zen Influence in Karate by Patrick McCarthy 294
The Torchbearer's Code by Patrick McCarthy 297
Postscript by Scot Mertz 302
Final Word by Patrick McCarthy 303
Pictorial Lineage 308
Lineage Chart 309
Informal Chronology 310
Source Images 312
Selected Bibliography 314
Recommended Reading 319
Oral Tradition [of] Kyan Chōtoku [*Chanmi*] 322

Acknowledgements

I am deeply grateful to several authorities who have graciously contributed to the work before you and would like to acknowledge them: First and foremost, is researcher, writer, translator, teacher, and dear friend, *Joe Swift* Shihan [Tōkyō, Japan]. In addition to so much else, it was through this gentleman that I first learned of Kyan's unpublished work. Next is, researcher, historian, master instructor and museum curator, *Hokama Tetsuhiro* Hanshi, and *Takeishi Kazumi*, owner of the *Youju Shōrin* bookstore in Ginowan [both from Okinawa, Japan]. It was from these two gentlemen that I first obtained copies of Kyan's unpublished work, along with just so much more. Historian, author, master teacher and 2nd generation Kyan lineage inheritor, *Shimabukuro Zenpo* Hanshi [Okinawa, Japan]. Zenpo Sensei's father was a direct student of Kyan Chōtoku and aside from being a walking encyclopedia of historical information, and opening many doors of opportunity for me here in Okinawa, I simply cannot say how much this remarkable gentleman helped me. Kyan Chōtoku specialist research historian [and author of, "*A Man Called Chanmīe*"], *Irei Hiroshi* [Okinawa, Japan], who unfortunately passed away during the research phase of this work, was of enormous assistance. Researcher, well-known author ["*Chanmīe-gwā*"] & Shōrin Ryu karate teacher, *Konno "Bin" Satoshi* [Tōkyō, Japan]. Researcher, Karate and Kobudo master instructor and *Tokushin* director, *Tokumura Kensho* Hanshi [Okinawa, Japan]. Researcher, historian, writer and friend, *Graham Noble* [UK]. Researcher, writer and teacher, *Charles Goodin* [USA].

Special thanks to *Dan Smith*, *Scot Mertz*, *James Pankiewicz*, *Miguel Da Luz*, *Thomas Feldmann*, *David Evseeff*, *Andy Sloane*, *James Hatch* and *Neal Simpson* for their support in various ways. I am especially grateful to American expatriate and fellow Karate-ka, *Brian Arthur*. In addition to being a permanent resident of Japan, he is also a Seibukan Tōkyō branch leader and equally passionate about karate, its history, and the life of Kyan Chōtoku. I seriously doubt that I could have presented the 1932 work in its entirety without his substantial contribution to the English translation.

Although many sources generously supported this project, there were a few who were not as forthcoming, possibly due to conservative thinking, protectionism based on style, cultural differences, misunderstanding, or politics. A potentially important source, who seemed eager to assist me in the beginning, and happily accepted a full-color copy of Kyan's unpublished 1932 work from me during my visit to his office in Tomigusuku, abruptly changed his demeanor before the project's completion. He not only declined to endorse my work but also requested anonymity and cautioned others to steer clear of me, labeling me as, "*dangerous*." Another local Kyan style-based instructor, indirectly associated with this unidentified source, also declined to meet with me, citing concerns about authenticity, format and potential misrepresentation in my work. Although I can only speculate as to how he may have been negatively influenced, I was at a loss to understand why he wouldn't jump at the opportunity to ensure its format, authenticity and potential for misrepresentation was completely accurate.

I would be remiss if I did not acknowledge other sources and authorities, from whom I obtained related information. My original research into the *Bubishi* and pioneers of the art, such as *Matsumura Sokon, Itosu Ankoh, Motobu Choki*, and *Miyagi Chojun*, among others, have been most helpful; In fact, it could very well provide the basis for an entire book on its own. While I did not originally interview *Uehara Seikichi, Nagamine Shōshin, Nakazato Joen, Miyahira Katsuya, Nakamoto Masahiro*, and *Kinjo Hiroshi* for this particular project, their previous contributions to my earlier work have, nevertheless, proved to be instrumental in the completion and publication of this new project. In fact, Nagamine and Nakazato themselves were actually personal students of Kyan and graciously conveyed much about the master and about studying with him during their youth.

As is often the case, countless fragments of information have been gathered from diverse sources, and I fear I have not adequately acknowledged them all. Nevertheless, it is my genuine hope that the amalgamation of these contributions resonates favorably with all who have played a part in shaping this project.

Preface
by Konno [Bin] Satoshi

Although Kyan Sensei's kata may appear rather simple, I believe they are highly functional with no superfluous movement. Deceptively simple, yet full of meaning; No matter how many years you practice them, there's always something new to discover.

My name is Konno Satoshi and, as a student of Shōrin-ryu Karate, I am very pleased that my research, on the founder of this style, Kyan Chōtoku [喜屋武朝徳,1870-1945], has been published. That said, I am also equally excited about [Canadian Karate researcher] Patrick McCarthy [a permanent resident of Okinawa], is now bringing together this [new and independent] study on the renown Okinawan pioneer of Karate, Kyan Chōtoku.

Born during the dawn of the Meiji Restoration, Kyan Chōtoku grew up during a time of great social transition in Japanese history; One which had a dramatic impact upon the Ryūkyū Kingdom. Witnessing diplomatic maneuvering, political transformation and cultural assimilation, a forceful annexation of his homeland by mainland Japan, amidst fierce local resistance from the Ryūkyūan authorities, brought to an end centuries of tributary relations with China, and social rediscovery. One should not find it surprising to learn that Kyan Chōtoku, aka *Chanmī* lived his life amidst unrelenting vicissitudes.

Kyan Chōtoku was from a family of wealth and position; his father, Kyan Chōfu [喜屋武 朝扶, 1839-1910], not only worked in the service of the royal family, he was actually an official part of the 1872 Ryūkyūan embassy to Tōkyō [sent to offer congratulations on behalf of the Kingdom for the success of the Meiji Restoration]. Later, in 1881, he also served as steward to Shō Tai, when exiled to Tōkyō. As such, the entire Kyan family were persecuted by the old guard. Of course, Chōtoku had accompanied him to Tōkyō where, as impressionable young man, one can only imagine the untold impact such an experience had upon him.

During my recent visit to his home, I was very excited to see that McCarthy Sensei possessed an actual copy of Kyan's [unpublished 1932], "Okinawa Kenpo Karate-do, Basic Kumite Illustrated 「沖縄拳法唐手道基本組手」." It's a remarkable book that has not been published for nearly a century and it was a dream come true to receive a copy of it from Patrick san. The photos and instruction in this book are not just a reference but a treasure for anyone who pursues Kyan Sensei's karate. It was also worthwhile conversation, discussing the social mindset, political agendas and diplomatic maneuvering, of that era, in which a handful of late 19th century newspaper articles, published by the Ryūkyū Shimpo, targeted Kyan Chōtoku with the purpose of defaming him.

In addition to the rare book, photos, and extensive research McCarthy has amassed, he also has many other "treasures" in his possession; A practice uniform worn by Kyan Sensei, the personal six-foot bo which belonged to the master, valuable calligraphy by his father [Chofu], and the personal testimony, which comes directly from his own disciples, such as Nakazato Joen, Shimabukuro Zenryō, Nagamine Shōshin and others; collectively, making this compilation uniquely invaluable.

McCarthy Sensei is not only a researcher, he is also an avid karate practitioner, too. As such, there are certain aspects of karate that only a practitioner can understand. The same goes for such things about the pioneers of this art, that only a practitioner can grasp, and these things are extremely important [to know/convey]. What was Kyan Sensei's motivation for training in karate? What were his thoughts as he developed his kata and passed them on? I believe that only those who have actually practiced karate can understand such things.

How will Karate researcher, practitioner and writer, Patrick McCarthy, use his experience and intellect to decipher and present the vast amount of material he has collected? I for one, am really looking forward to it.

Exordium
by Irei Hiroshi

As a local resident of Kadena, I have spent considerable time researching, studying and writing about the life of Kyan Chōtoku. Therefore, I believe I am qualified to speak, with some degree of accuracy, about this former local resident and historically important pioneer of Okinawan Karate.

While I have not known Patrick McCarthy very long, I've enjoyed the pleasure of having him as a guest here at my home, on a couple of occasions in 2021. He was introduced to me through my good friend, Shimabukuro Zenpo, head master of the Seibukan, who vouched for his character, dedication and credibility. After meeting him on the first occasion, it became immediately obvious just how passionate he was, and not just about Kyan Chōtoku, his life and fighting art, but also about Okinawan people, our culture, customs and language, too. I enjoyed spending many hours with him discussing just such topics and felt there was something special about him. So, I was even more pleased to learn that, because of this passion in embracing our unique, and seemingly vanishing, lifestyle, his journey has compelled him to immigrate here and live among us, as an Okinawan.

I was also deeply impressed that he's gathered so much support for this compilation, including that of the revered Japanese novelist, Konno Bin; himself also authoring a bestselling book on, Chanmī. Believing that Patrick san's enthusiasm, might also help rekindle interest in reviving a previous Chanmī related project [*I was involved with before being diagnosed with stage #4 cancer*], I gave our meeting serious consideration. In the time that elapsed between our first and second meetings, I was able to arrange a special gathering of influential people. Inviting members of the Motonaga family, and senior Kadena politician, Nishida Kenjiro, to join Zenpo Sensei, Patrick san and I, we met here at my residence again in November 2021. With Nishida san serving as Secretary General for the Okinawa Prefectural LDP, and Emeritus

Professor at Okinawa National Chengchi University, I sincerely hope his support will lend extra exposure to the project.

I am convinced, the contents of this new book, *"Kensei, Kyan Chōtoku, The Man & His Art,"* will have far-reaching value. I'd like to believe that this work might also help inspire a revival of interest in rebuilding *Chanmī's* original house on the Hija River, as a historically important landsite, commemorating the legacy of this venerable pioneer. To this end, I enthusiastically lend my name, research and support to McCarthy Sensei. I hope this new work of his will be welcomed by both local Okinawan supporters and Karate enthusiasts around the world. I hereby highly recommend this book.

Congratulations

by Hokama Tetsuhiro

My congratulations to Patrick McCarthy Sensei on the publication of this work about *Kensei* [拳聖] Kyan Chōtoku [喜屋武朝徳, 1870-1945] aka Chanmī [チャン ミー]. McCarthy sensei is a well known researcher of Ryūkyū Karate and Kobudo history and its cultural heritage. As a world ambassador, I applaud his efforts at helping to study, preserve and promote the arts of Karate and Kobudo throughout the world.

His independent studies over the past forty years have brought him into contact with many of the most senior authorities of our fighting arts. In this time he's also visited all the most historically significant sites here in Okinawa. His many publications are a testament to his dedication and extensive fieldwork. His research and translation of the Bubishi [武備志], Okinawa's ancient book of knowledge, is amongst his best known work.

Together, we've travelled to various places during his visits here from the mainland, where he used to reside. I remember on one occasion we went over to the *Furuferin Dokutsu* [フルフェーリン洞窟] in *Tomari* [泊村], followed by *Shinyashiki Park* [新屋敷公園] and then to visit the curator at the *Seigenji* [聖現寺] while researching *Matsumora Kōsaku* [松茂良 興作, 1829-1898]. On the same day, we also visited the family of *Yabu Kentsū* [屋部 憲通, 1866-1937] in Shuri, the former residence of *Matsumura Sōkon* [松村 宗棍, 1809-1899], and the original *Ochayagoten* [御茶屋御殿] site at *Shuri's Sakiyama-cho* [首里崎山町], all in one day! That was about forty years ago although, it seems like only yesterday.

Wonderfully gifted, with a deep respect for tradition, McCarthy Sensei is charismatic, with an extraordinary memory; In fact, he's like a walking encyclopedia. For example, when discussing historical events, early documents and or the contributions of various pioneers, he's able to instantly cite exact dates and places, quote unique literary passages and describe historical events with remarkable accuracy. I've never seen anything like it. Most importantly, he values loyalty above all else, and is trusted and respected as a man of integrity.

As the director of the *International Ryūkyū Karate Research Society* [琉球唐手国際研究会], he's travelled all over the world teaching seminars and lecturing for many notable groups and instructors. I often receive Karate books from various authors around the world and frequently find forewords by Patrick McCarthy in many of them. Highly regarded for his pioneering studies, and Kata-application practices [型分解術], in the Western World, his work is frequently referenced by many other serious researchers and authors and forewords by him abound many other important works.

Including never before seen research, this new compilation on Kyan Chōtoku is just another example of McCarthy Sensei's ability to deliver something totally unique. I am confident you will find it highly interesting and most informative. As such, I am pleased to lend my name in support of this work.

Preamble

by Joe Swift
Standing Director
All-Japan Ryūkyū Kobudo Federation
Tōkyō, Japan

It is my distinct pleasure and honor to write this brief foreword for *"Kensei, Kyan Chōtoku: The Man and his Art,"* by long-time mentor and friend, Patrick McCarthy Sensei. I can think of no one better to present the material contained within these pages.

My own Karate journey began at the age of 12 in an Okinawan style known as Isshin-ryu. This system was founded by a man by the name of Shimabuku Tatsuo, who himself was a direct student of Kyan Chōtoku, Motobu Choki, Miyagi Chojun and Taira Shinken. The technical content of Shimabuku's system shows the greatest number of Kata to have come from Kyan. Hence, I have a bit of a personal lineage connection to Kyan which makes this opportunity even more poignant.

When I first began learning Karate there was little reliable information in English on Kyan, and I would later come to learn, in Japanese either. There were a few fantastical stories of martial heroism in a smattering of books, but it probably wasn't until McCarthy Sensei's excellent English translation of Nagamine Shōshin's *Tales of Okinawa's Great Masters* that some reliable detailed information came about.

In Nagamine Sensei's book, details of Kyan's early life, training and stories of his martial prowess came to light. Of particular interest is his rendition of a now-famous story about a bout between Kyan and a Japanese Judo expert in Taiwan. More details about this legendary fight will be shared in the main part of this book, and which should substantially delineate the differences between the old-school Ryūkyū Karate ideals of interpersonal violence as against the modern fair-competition-based mindset that befell the sport of Judo even by the 1920s.

Over the next two decades, a deluge of primary and reliable secondary source based information has become available, such as *Shōrin Ryu Seibukan (Kyan's Karate); Okinawan Karate, a Man Called Chanmīe;* the historical novel *Chanmī;* early newspaper articles by and about Kyan; and the icing on the cake, the rediscovery of a 1932 manuscript on Karate by Kyan entitled *Okinawa Kenpo Karate-do Kihon Zukai Kumite*, the full translation of which is available in this presentation.

From these newer publications we can come to paint a more comprehensive picture of the man and his legacy. For example, we know that his father, Kyan Chōfu, was such a trusted member of the last Ryūkyūan King, Sho Tai's, retinue that he was part of the delegation that was sent to Japan to congratulate the new Emperor Meiji on his ascension to the Japanese imperial throne; and that Chōfu was also one of the members of the entourage of Sho Tai when he was "invited" to come live in Tōkyō after the abolishment of the Ryūkyū Kingdom.

Whilst there, Chōtoku studied for a while at the Nishogakusha, one of the premier institutes of higher learning in Meiii Era Japan, that still exists under the name Nishogakusha University. Many luminaries from modern Japanese history were alumni of this school, such as author Natsume Soseki, prime minister Inukai Tsuyoshi, Kodokan Judo founder Kanō Jigorō and women's rights activist Hiratsuka Raicho. It is obvious that Chōtoku was in good company, likely due to his royal heritage in a day and age where discrimination against Okinawans in mainland Japan was open and brutal.

Next, I would like to touch upon the exciting discovery of Kyan's text on Karate fighting techniques. I was first alerted to its existence back in March 2017 by my friend and colleague, Mr. Aihara Shinya, the chief editor of the *Shin Karate-do* magazine. During a trip to Okinawa, he received a photocopy from Mr. Takeishi Kazumi, the owner of the Yoju Shōrin used bookstore in Ginowan, who was in talks to reprint the book in its entirety. The Yoju Shōrin is the entity who undertook the republication of many of the early books on Karate, including Funakoshi, Mabuni, Miki and Mutsu's works. Mr. Aihara also sent a couple of photos of his new treasure.

A few months later, Mr. Aihara held an exhibition of part of his extensive collection of martial arts related books in Tōkyō. I called him up and made an appointment to meet with him at the venue and asked to see the Kyan book. He obliged, and I was not disappointed. In the meantime I also contacted Mr. Takeishi about the publication of the Japanese reprint, and was told that, *"there were issues with the family of the man who funded the book to get the rights to reprint and that the project was suffering from major delays."*

In the meantime I also shared this discovery with McCarthy Sensei, who was in the process of planning his relocation from Los Angeles to Japan, with an eye on moving to Okinawa with his wife. Jump forward to December, 2020, McCarthy Sensei made his final move to Japan. Staying in Tōkyō prior to arriving at his final destination of Okinawa, we had the opportunity to meet up a few times and discuss many issues, one of which was the Kyan book.

Once in Okinawa and settled down, McCarthy Sensei brought his extensive list of local and overseas contacts to bear on the issue. Before long he was meeting and interviewing many Okinawans with direct Karate or familial lineages to Kyan Chōtoku. Meeting with Mr. Takeishi to discuss an English presentation of the book, he obtained a high-resolution color copy of the book itself to work from. Being a proverbial "badass" in the realm of quality Karate research, the results of his efforts rest comfortably in the book, which you now hold in your hands.

Kyan's book, probably inspired by that of his cousin Motobu Choki, focusses mainly on the fighting applications of the art. This sets it apart from the books of Funakoshi Gichin, which focused mostly on the solo performance of the various Kata of Karate. It consists of introductory sections on such issues as the goal of Karate, training maxims and precepts and other preparatory knowledge.

However, the meat of the text is photographic and textual explanations of some rudimentary Kata fighting applications. This section shows not only the defensive maneuvers and counter strike and kicks, but also delves into the throwing and grappling realm of Karate as well. Although short and with only a few photos, this book should be more than enough for the discerning Karate practitioner to use as inspiration to delve further into their own Kata practice.

In addition to this Kumite text, there is also a persistent rumor of a Kata edition as well, but as of this writing, it has not been found. There is one photograph in the public realm that seems to hint at being from a similar publication as the 1932 Kumite booklet, but this is only speculation on my part.

With apologies for the length, and somewhat rambling nature, of this foreword, I invite the readers to step into a bygone era, and learn directly from the lessons the pioneers of traditional Karate. In doin so, you are sure to enhance not only your appreciation for the technical tactics and strategies found within the Kata, but also enrich your daily life through the philosophy underlying this wonderful cultural heritage.

Prologue
by Patrick McCarthy

The work, which lies before you, "*Kyan Chōtoku, The Man & His Art*," provides a comprehensive account of the life and contributions of Kyan Chōtoku, one of the early innovators of Karate in Okinawa. Despite his undeniable skill and impact on the art, Kyan's legacy has been overshadowed by that of his contemporaries. However, as documented in "*Haihan toji no jinbutsu*" (1915), Kyan was not only a skilled practitioner of empty hand karate, but also a man of great physical strength and skill in other martial arts. Even during his time in Tōkyō, he continued to refine his martial skills, including karate and *kenjutsu*, by practicing in his garden during the harsh winters.

The book features rare photographs, articles, commentary from Kyan's personal students, and excerpts from his own writings, along with the recently discovered 1932 unpublished work, providing readers with a deeper understanding of Kyan's life, art, and the historical context in which he lived and worked. Despite the challenges faced during the translation project, I feel the final result accurately captures Kyan's words and ideas.

Motobu Choki

Having spent considerable time learning, practicing, researching, studying, and translating the work of Motobu Choki [1870-1944], as detailed in my 2002 publication "*Karate My Art*" (ISBN 9781723105609), I was captivated by the remarkable parallels that emerged when exploring the mindset and practices of Kyan Chōtoku [1870-1945], and the nature of his 2-person drills contained in his recently discovered 1932 publication.

It is noteworthy that these two Okinawan Karate pioneer legends shared more than just the same dates of birth [and approximately time of death], the 3rd born sons from aristocratic families and childhood friends; they were actually blood relatives from Shuri and enjoyed the privilege of studying the fighting arts under many of the same sources, albeit at different times. Through an examination of their lifestyles, reputations, the writings they left behind, and the ability to contrast their 2-person practices, it becomes evident that their karate styles were incredibly alike, with the primary distinction lying in their physical sizes. This divergence in stature likely influenced their respective areas of specialization within the martial arts framework. By unraveling the intertwined narratives of Motobu Choki and Kyan Chōtoku, we gain insight into the rich heritage they shared and the lasting impact they left on the world of Okinawan Karate.

It's important to note that these conclusions are based entirely upon my observations. Further research and analysis by others in this area could provide additional insights and a more comprehensive understanding of the relationship between the two pioneers.

In my endeavor to capture the essence of the man and his art, I have carefully curated a collection of photographs, information, and articles from sources widely recognized for their credibility and reliability. These meticulously selected pieces provide a multifaceted perspective, offering a comprehensive portrayal that I believe best illustrates his remarkable talent and enduring legacy.

Kyan's legacy has been clouded by a complicated history, politics, and propaganda. In this work, I invited contributors to share insights on different aspects of Kyan's life while reflecting on his legacy myself. By looking beyond labels and styles, I believe that Kyan's teachings have much to offer modern learners of Karate, and we can rediscover the true essence of Karate as it was originally intended.

In the vibrant tapestry of Kyan Chōtoku's life, the cultural and political climate of his era cast a shadow of radical militarism and escalating nationalism. As we delve into the pages of history, a question arises: Was Kyan himself influenced by these forces? Did they shape his beliefs and behaviors, or did he remain steadfast in his dedication to the art of karate and its inherent values?

The backdrop against which Kyan Chōtoku lived and practiced his art was one of significant political change and nationalistic fervor. Imperial Japan was experiencing the growing pains of its radical military and nationalist aspirations. As the nation sought to assert its dominance and establish a unified Japanese identity, Okinawa, with its unique cultural heritage, found itself at a crossroads.

But amidst this charged atmosphere, it is worth exploring whether Kyan, a practitioner of karate renowned for its emphasis on peace and self-defense, was swayed by the prevailing militaristic sentiments of the time. Did he find himself pulled towards the path of conformity, or did he steadfastly hold onto the core principles that defined his art? Or, are we misunderstanding the origins and nature of the art as it was meant to be?

As we trace the footsteps of Kyan Chōtoku, we encounter intriguing glimpses into his character and choices. While the political and nationalistic forces of the era may have cast their long shadows, Kyan's actions and demeanor suggest a man who remained true to the spirit of karate, transcending the superficial trappings of the time.

Through meticulous research and analysis, we aim to unravel the intricate relationship between Kyan Chōtoku and the political ambience that enveloped his world. We will scrutinize the historical records, anecdotes, and testimonies that offer insights into his beliefs, interactions, and personal convictions. By examining his choices within the broader context of the era, we strive to determine whether he resisted the tide of militarism or whether he, too, was influenced by the prevailing currents.

Our exploration serves not only to shed light on Kyan's character but also to deepen our understanding of the complex interplay between personal conviction and societal pressures. We invite you, the reader, to accompany us on this journey of discovery and contemplation, as we seek to discern the true essence of Kyan Chōtoku and the impact of that era on his path.

Within these pages, we will navigate the historical landscape with a keen eye, constantly pondering the question: Did the political and nationalistic atmosphere adversely affect Kyan Chōtoku, or did he carve his own path, resolute in his dedication to the art of karate and its principles of harmony and self-improvement?

As we embark on this exploration, let us remain open to the complexities and contradictions that may arise, for history often reveals multifaceted truths. Together, let us delve into the life of Kyan Chōtoku, a man shaped by his era yet standing as a testament to the enduring spirit of karate.

Skeletons in the Closet!
Thought lost, in the sands of time, a glimpse into Kyan's past was brought to light in a 2018 publication entitled *'The Downfall of a Ryūkyū Samurai.'* Describing some less than admirable behavior associated with Kyan Chōtoku, I thought it important to note that the entire story lacked factual evidence to substantiate any claims of wrongdoing! While it is acknowledged that Kyan was most certainly involved in the matter, the specific nature of his involvement was never clearly defined. Considering his reputation and standing, it is most likely that someone of his caliber and skills was contracted by a third party to safely escort the said passengers from Okinawa to Kobe, presumably to begin their employment as indentured workers. Despite the existence of five newspaper articles from 1898 that implicate Kyan, they fail miserably to provide substantial proof to support the allegations. However, it is crucial to approach this topic with genuine respect and empathy, acknowledging the complexity of the situation and the absence of definitive evidence.

The book also delves into how rumours and hearsay about Kyan have been presented as fact over the years. Unfortunately, good or bad reputations are often based on hearsay evidence rather than documented proof, further emphasizing the challenge of separating fact from fiction in Kyan's story. I acknowledge that much of the information presented may not be new to devoted Kyan enthusiasts, with the exception of a 1932 discovery that will be discussed in more detail later.

Ultimately, the legacy of Kyan Chōtoku is a complex and multifaceted one. He was a skilled martial artist, an innovator, and a pioneer in the development of Okinawan Karate. At the same time, he was also a man with flaws and contradictions, and his legacy has been overshadowed by rumors and hearsay. By exploring Kyan's life and legacy in a more nuanced and comprehensive way, we can gain a deeper understanding of his contributions to the art of Okinawan Karate and the historical context in which he lived and worked.

The Motonaga House
Introducing Kyan Chōtoku makes it necessary to also mention his family lineage, as it holds historical importance, influence and prestige. Associated with Shuri nobles, the Motonaga House was a part of the Princely Shō clan and an integral part of Chōtoku's story. Its founder, Motonaga Chōgi [1784–1829], was his ancestor and the fifth son of the Motobu Udun family. Motonaga Chōgi's marriage to Manabi, from the Kyan House, represents the link to this history. Notably, Chōtoku's father, Chōfu, was initially from the Motonaga House but inherited the Kyan House due to its lack of male heirs. This intriguing historical twist is how Chōfu became adopted into the Kyan House and not only reveals Chōtoku's ancestral connection to the Motonaga House, but also that Chōtoku's true family name was, Motonaga. This narrative highlights the intricate familial connections that shaped Kyan Chōtoku's identity and sets the stage for a deeper exploration of his contributions to the world of karate.

Through this book, I hope to shed light on Kyan Chōtoku's life, art, and legacy, and encourage readers to question preconceived notions and myths surrounding his story. By doing so, we can better appreciate his place in martial arts history and the lasting impact he has had on the development of Okinawan Karate.

A Moment with a Student of Kyan Chōtoku
by Patrick McCarthy

My first lesson with Nagamine Sensei during the summer of 1985

I first met Nagamine Shōshin [1907-1997], in the summer of 1985 during my inaugural visit to Okinawa; Not long thereafter, I immigrated to Japan, married and settled down in Kanagawa Prefecture. Over the next decade, I traveled to Okinawa frequently as an independent researcher and enjoyed cross-training opportunities with many of the most senior authorities of Karate, including Nagamine Sensei at his Kodokan dojo in Naha's Kumoji district. To learn from a master, who had himself been taught by such legendary figures as Motobu Chōki, Shimabuku Taro, Aragaki Ankichi and Kyan Chōtoku, etc., was a privilege words can hardly describe.

I deeply cherished the amicable bond I shared with the master and his son, Takayoshi Sensei. I treasured our friendly relationship, holding them in the utmost respect and recognizing their unparalleled expertise and wisdom. I was always mindful of my position and role within our interactions. As such, it came as quite a surprise, and an honour, when I was asked to undertake the translation of such important research, as his 1986 book, "*Tales of Okinawa's Great Masters*" [aka "*Shijitsu to Kuden ni yoru Okinawa Karate Kakutō Meijin-den*" ~ 史実と口伝による沖縄空手・角力名人伝].

The irony was that the very first book on the history of karate I ever bought in my youth was, Professor Shinzato Katsuhiko's wonderful English translation of Nagamine Sensei's 1976 publication; "*The Essence of Okinawan Karate-do.*" Having made quite an impression upon me at the time, I never thought that I would one day befriend such a man, much less be petitioned to translate his research, and asked to also write a foreword for its publication. As I have said many times since then, "*it just proves that anything is possible.*"

During my lengthy analysis and English translation of the "*Bubishi*," Nagamine Sensei was also very helpful and wrote a testimonial-like foreword for it. During the time I was conducting my research into the Bubishi, and translating his book, we spent considerable time discussing the history to the art, his early training and the instructors under whom he'd studied. As I had previously written, in the English translation of his book, "*It's no secret that his guidance had a profound impact upon the way I came to embrace karate, assess its evolution, value to society, and my personal understanding of its application.*"

I believe that Nagamine Shōshin was a rare individual who, in an effort to keep his collective knowledge a living experience for the community he served, successfully reinterpreted the common principles he'd gained from his mentors, and generated a contemporary vehicle through which to impart them; As such, his art, Matsubayashi Shōrin Ryu became a living testament to his impeccable background, innovative approach and inspirational leadership. Beyond the introduction to Kyan Chōtoku's art, I'd gained through the guidance of Richard Kim during the 1970s, the informal training encounters I enjoyed with Nakazato Joen and Shimabuku Eizo in the mid-1980s, much of what I came to know about this pioneer comes to me by way of Nagamine Shōshin.

The first Kyan Chōtoku article to be featured is my personal Japanese-to-English translations found in Nagamine Sensei's [*now out of print*] book, "*Tales of Okinawa's Great Masters.*"

Chapter 1
Unveiling the Enigma
Exploring the Life of Kyan Chōtoku

"If you train extensively in karate, but never have to use it, you have achieved the essence of its practice."
~ Kyan Chōtoku

Kyan Chōtoku
by Nagamine Shōshin

The Fighting Spirit of the Small Framed, Self-Trained, Kyan Chōtoku Sensei
The Lesson of a Strict Father

"Keep your Vow of Modesty"
Kyan Chōtoku was born in December of 1870 in Shuri's Gibo village. The son of a very strict father named Chōfu, their family were descendants of *Shō En* [正圓, 1415–1476] and related to *Shō Sei* [尚清, 1497–1555], the 4th king of old Ryūkyū Kingdom. Employed by *Shō Tai* [長泰, 1843-1901], the last king of the Ryūkyū kingdom, Chōfu was responsible for the keeping of the royal "hanko" (official seal of the king) and was schooled in the study of ancient Japanese & Chinese culture and thought. Moreover, Chōfu was also regarded as a scholar warrior, a man who was well trained in the fighting traditions and equally recognized as an intellect.

Leaving Okinawa for nearly four years, Chōtoku resided in Tōkyō with his father between the ages of 12 to 16 where he studied Kangaku (the study of Chinese Culture and Thought) at the Nishogakusha. Being born a descendant of royalty meant that Chōtoku, the son of a nobleman, was destined to walk in the footsteps of his ancestors. Compared to when his father was young, Chōtoku was far smaller and weaker too, in both size and strength. Being so small, Chōtoku would certainly need such skills in his future, hence, his years in Tōkyō were also spent diligently pursuing karate and grappling training in both the heat of summer and cold of winter.

Back around 1932 I used to work at the Kadena police station. The head of that station in those days was a man named *Hiyagon Ankoh*. I remember Mr. Hiyagon once telling me a story about when Chōtoku and his father lived in Tōkyō. The father of Hiyagon Ankoh, like Chōtoku's father, had also once been employed by the Sho family and were former Pēchin. If and when it got cold in Tōkyō, Hiyagon Ankoh and his brothers often snuggled together under the kotatsu (a table covered by a blanket to contain the heat source from underneath) to keep warm. During the times they did this, Hiyagon's father would scold them by saying "*You are the son's of a Pēchin, don't be such cowards! Did you know that Chōtoku and his father always train outside on such miserable days?*"

After completing his assignment in Tōkyō, the Kyans' returned to Okinawa and lived between Shuri and Mawashi in Naha's Takaraguchi district [*the old 4-chome section of Gibo*]. One day not long after their return Chōtoku stood in front of the altar in their living room listening to his father. "*You're small but have a competitive spirit Chōtoku*," said his father. "*Even though you do not have the body of a martial artist, you can still develop effective technique depending entirely upon how diligently you train yourself*," he continued to say. You can be second to none, his father told him, "*if you develop the technique suitable for a person of your body size, and, master the application of the kata.*"

There was a famous 17th century general named *Kabayama Hisataka* who once served the Shimazu warriors in Satsuma. Gaining the nickname "*Oni-Shogun*" (devil general) at the battle of Keicho, like Chōtoku so too was he quite small only about 5-shaku (150 cm). However, in spite of his tiny size he became regarded as a bold hero. In fact, so fierce was Kabayama that people of that era often said that trying to defeat him was like trying to swallow a needle.

Often when a person first becomes strong through Karate training, they can become arrogant and develop into a show off. It is very important for one to transcend this affliction. If one is to truly understand the fighting traditions and become a Bujin (person dedicated to "Bu") they must first embrace *Matsumura's 7 Virtues of BU*: 1. Forbids willful violence, 2. Governs the warrior, 3. Fortifies people, 4. Fosters virtue, 5. Appeases the community, 6. Brings about a general harmony and 7. Prosperity.

In the ancient words of his predecessors, handed down in a poem, Chōtoku's father willed him the following verse and asked him to never forget to the value of its contents.

Poem
Chichishi no ishiji toimamuteuriba. Noyodesukunayuga kamin shimun

Interpretation:
Accomplishment is not limited to rank or position, and can be realised by everyone. How can you ever fail if you maintain a serious commitment to be prudent?

Back home Chōtoku ultimately studied under such great masters as Bushi Matsumura Sokon and Itosu Ankoh in Shuri, and Oyadomari Kokan in Tomari. He became so entrenched in pursuing the fighting traditions in and around the districts of Shuri and Tomari that he finally transcended his weakness; *How to use his tiny body to overcome a larger opponent*. Often caught with his back to the wall, Chōtoku created innovative ways of escaping injury by moving laterally rather than moving forward or backwards.

Once he discovered the importance of shifting and moving his small body to gain a position superior in an effort to subjugate an opponent, he focused his training on *ashi-sabaki* (foot work), and often trained down at the riverside, or sometimes on the back of the bridge railing. Within a few years of training Chōtoku mastered the secret essence of karate by reinterpreting its principles and applying them to his small body. In fact, so diligent did Chōtoku practice karate that by the time he turned 30 years old, he was well known in and around Shuri and Naha by the name of "*Chanmī-gwā*" ("*Small-eye Kyan*.")

During the establishment of the *Haihanchiken* (when prefectures replaced feudal domains) most *Kemochi* (aristocratic families) lost both their position and stipend too. The Kyan family was among those who were effected by the transition and knew only hard times after that. A biting poem describes a feeling prevalent during that time.

Poem:
"Ugade nachikasaya haiban no samure meetariyakante umagwā sunchi"

Interpretation:
Before the Haihanchiken Ryūkyū Bushi strut about. Now, however, after losing both their position, and stipend, they have been reduced to hiding their faces under their hats as coachmen pulling carts. It's a pity to see them as such.

I can imagine that Chōtoku Sensei grew up knowing only too well what hard times really meant. Finally, and for financial reasons, Chōtoku Sensei had to relocate to *Makihara* in *Yomitan Village*. As a descendant of the Sho family he was still privileged to some inheritance and got use of a small plot of land located in Makihara handed down by the Sho family. Cultivating silkworms and hauling a cart, Chōtoku was able to carve out a meagre existence. Yet, in spite of his difficult times, he never once gave up his practice of the fighting arts. It was during that time that Chōtoku Sensei learned the *Kusanku* tradition (kata) from master Yara of Chatan, the man who managed the Sho family's riding stables in Makihara.

Known in the history of Karate as *Chatan Yara*, he was a public official who was sent to Nakagami-Yomitan, by the Sho administration to manage their private riding stables. In spite of being younger than Matsumura Sokon, Yara was certainly not inferior to him in technique and was regarded as a prominent *bujin* by all those who knew him.

Kyan Sensei often talked about Chatan Yara to his student, *Aragaki Ankichi*. This I know because Aragaki Sensei told me directly. According to him, "*Chanmī-gwā*" said "*When Yara was young, he developed remarkable agility and had really powerful legs.*" One story maintained that in his youth he once jumped off one end of the Hijabashi (Hija bridge) and then leaped back up on the other side like a bird in flight. However, when I (Aragaki) learned from him, his strength had declined considerably and he needed a stick for walking about.

One evening while Chōtoku Sensei was lecturing a couple of us in his yard he swung his walking stick around and abruptly shoved it at my chest and asked how I might handle an encounter like this. Ankichi Sensei told me that *Chanmī-gwā*, in spite of his age, was still really intense, and that his stable posture controlled his very *maai* (distance) which resulted in his inability to respond at all. All he could do was break out into a cold sweat after being provoked by Master Kyan.

Up until that time Aragaki been somewhat of a braggart because he had quite a positive opinion of his own skills. However, the old master really hit home with his precision. He always maintained that well-trained bujin always had something which transcend age and physical technique. There was no question that Kyan Sensei, in his lifetime of training, had established powerful *ki* energy. So impressed with Master Kyan's skill, Aragaki Sensei trained even harder from that point on.

Deeply moved after hearing that story from Aragaki Sensei, I too intensified my resolve to train even harder. The Kusanku tradition was the principal vehicle through which Yara transmitted the secret applications of karate to Kyan. Kyan taught it to Aragaki, who taught it to Shimabuku Taro, who taught it to me. The tradition has come to be called "*Yara no Kusanku*" (Kyan's interpretation of the Kusanku tradition) and, highly regarded, it is also the last kata learned in the Matsubayashi school.

Karate Enlightenment
30% Inspiration ~ 70% Perspiration
Continuing on with Master Kyan I would like to introduce an episode about sensei when he had to lowered himself to haul a cart. At that time there was a huge man named Matsuda who had a rough reputation with young villagers. One day Kyan Sensei scolded Matsuda about his rough behaviour. Matsuda responded by telling Kyan that in spite of his great physical talent he knew nothing about real confrontations as kata and actual fighting were completely different. Moreover, Matsuda continued to say, I would be happy to take this opportunity to give you a demonstration of exactly what I mean.

They met on the banks of the Hija river where a crowd of villagers anxiously awaited. In an open space just beside the river the young villagers gathered with great excitement as Chōtoku Sensei faced the giant Matsuda. Without delay Matsuda lunged at the tiny Kyan in an effort to strike him with his fist into the solar plexus. Just at that moment however, Kyan quickly side stepped and responded by driving his shin into the sciatic nerve of Matsuda's leg which resulted in howling in tremendous pain and his huge body falling down into the river. So quickly had the encounter happened that everyone was astonished, including Matsuda himself, who, in spite of his damaged leg, became an instant believer. Apparently, the encounter also caused Matsuda to reconsider his nasty attitude.

In spite of his poverty Kyan Sensei managed to build his own house near the Hijabashi. There he taught karate to many young villagers in his yard. Additionally, Master Kyan also taught karate at the Kadena police station and the College of Agriculture and Forestry, the school where *Nakazato Joen*, the current head of the *Okinawan Karate-do Remnei*, first learned under him.

Even to this day I still value and keep Kyan's teachings alive: *"First of all you must achieve inner-stability, if you are to ever truly embrace karate throughout your entire life. Find an occupation suitable to your character, and one which will provide you with the opportunity to pursue karate;"* In my case, I became a policeman.

After gaining employment as a prefectural law enforcement officer, I was transferred to the Kadena police station in December 1931. I danced for joy because I could be near where Kyan sensei lived. However, before I was able to actually study under Kyan sensei himself, I first learned his favorite kata: Passai, Chintō, and Kusanku, from Aragaki Ankichi and Shimabukuro Taro. Having been so small, Kyan sensei had always trained much harder than everyone else. He always said that training was, *"*30% inspiration and 70% perspiration!"* [* *I've also heard 30% aptitude & 70% effort...*]

Another example which Kyan sensei often used to describe the importance of consistency in practice was about hitting the makiwara. *"If one trains everyday,"* said Kyan, *"one can actually break boards or tiles effortlessly. However, by the same token, if one discontinues their makiwara training, one's fist will lose its conditioning. So too in karate: if one trains hard one will achieve remarkable results. However, and like makiwara training, if one discontinues one's training, one's ability will wither away. Superior conditioning can only be built upon relentless effort. The size of one's body is irrelevant."* The words of master Kyan are still very much alive in the privacy of my mind. Just look at me, I am a perfect example of his wisdom. Although I never had the physique or talent, I always adhered to his advice and trained hard.

During master Kyan's era *"kakedameshi"* (*the test of one's skill and spirit through actual contact grappling/striking*) was a popular practice among confident men of karate. *Chanmī-gwā* rarely, if ever, refused any challenge from hot-blooded young men, and never lost a single match. In spite of people in the old days saying that such men of karate did not live long lives, Sensei lived until the ripe old age of 76 years old. His death at

76 must certainly be testimony to the fact that men of the discipline can, and do, live to ripe old ages if and when they take good care of themselves. His technique was equalled only by his passion to improve it.

Unfortunately, Kyan sensei was born during a rather tumultuous generation and lived his life out in humble poverty under less than perfect conditions. Perhaps then, it is in those "*less than perfect conditions*" that we can find the circumstances conducive to master Kyans' penchant for karate.

The Taiwan Incident
I would like to introduce another episode about master Kyan's life. Incidentally, this story was passed onto me through the late *Kudaka Kori*, a man I knew since my childhood. Kudaka Sensei first told me this story in the summer of 1975 when he was back in Okinawa on vacation from his home in Tōkyo where he headed up his *Shōrinji-ryu* dojo in Tōkyō's Shinjuku district.

Kyan sensei, Kuwae Ryosei (the last disciple of Bushi Matsumura) of Shuri, and Kudaka Kori, all demonstrated Karate-jutsu at the Butokuden in Taipei. Before the demonstration began a big Japanese named *Ishida Shinzôu*, a Judo 6th dan, came to the dressing room to pay them a visit. Looking to test his skill against a karate-ka, Ishida was the Judo teacher at the Taipei (Japanese occupied) police station. "*I want to fight with a karate-ka for the purpose of studying its value*" announced Ishida. "*I am not interested in trying to kill anyone,*" insisted Ishida, "*therefore, in the interest of research, please consider my challenge.*"

In spite of being surprised by Ishida's unexpected proposal, they reasoned that there could very well be a bigger problem if they declined his offer. Then there was also the loss of face which would not go over very well back in Okinawa. It would do nothing to enhance the image of the art if they refused to fight with the judoka. They realized that there was much more at stake than a simple bout between a judoka and karate-ka, it was a matter of honour.

Deciding to accept the offer the three needed to choose who would fight the judoka. A brief discussion resulted in Kyan sensei deciding that he would take on the Japanese judoka simply because *Kuwae was too old*, and *Kudaka was too young*. Removing his good demonstration gi, for fear of damaging it, Sensei stood, ever so thin by comparison, before Ishida, dressed in only his flimsy underwear.

Totally relaxed, Kyan stood in a natural, but ready stance, fully prepared to engage the younger and more powerful opponent. Concentrating upon his Ki (energy) he patiently waited for Ishida to move into his combative posture. As Ishida lunged forward to grab Kyan (*the way in which a judoka often attacks*), Sensei faded back into a *neko-ashi datchi* (*cat-paw stance*). Just as the judoka was about to grasp onto the smaller karate-ka, Kyan drove his left thumb into the mouth of his attacker. A dangerous move under normal circumstances, but Kyan knew just exactly how to place his thumb, between the outside of the teeth and the inside of the cheek, so that it would not be bitten off. Seizing onto the outside of the cheek with the other four fingers in an attempt to separate the skin from the bone, sensei stomped down on his right foot which rendered the judoka off balance and immobile. Pulling him down to the ground by the inside of the cheek sensei thrust a good clean hammer fist punch down to the jaw near the mastoid process, stopping it just before making contact. Never having experienced anything quite like that, the terrified Ishida instantly submitted, as victory and defeat was obvious. Following the bout Kudaka, Kuwae and sensei put on a successful demonstration. Ishida, in good spirits, asked and received daily instruction from sensei until his return to Okinawa.

Never having heard of this kind of gruesome technique, I wondered how effective it would be if used in an unexpected way. Hence, I tried it with a couple of my students and found that it was really effective especially when being grabbed. Kudaka sensei also believed that the real reason sensei stripped down into his underwear was to reduce the possibility of being thrown if the judoka actually was able to grasp onto him. The thin underwear would be an effective tool simply because it would rip when powerfully grabbed.

I don't think that it was an easy task to think up such an effective response under that emergency situation. Nonetheless, Kyan sensei did it. His knowledge of such things clearly demonstrated his understanding of technique no longer practiced in modern karate. This kind of technique resulted from the deep study of aggressive human behaviour at Shaolin generations before. Studied, further enhanced, indiscriminately reinterpreted, and finally codified into application practice, such principles have all but disappeared in modern karate. It is deeply important that we study the true value of ancient kata in an effort to fully understand the magnitude of its actual application. In doing so we can come to know that which was obvious to men like Kyan Chōtoku.

I built my own 12 tsubo (1 tsubo equals 2 tatami mats) dojo in Naha's Sogenji district in May 1942. At that time it was the biggest private school of karate in all of Naha. During the grand opening demonstrations I was deeply honored by the presence of many great guests which included Major General Kanna Kenwa, Matayoshi Kenwa from the Ryūkyū Shinpo Newspaper Co., and Dr. Tomoyori Hidehiko, etc... However, the greatest guest of them all was Master Kyan Chōtoku. He came all the way from Yomitan village, with his assistant Aragaki Ansei (the brother of Aragaki Ankichi), and demonstrated both Passai kata and the Bo (6' wooden cudgel). Master Kyan was then 73 years of age. Watching the old master perform filled my eyes with tears because I was so deeply moved by his obvious mastery of budo, determination to support me regardless of the great distance and his age, and his life long dedication to karate.

Even at his advanced age, the other guests were in awe of not only Kyan's sharp and powerful movements but also the master's indomitable spirit. Sensei really looked great at that time. It was, nonetheless, the last official demonstration of his life. That, for me, was also a very meaningful consideration. Scarcity of food and the widespread destruction of war forced Kyan sensei to evacuate his home in Yomitan to Ishikawa city. How much the wear and tear of war had upon his deteriorating health and mental stability remains unknown, but the great master of karate, Kyan Chōtoku, died on 20 September, 1945 at 76 years old.

Because of his tiny size, Kyan Sensei spent considerable time and effort developing his jodan-tsuki. Never having altered this technique, his jodan-tsuki represents his own interpretation of using the strike in a practical way for a person his size. It can be said that his unique jodan-tsuki exists in no other ryuha and must therefore illustrate his own understanding of karate. For a man his size, sensei knew his strengths and weaknesses well. His personal motto was always "*Effort is everything*." In many ways, so too was my training motto based upon master Kyans' originality and ideas.

Motto for Training Karate-do
1. We are all children of God
2. The boundaries of human achievement lie only in the mind
3. Seek to always improve the intensity of your training
4. If he practices 5 times, I'll do 7 times or 10 times.
5. Never depend upon others. Miyamoto Musashi said, "*Respect the gods and Buddha too, but never depend upon them.*"
6. Believe in yourself, and embrace the principles of, "*Shingitai.*"
7. Karate teaches that the real enemy lies within. Get interested in the pursuit not just the possession, the race not just the goal; Effort is everything!
8. Learn to live in harmony with nature, and your fellow man, rather than frivolously trying to destroy it, or dominate them. Travel the middle path.

Trans. Note: Taiwan Incident
When undertaking the original translation of Nagamine Sensei's book, the incident in Taiwan was described as August of 1930. This information was also confirmed in my personal conversations with *Hisataka Masayuki*, the son of *Kudaka Kori*, who initially shared the story. However, I have since discovered that *Kuwae Ryōsei*, who was involved in the incident, actually passed away in late 1926. Therefore, the previously mentioned date must be incorrect. In my further research, I came across information about Kuwae having a son named *Ryōkei* (1886–1966) who resided in Taiwan. Initially, I considered the possibility that it might have been *Ryōkei* involved in the incident. However, the story clearly describes the individual as, "*the last student of Matsumura*" in the third person, indicating that it couldn't be the son. While there are several potential explanations and avenues for exploration, I wanted to highlight this issue as I haven't been able to find a definitive source to corroborate the correct time frames. Perhaps this could be a task for another researcher to delve into and find more conclusive information..

* *Ishida Shinzô* ~ Born 1881 Miyagi Prefecture [Japan]; DNBK Kyôshi and Kodokan Judo 6th dan. A professional Judo instructor residing in Taipei [Taiwan] in 1930.
* Source: *Budo Hōkan*, Dai-Nippon Yūbenkai Kōdansha; 1930 Tōkyō p329

* There's another story I came across, which I believe originally comes from Mochizuki Minoru and/or Kudaka Kori [as they both have history with Toku Sanpo]. Described in a magazine article entitled, "*Kyan Chōtoku ~ Profile of a Karate Pioneer*," by British Karate instructor, Phil Snewin; "*Kyan's Karate must have been effective as there are more than a few instances of his being challenged and according to the Okinawans, he was never beaten in a fight. Due to his build, Kyan chose not to try to win by brute force, but would defend using evasive tactics and then counterattack quickly. On one occasion when Kyan and his two disciples were on a trip to Hokkaido in northern Japan, they were challenged by a local fighter, Toku Sanpo [actually a famous Judoka]. Kyan's advice to [his student] Arakaki, was for him to use a one-strike knockout punch after having stepped back carefully to the edge of the arena, should the protagonist make a move against him. Sadly, however, the outcome was not recorded and little more is known about the incident.*"

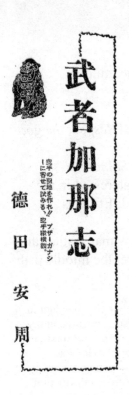

Busaganashi
by Tokuda Anshu
Source Gekkan Karate-do, Vol. 1 Issue 2
Published: 1 June 1956
Pp 44-45

Small-Eyed Kyan

The first time I experienced the actualities of Karate was when I began going to this man's Dojo. In 1928, the mood of celebration for the Enthronement of the Japanese Emperor reached as far as the southern islands, and elementary and junior high schools throughout the prefecture held flag parades and lantern processions in each municipality where the schools were located. Around this time, Kyan Shihan lived in a thatched hut in the fields near the Hija River, which runs across central Okinawa, and taught (Karate) to the students of the Prefectural Agricultural College.

Kyan Migwā was his nickname, called so because his eyes were so narrow. His full name was Kyan Chōtoku, and he was from an aristocratic family from Shuri.

Kyan Sensei's wife saved me once when I was surrounded by ruffians from another school. From that strange beginning, I became a student of Kyan Sensei. The first thing I learned was Seisan. I thought it had to be the most boring, redundant Kata in the world, but it was said to be the basic Kata of Shōrin-ryu, so I studied it with zeal. The next thing I learned was Wansu, but again it was not very impressive. Next was Passai, which had somewhat flashy movements, and was pleasing to the young me. After that came Chintō, Gojushiho, Ananko and Kusanku; all we did was practice Kata. It seemed to me that Sensei's instructional direction was to aim at having beautiful Kata all the way through.

One moonlit night, I was accompanied by my teacher and a group of agriculture and forestry students I once gave a demonstration at a branch school in Nakadomari, Onna Village, 10 kilometers north by passenger carriage. The branch school was located on the outskirts of a fishing village facing the East China Sea. We were treated exceptionally well that night. We were invited to the guest of honor's table by the village mayor, village council members, and other village dignitaries, who treated us to pieces of giant octopus sashimi the size of an adult's wrist.

After some Awamori was added and both the hosts and guests were in a good mood, the demonstration began. This Nakadomari village is located almost in the middle of the long and narrow Okinawa, and is the narrowest part of the island, with only about five kilometers between the Pacific coast to the east and the East China coast to the west.

The demonstration took place in the playground. A number of square lanterns were placed under the tables for lighting, and I, the youngest, was instructed to perform Seisan first. It was the first time I revealed my skills to the public. My heart was pounding. The grass on the playground was wet with dew, and fishing lights flickered on the beach. "I wonder if this little boy can do Karate?" "That's unusual."

The crowd around us laughed mouth to mouth, and as an eleven-year-old boy, my knees shook. But it was do or die time, and I had to go all in. In desperation, I bowed, put on my headband, and began the Seisan kata. When my performance started, there was no more crowd, no more teachers, no more wardens, no more anything. I just mindlessly faced the shining moon and continued to perform to the best of my ability, even though I was very young. When I dropped my hips and finished the last kata, I was greeted with thunderous applause. Then, after four or five high school students from agriculture and forestry did Kata and Kumite in succession, Kyan Sensei stood up and walked to the middle of the playground.

He said, "Now, whoever is willing, try and stretch out this bent arm of mine." At the sound of his voice, the mayor of the ward, wearing a traditional Japanese kimono, yanked on the Sensei's arm, but it didn't falter. Then a couple of strong young men tried it, but Sensei's arm was as stable as a rock, and the same thing happened when two or three of them pulled in tandem. Even to my young eyes, just like the crowd, it was a miracle that such power could be hidden in the small, skinny Sensei. On the way home, we took a coach again, which made the sound of pounding hooves. My grandfather was waiting up for me to come home. When he heard what I had to say, he told me to do the same Kata as I had done in Nakadomari. When I showed him, my grandfather was completely delighted and said he would buy clogs made of paulownia wood as a thank you gift for Sensei.

Brief history of the author; Tokuda Anshu
Born in Shuri City, Okinawa Prefecture in 1919. Graduated from Second Prefectural Junior High School in 1936. 1942 Graduated Faculty of Political Science & Economics, Waseda University Currently; Reporter for the Sun Photo Newspaper

Gekkan Karate-do Magazine
Vol. 1 Issue 2 1956

Deeds of Valour
by Shimabukuro Eizō

English Translation by P. McCarthy

On pages 12-15, of his 1964 book, "Okinawa Karate-do Ou Touki" 沖縄空手道王統記, Shimabukuro Eizō [島袋永三, 1924-2017], recounts a story about Kyan Chōtoku, defeating four villains under the title, "Deeds of Valour."

Kyan Chōtoku, a native of Shuri, devoted himself to karate training and discipline from a young age, and remained in Shuri until he reached his thirties. During that time, a gang of four villains plagued the people of Shuri and Naha, instilling fear through robbery, violence and even murder against travelers on the road between the two villages. The citizens of Shuri reported these incidents to the police, but the authorities, armed with long sabers reminiscent of Japanese soldiers, seemed more interested in asserting their authority than capturing the criminals. Despite an incident with the authorities one night, the villains were not apprehended and got away! As a result, the roads became unsafe and traffic came to a halt.

Desperate to find a solution, the concerned citizens of Shuri realized that only the most skilled karate masters in Okinawa would stand a chance against the villains. They learned about the renowned Master Kyan and approached him, sharing the details of their predicament and seeking his help. Initially, Kyan refused their request for unknown reasons, but the persistent and heartfelt pleas of the townspeople eventually convinced Kyan to accept the challenge. From that day forward, every evening Kyan travelled the highway, carrying a fighting cock under each arm and singing his favorite song [*the reasons behind these actions remained known only to him*].

One evening, as Kyan made his way along the highway, he found himself surrounded by four masked young men—the very gang of villains he sought. Confronting him as if he was harmless, they demanded to know where he came from and where he was going. Kyan calmly replied that he had just purchased the chickens in the countryside and was on his way home. The villains threatened to take his life if he didn't hand over his money. Claiming to have only leftover change from the purchase, he explained that he couldn't give them the money as it would leave his poor family destitute. Considering him impudent, the villains renewed their threats along with an ultimatum—"*your money or your life!*"

In a display of quick thinking and skill, Kyan handed over the small change and feigned an attempt to escape in the direction he had come from. However, they stopped him, brandishing a large knife and demanding the chickens, too. Appearing as if he was handing over the chickens, Kyan darted out with lightning-fast movement knocking down three of the villains with powerful strikes. With the three incapacitated Kyan quickly closed in on the remaining villain, to face him head-on. Overwhelmed by fear, having just witnessed his comrades get dropped, the fourth villain fled. Kyan yelled out, letting them know who he was and that they would do well to abandon their wicked ways or run the risk of encountering him again. He warned them not to mistake his leniency, as others wouldn't have shown them such mercy. He sternly admonished the men and emphasised choosing a path of righteousness and earn respect. Following the encounter, the townspeople could now travel the highway without fear. The courageous actions of those who sought Kyan's help were praised and admired. Not surprisingly, the song Kyan sang as he strolled along the highway became widely known and spread far and wide, adding to his reputation.

The encounter with the four villains marked a turning point for both Kyan and the townspeople. With the highway now safe to travel, people expressed their gratitude and admiration not only to the Master but also to those who had sought his assistance, when the police were unable to resolve the issue. News of his remarkable skills and courageous deeds spread throughout Okinawa.

Kyan resided near the Hija Bridge in Kadena, which was a bustling community before the war and a major trading hub in the central part of Okinawa. As such, he established a karate dojo in the area and became known as a revered master. One notable skill he specialized in was the

"*Art of Leaping.*" To demonstrate this skill to his students, he would sometimes leap backward from a small platform onto the handrail of the bridge, which stood about nine feet high, and land in a ready-to-attack posture. Kyan's dojo became a gathering place for aspiring young men who sought to learn from his expertise. His teachings went beyond physical techniques, emphasizing the importance of discipline, respect, and moral integrity. He was known not only as a skilled karate practitioner but also as a mentor and role model for many.

As the years passed, Kyan's influence grew, inspiring countless individuals to pursue the path of righteousness through karate. His exceptional abilities and unwavering commitment made him a legendary figure in Okinawan fighting arts.

His triumph over the four villains became a symbol of bravery and resilience, reminding everyone that determination and skill could overcome adversity. Kyan's legacy extended far beyond Shuri and Okinawa, shaping the development and global recognition of karate as a respected martial art.

Today, Kyan's name symbolizes excellence and honor in the world of karate. The story of his victory over the four villains remains an integral part of Okinawan folklore, cherished for its demonstration of valor and the indomitable spirit of a true karate master.

Kyan Folktales ~ Youtube

In Yomitan Village, numerous old folk tales have been passed down through generations, including stories about the renowned karate master Kyan Chōtoku, who is also referred to as Chanmī-gwā. This video was recorded and compiled based on the audio materials of traditional folk tales collected in 1976 by Matsuda Nobumasa (DOB 1896). The selected folk tales were recorded with subtitles in the local "*Shimakutuba*" dialect. Shimakutuba, literally 'Island Speech', is a term used to describe various *Ryūkyū-goha* [琉球語派 aka 琉球諸語]; i.e. Ryūkyūan languages spoken in the southernmost parts of the Japanese archipelago, especially in Okinawa.

The two Kyan folktales are only three minutes in duration but the entire video [*16 min 23 sec duration*] can be located on YouTube; See here ...
https://www.youtube.com/watch?v=g9MHSPcmEAM&t=3s

Presented here is an informal overview rather than a sentence by sentence direct translation and I have purposely omitted the episodes not related to Karate:

Episode #1
Once upon a time in Yomitan Village, there lived a man named Chanmī-gwā. At first glance, Chanmī-gwā appeared slender and not particularly strong, weighing around 50kg. However, he possessed incredible martial arts skills and was known for his immense power.

In the days before the war, there was an event called Harayama Shobu, where Chanmī-gwā would showcase his karate skills in front of the Yomitan village office. Whenever he performed, his arms and entire body would tense up, resembling steel. The onlookers were astonished by his exceptional expertise.

Outside of his martial arts prowess, Chanmī-gwā worked as a horse carriage owner near Hīja Bridge. It was during one of his rice-charging expeditions that he encountered a group of rough carriers from Yonabaru.

As Chanmī-gwā calmly loaded his rice bags onto the carriage in his usual unhurried manner, the boisterous carriers from Yonabaru grew impatient. They rudely demanded that Chanmī-gwā step aside, asserting their right to charge their rice bags first.
Chanmī-gwā's temper flared at their self-centered behavior. "What are you saying? There is a proper order to things. Don't act selfishly!" he retorted.

Driven by his anger, Chanmī-gwā swiftly kicked the rice bags, skillfully loading them onto the carriage in no time. The Yonabaru carriers watched in awe as they realized they were facing a man of extraordinary power. Overwhelmed by Chanmī-gwā's remarkable abilities, they scattered in fear, fleeing from the scene.

And so, the legend of Chanmī-gwā's incredible strength and skill spread throughout the village, leaving a lasting impression on all who witnessed his extraordinary feats.

Episode #2
In the village of Yomitan, Chanmī-gwā, known for his exceptional karate skills, took on a new student—Yara Rindō's daughter. As he taught her the ways of karate, a deep bond formed between them, blossoming into love.

One fateful day, as Chanmī-gwā made his customary visit to Yara Rindō's house, a group of men appeared, pretending that he intended to take away the young Yara daughter. Outraged by this perceived threat, the young men of Yara armed themselves with sticks, ready to confront Chanmī-gwā.

Realizing the danger he faced, Chanmī-gwā swiftly reacted. Being near Hīja Bridge at the time, he scooped up the daughter and leaped onto the bridge's parapet. The determined young men pursued him relentlessly, but Chanmī-gwā's agility and speed evaded their grasp. With a nimble escape, he managed to flee from their pursuit.

In the aftermath of this daring escape, Chanmī-gwā and the Yara Rindō's daughter became husband and wife, sealing their love with marriage. It became evident that Chanmī-gwā's remarkable martial arts abilities were complemented by his light-footedness, despite his smaller stature. Stories circulated of his extraordinary agility, with one tale recounting how he effortlessly leapt from one roof to another, resembling a bird in flight.

And so, the legend of Chanmī-gwā's prowess in both martial arts and nimbleness lived on, inspiring awe and admiration among the villagers who witnessed his remarkable feats of strength and grace.

* Another English translation by the OKIC can be located here
http://okic.okinawa/en/archives/news/p4192

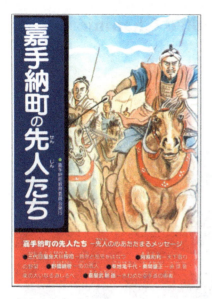

The 1993 book "Kadena Town's Pioneers," [shown here], published by the Kadena Town Board of Education, examples a chapter dedicated to Okinawa karate and Kyan Chōtoku; The episodes are recounted over 18 pages. The story begins with Chōtoku, who resided near Hīja Bridge, deciding to venture into the business of transporting goods from the port to Naha port's warehouse, known as Tundō. During this time, goods were transported using horse carriages, and those involved in this trade were called "*Basha-muchā*," or horse coach owners. The work of a carriage owner was physically demanding and labor-intensive. Consequently, many of these owners were rough individuals, often imposing figures who were not easily approached. Among them, there was little consideration or regard for one another. On the journey to Naha, where the roads were narrow, conflicts between carriers would often erupt due to a lack of prioritization. Upon arrival at the warehouse, disputes would arise over the order in which freight was to be delivered. These robust men took pride in their skill and agility.

Following this explanation, the narrative introduces a similar episode involving the formidable men from Yonabaru. However, in this particular instance, it is mentioned that Kyan Chōtoku, instead of carrying rice bags like the others, would shoulder bags of sugar. Furthermore, he showcased his dexterity not by using his feet but by skillfully wielding a rokushaku-bō staff.

Okinawan Karate ... A Man Called Chanmie

by Irei Hiroshi
20 September 2010

In this chapter, we embark on a journey into the captivating world of Okinawan Karate, guided by the extensive research graciously shared with me by the late *Irei Hiroshi*. *Irei san*, a renowned authority on the life of Kyan Chōtoku, has played a crucial role in shedding light on the remarkable achievements and enduring legacy of this karate pioneer.

Irei's passion for unraveling the intricate tapestry of Okinawan martial arts was evident in his tireless pursuit of knowledge. Introduced to him by Grandmaster Shimabukuro Zenpo, I had the privilege of meeting *Irei san* on several occasions. During these meetings, he generously shared his wealth of research and insights, contributing greatly to my own quest for understanding.

The cornerstone of this chapter is *Irei's* small book, "Okinawan Karate, A Man Called Chanmie." Within its pages, *Irei* masterfully weaves together historical accounts, personal anecdotes, and profound analysis to present a comprehensive portrait of Kyan Chōtoku's life and contributions. His meticulousness in approaching his research is evident as he painstakingly unearthed hidden details and shed new light on the enigmatic figure of Chanmie.

With deep gratitude and admiration, I present this chapter, drawing extensively from the research gifted to me by *Irei Hiroshi*. His unwavering support, belief in the importance of sharing knowledge, and encouragement to expand the horizons of understanding have been a guiding light in my journey.

Through the exploration of *Irei's* research and the intriguing tale of Chanmie, we aim to honor the legacy of Kyan Chōtoku and provide a deeper appreciation for the rich heritage of Okinawan Karate. Together, let us delve into the pages that lie before us, embracing the spirit of martial arts and the wisdom imparted by those who came before us.

With the utmost respect for the late *Irei Hiroshi* and a profound appreciation for his invaluable contributions, I invite you to join me on this enlightening expedition into the life and legacy of "*A Man Called Chanmie.*"

Enrollment in Nishogakusha College

Mishima Chūshū

二松學舍大學

Nishogakusha College was established in 1877 [by *Mishima Chūshū*, 1828-1911], coinciding with significant events of that time such as the establishment of Tōkyō University and the occurrence of the Satsuma Rebellion.

During the Meiji Era, Saigo Takamori, a prominent figure, led a civil war alongside disgruntled samurais against the Meiji Government. However, they were suppressed. This occurred ten years after the transformative Meiji Restoration.

At the age of seven, Kyan Chōtoku, later known as Chanmie, was a physically frail and shorter boy compared to others his age. His eyes were smaller as well. Despite these characteristics, nobody anticipated that Chōtoku would later enroll in Nishogakusha College after ten years. Following the tradition of the Shuri Bushi family, he studied Confucianism at the age of seven with his older brothers Chōho and Chōhitsu. This daily routine became monotonous and dull. Chōtoku was born in 1870.

In the year of his birth, 1870, the New Meiji government selected the Rising Sun flag (Hinomaru) as the national flag of Japan. While this might have been considered good fortune for regular Japanese families, such an event went unnoticed in the foreign land of the Ryūkyū Kingdom at the time.

Chōtoku's father was 31 years old at the time of his birth and his mother, Mamatsu, was the daughter of the Katsuren-Mo Clan. Chōtoku was the third son of the Kyan family, which was quite typical for a Shuri noble family; dependents of Prince Haneji Chobu. The Kyan family had twelve children, six sons and six daughters.

During that year, there was a national slogan promoting the encouragement of new industries, wealth, and military strength. The aim was to build a modern country modeled after the West. In Japanese society as a whole, the introduction of Western civilization was blindly followed without much reflection or doubt. Fukuzawa Yukichi [1835-1901], a Japanese author, writer, teacher, and political theorist, and his Keio Gijuku University symbolized this trend. They strongly discouraged oriental cultures but admired Western cultures. Japanese society was undergoing a transformation, embracing the concept of, "*survival of the fittest*" brought about by the introduction of Western civilization.

Amidst this cultural shift, Mishima Chūshū, an academic specializing in Chinese studies, felt a sense of crisis regarding the excessive integration of Western civilization and Western philosophies. At the age of 47, he decided to establish a Chinese Studies School, emphasizing the importance of studying Oriental culture for the nation's development.

Mishima Chūshū proved to be an influential figure as he developed numerous human resources since the establishment of Nishogakusha College. He held prominent positions such as a literature professor at Tōkyō University, an officer at the crown prince's palace, and an advisor to the imperial palace. Nishogakusha, Keio Gijuku, and Dojinsya were referred to as the "*Big Three Schools of the Meiji Period*" around that time.

Shō Tai

Returning to the year 1872, when Chōtoku was two years old, King Sho Tai, the last king of the Ryūkyū Kingdom, was demoted to the lord of Ryūkyū Han. Previously, he held the title of King of the Ryūkyū Kingdom.

Ryūkyū entered into a vassal relationship with Emperor Meiji, effectively becoming a protectorate. This was the second instance of the Ryūkyū Kingdom falling into a vassal relationship, the first being its relationship with China.

For the Ryūkyū Kingdom, it was a national crisis as the Meiji government exerted direct control over it through Satsuma domination, treating it as a puppet state. The Ryūkyū Kingdom's autonomy was significantly diminished, and it faced challenges under this new arrangement.

Kyan Chōfu; Father of Chanmie

Chōfu

From the depths of this national crisis, the appearance of Kyan Chōfu [喜屋武朝扶, 1839-1911], who the people knew and loved, became a man of some importance.

He was selected as a member of diplomatic delegates to Japan. His official title was *Sangikan Kyan Pēchin Chōfu* [賛議官 (さんぎかん) 喜屋武親雲上朝扶], father of *Chōtoku.*

Trans Note:

Sangikan (賛議官): The Sangikan, also known as the "*Counselor of State,*" was another counselor position within the Ryūkyūan government. The Sangikan served as an advisory council to the king and provided guidance on important matters. They were responsible for discussing and deliberating on various issues, offering recommendations, and assisting the king in decision-making. While the Sanshikan had more executive powers, the Sangikan focused primarily on providing counsel and guidance to the monarch; Kyan Chōfu was also known as *Shō Ishin*/向維新)

Sanshikan (三司官): The Sanshikan, also known as the "*Three Great Ministers*" or "Three Principal Officers," was a high-ranking council within the Ryūkyū Kingdom's government. This council consisted of three ministers who held administrative and executive powers. The Sanshikan played a crucial role in policy-making, advising the king, and managing state affairs. They were responsible for the day-to-day governance of the kingdom, overseeing matters related to diplomacy, finance, military affairs, and internal administration.

In summary, the Sanshikan held significant administrative and executive powers, whereas the Sangikan was an advisory council without direct executive authority. Both positions were important in the governance of the Ryūkyū Kingdom, but their roles and responsibilities within the government hierarchy were distinct.

Chōfu, the father of Chōtoku, remains a relatively unknown figure, even within the Okinawa karate community. Okinawan historians have not given much attention to Kyan Chōfu, who was one of the prominent masters of Okinawa karate during that time. Due to this lack of attention, there are no existing books that delve into the father and son relationship between Chōfu and Chōtoku. However, with this new publication a more detailed account of their lives has emerged. Hopefully, this work might highlight the vast potential for further study and research in Okinawan karate history. The pursuit of historical documentation relating to karate-ka remains an important avenue for our continued learning and understanding.

Chōfu is documented in Ryūkyūan historical records for his appointment as Sangikan in 1872. He held a prominent position as a delegate alongside Sho Ken (Prince Ie), who served as the ambassador to the Refurbished Coronation Congratulatory Delegates to Emperor Meiji. Chōfu occupied the third position among the Sangikan and next to the vice ambassador Ginowan Uekata Chōho [aka Giwan Chōho]. Most notably, he had the distinction of being personally presented to Emperor Meiji.

In recognition of his role and accomplishments, Chōfu received various gifts, including 2 rolls of brocaded cloth, 5 rolls of silk, 2 rolls of fine red and white crepe, a set of gold lacquered ink stone box, two cloisonné pots, and new currency amounting to 100 yen. These lavish gifts underline the significance of his position and the esteem with which he was regarded.

It is also noteworthy that out of the numerous delegates from Ryūkyū, only three representatives had the privilege of an audience with Emperor Meiji. This fact underscores the exceptional distinction and honour bestowed upon Chōfu in his role as a Sangikan delegate.

These details shed light on the historical significance and accomplishments of Chōfu, as well as the broader context of Ryūkyūan delegates during that period. The available historical records and documentation provide valuable insights into the lives of Chōfu and, my extension, Chōtoku and help contribute to our understanding of Okinawan karate history.

A party of congratulatory envoys sent from Ryūkyū to Tōkyō, the seat of the new Meiji government, in 1872. Front row from right: Kyan Pēchin Chōfu (Councilor and Chōtoku's father), Prince Ie Chojiki (the Chief Envoy), Ginowan Uekata Chōho (aka Giwan Chōho; Vice Envoy). Back row from right: Yasuda Pēchin, Junior Recorder Horie (the translator from the Ministry of Foreign Affairs).

Chōtoku was only two years old when his father, Chōfu, began his career as a statesman in the Ryūkyū Kingdom. During the same year, the first steam locomotive railway opened on the mainland of Japan, running from Shinbashi to Yokohama. This momentous event, with the Japanese locomotive train emitting smoke, symbolized a cultural enlightenment that followed the railway's path. The train completed the 23.8 km distance between Shinbashi and Yokohama in 53 minutes, making six round trips per day. Crowds gathered around the stations, eagerly awaiting the sight of the train. At 10 a.m., the first train, carrying Emperor Meiji, departed from Shinbashi station and arrived in Yokohama after 53 minutes. The opening ceremony was attended by other distinguished guests, including Ambassador Sho Ken and Vice Ambassador Ginowan Uekata Chōho. Although there is no record of Kyan Chōfu's presence as a guest, it is reasonable to assume that he occupied a distinguished seat at the ceremony.

During the end of the Edo Period, notable individuals such as Sakamoto Ryōma from Tosa, Takasugi Shinsaku and Hirofumi Ito from Chōshū, and Godai Tomoatsu from Satsuma, who were radical activists and supporters of the imperial regime, defied the national ban and secretly traveled to Europe. Witnessing the power of modern Western nations left an indelible impact on them.

It is conceivable that Prince Ie, Ginowan Uekata, and Kyan Chōfu, as representatives of the Refurbished Coronation Congratulatory Delegates to Emperor Meiji, were equally astonished when they observed the impressive locomotive departing from Shinbashi Station in Tōkyō, the capital of Japan. They likely found themselves deeply divided over the issue of whether Ryūkyū should align with Japan or the Chinese Qing Dynasty.

While Japan was rapidly gaining power in Asia, the Suzerain state of the Qing Dynasty was in decline. Prince Ie, Ginowan Uekata, and Kyan Chōfu, three delegates, were set to attend the grandest event in the Empire of Japan, celebrating its modernization with countless hopes and dreams. Ginowan Uekata Chōho was known for his strong admiration for Japan, wholeheartedly supporting the homeland's modernization efforts. However, upon returning from his role as a delegate, he faced a storm of criticism for betraying the Ryūkyū Kingdom, and was labeled a traitor.

In his later years, Chōtoku recalled, "*My father Chōfu was very strict. Even when it was snowing outside, I could only have breakfast after my karate lessons in King Sho Tai's royal garden. "My father, Chōfu, stood 5'6" tall, weighed 75kg and possessed great strength with a deep passion for the fighting arts. He was a man of few words and strict discipline but faithfully served the King's Family.*"

During that time, *Bushi* serving the Ryūkyū Kingdom were required to study Confucianism and train in *Ti/Di* [i.e. 手/karate] as part of their cultural refinement. Chōfu was taught karate by Bushi Matsumura [1809-1899], who was a regarded as a mentor of the fighting arts during his time. It is well known among the local karate community that Matsumura's teacher was Sakugawa Kanga [佐久川 寬賀, 1786-1867]; aka as *Todi* (唐手/*Karate*) Sakugawa. The very roots of this art can be traced back to him. Hence, the art has been passed down from Sakugawa Kanga to Matsumura Sokon and then to Itosu Anko, although some may consider this lineage to be a subject of controversy.

Chōfu received direct training from Matsumura Sokon for two years, starting when he was 16 or 17 years old. Matsumura Sokon resided near Shikina-en, the largest villa of the Ryūkyū Royal Family at the time. Chōtoku, too, became a disciple of Matsumura Sokon. Chōtoku vividly described the day he met the renowned karate teacher: "*In the spring of my sixteenth year, I went to Shikina Garden with my father and met the great karate teacher Matsumura Sokon. Through him [my father], I requested to learn karate.*" Chōtoku personally wrote this account in his, "*Memories of Karate,*" the Okinawa Shimpo newspaper on 7 May, 1942. While this evidence supports the understanding that Chōtoku was a direct student of Matsumura Sokon, additional verification would be welcomed.

Chōtoku's childhood was marked by turbulent times, as the Ryūkyū Kingdom underwent significant societal changes under the jurisdiction of both Imperial Japan and the Chinese Qing Dynasty. Despite constant appeals from Ryūkyū, the new Meiji government of Japan repeatedly rejected the request for dual jurisdiction under Japan and the Chinese Qing Dynasty, resulting in a challenging situation for the Ryūkyū Kingdom.

Kamegawa Uekata, a leader of a pro-Qing dynasty group, targeted Ginowan Uekata Chōho, accusing him of betrayal and treason. They labeled him as the Japanophile who had recently returned from Japan as a member of the Refurbished Coronation Congratulatory Delegates to Emperor Meiji. The main reason for criticizing Ginowan Uekata, as a Japanophile, was because OF the significant change brought about by the reformation of the Ryūkyū Kingdom to the Han system, which occurred three years after the delegates' return to Okinawa. This change resulted in a substantial loss of income and salary, which adversely affected more than 2,600 Shuri-based Bushi and their families.

In response to Ryūkyū Kingdom's strong request, the Qing Dynasty dispatched *He Ruzhang,* a Chinese minister, to Japan; *Trans. Note: He Ruzhang was China's first minister to Japan, to re-establish Ryūkyū's tributary relationship with China and maintain Ryūkyū's independence. He* protested to Terashima, the Meiji government's Foreign Minister, arguing that exclusive Meiji rule contradicted the treaty of amity between China and Japan. The Ryūkyū Kingdom desired to maintain its vassal relationship with the Chinese Qing Dynasty, but Japan refused to acquiesce. Ultimately, the new Meiji government decided to place Ryūkyū under exclusive Japanese control.

Japan had concerns about potential intervention from Western Europe if negotiations with China were prolonged. In 1878, the Meiji government appointed Matsuda Michiyuki [松田 道之, 1839-1882], as the Ryūkyū disposition government clerk. At that time, Chōtoku was only eight years old. In the same year, Kanō Jigorō [嘉納 治五郎, 1860-1938], who would go on to pioneer Judo, enrolled in Nishogakusha at the age of 19. Around this time, Chōtoku was studying and practicing sumo wrestling in Okinawa with his older brother Chōhitsu. Their father, Chōfu, held a highly trusted position with King Sho Tai and struggled to comprehend the international situation amidst Japan's ascent and the declining Chinese Qing Dynasty.

Kyan Chōfu & Matsuda Michiyuki

In 1879, Matsuda Michiyuki, a government clerk of the Ryūkyū Disposition, traveled to Ryūkyū and arrived at the port of Naha. At that time, Chōtoku was nine years old. On 25 March, 1879, Matsuda presented 20 items outlining the plan for the disposition of the Ryūkyū Kingdom. He brought along 160 policemen and 400 soldiers and requested that Shuri Castle be vacated.

Fifty-nine days prior to his arrival in Ryūkyū, Matsuda delivered *Notification 13*, to Prince Nakijin (Sho Hitsu). Issued by the Meiji Government, the notification prohibited any tribute delegations and ordered the cessation of Coronation Congratulatory Delegations to the Chinese Qing dynasty within the main conference room of Shuri Castle; i.e. *Dai-Seiden*.

During this decision-making conference, Prince Nakijin, Urasoe Uekata, Tomikawa Uekata, Yonabaru Uekata, and Kyan Chōfu were seated adjacent to Yonabaru Uekata.

According to the Naha City Historical records - *Data & Materials Edition No 2, Mid 4, P192*, it was recorded that "*Kyan Uekata was present and seated on the lower right, facing left.*" His name, and formal title, within the new Meiji government, is significant.

Kyan *Uekata* [上方], was also known as Kyan *Sangikan* [賛議官, and *Shō Ishin*, 向維新, according to Ryūkyūan documents], was unquestionably the father of Chōtoku. It is reported that the Ryūkyū Kingdom appealed for "*dual jurisdiction of China-Japan*" until they were eventually forced to vacate Shuri Castle by the order of Matsuda Michiyuki, the Ryūkyū Disposition Government Clerk, in 1879.

At that time, the Ryūkyūs could not refuse the will of the new Japanese government. Ironically, even now, Japan seems to be unable to refuse the will of the United States of America. This serves as a cynicism of the current political situation. Essentially, it can be said that the same situation between Japan and the Ryūkyūs is now recurring in the Japan-U.S. relationship. The relationship between Japan and the Ryūkyūs, which was once based on hard power, has transformed into a relationship between Japan and the U.S. based on soft power, but the essence of relations between nations remains unchanged.

Sho Tai, the last king of the Ryūkyū Kingdom, was ordered to move promptly to Tōkyō. Police Headquarters were established, and precinct police stations were deployed in Shuri and Naha to control local rebellions by groups affiliated with and under the jurisdiction of the Qing dynasty. Former U.S. President Ulysses Grant happened to visit Japan in the middle of an around-the-world trip. He suggested to Japan a proposal for arbitration to divide Ryūkyū into two, but it never materialized. King Sho Tai was demoted to become *Marquis Sho Tai*, and all his property was confiscated by Emperor Meiji.

Along with King Sho Tai, who was ordered to move to Tōkyō, Chōfu, the father of Chōtoku, also relocated to a large house of two thousand *tsubo* (66,000 square meters) in *Kojimachi Fuimicho*, Tōkyō, where *Kudan* Middle School stands today.

At that time, Chōfu held the status of *Kafu* [家婦]. The Kafu status was lower than *Karei* [家令], and the purpose of those in this class was to take care of noble people. Chōfu did not provide personal care but instead provided financial support for "*Marquis Sho Tai*." Marquis Sho Tai received an annual payment of ¥200,000 from the Meiji government, while an officer employed in the Okinawa Prefectural Government received a very modest ¥60 per year. During that era, the number of *Bushi* in the Shuri district was 3000, however, only 367 such Bushi were actually salaried. The remaining Bushi received no salary and were treated as unemployed individuals. This policy abolished the "*Chitsurokusei*," which was seen as a desperate resistance by Kamegawa Uekata.

Lower ranked Ryūkyū Bushi in the early Meiji Period; c. 1880s

* *Trans. Note: The term "Chitsurokusei," reflected the narrative propagated by the Japanese government to justify their actions and assert control over the Ryūkyū Islands. It portrayed the Ryūkyū Kingdom as lacking the ability to govern independently and suggested that Japan's intervention was necessary for the stability and progress of the region.*

This resulted in 90% of the Shuri-based Bushi becoming unemployed and relocated out from the urban centre to more distant rural areas, learning and taking up new skills, retiring and/or relying upon the financial assistance of family members and/or relatives, when and wherever possible.

During that time, such [unemployed] Bushi, became known as "*Yahdui*," were identifiable by their origins. A known Ryūkyūan poem described them as "*Ugadi nachikasaya Samureih me-e-ta-a-ri haiban-nu kanti nmmagwā sunchi*" ("*At the end of the old dominion days, a pitiful and destitute Samuree (サムレー) hides his face with a cloth as he pulls a coach and horse, overwhelmed with shame*"). This term, referring to unemployed individuals resembling poor, unpaid Bushi, is still used today. However, it is important to note that not all Bushi were in this unfortunate position. Some Bushi received substantial salaries ranging from 100 yen to 2,000 yen per year. The Kyan family, owing to Chōfu's dedicated services, was expected to be among the well-paid Bushi [aka *Samuree*]. Chōfu had a successful career as a statesman during the end of the Meiji Era, received generous gifts from Emperor Meiji, and held a strong faith in King Sho Tai. He was even promoted to a property administrator for the king's family.

Contrary to the belief, the idea that the Kyan family would end up as pitiful and poor samurai was simply a rumour rooted in misunderstanding, primarily spread within the Kadena and Yomitan areas. Chōtoku, being a man of few words, maintained a reserved demeanor after mastering self-discipline as a guiding principle in his life. He paid little attention to rumours or others' opinions. He allowed the rumours to persist, claiming that he was a pitiful, poor Bushi in the waning days of Ryūkyu Kingdom. At the age of 38, he moved to Makibaru in Yomitan Village. He married Kama from the Rindo family, and they had their first daughter, Yasuko. Chōtoku never disclosed his previous *Samuree* status or academic background to his wife, daughter, or grandson, Nishihara Morichiro.

Just two years after the Satsuma Rebellion, a violent conflict known as the Seinan Civil War, the animosity between the "*Ganko-to Party*" (pro-China party/Stubborn Party) and the "*Shinpo-to Party*" (pro-Japan) continued. Both parties expressed dissatisfaction with the transition from a dominion state to a prefecture. Meanwhile, temporary residents, mainly

Kagoshima merchants, flocked to the area, while the common people still suffered from the scars left by the Satsuma Rebellion.

---

*Trans. Note: The term **"Ganko-to Party"** refers to a political faction that existed during the Meiji era in Okinawa, Japan. The name "Ganko-to" can be written in Japanese as "頑固党" (Gankotō), where "頑固" (ganko) means "stubborn" or "inflexible," and "党" (tō) means "party" or "faction." The Ganko-to Party was known for its conservative stance and strong support for maintaining close ties with China. They opposed the modernization efforts and reforms promoted by the Kaika-to Party, which advocated for closer integration with mainland Japan and adopting Western ideas and institutions. The Ganko-to Party's influence declined over time as Okinawa gradually underwent modernization and transitioned from a kingdom to a Japanese prefecture. The party's ideals and traditionalist views faced challenges in the changing political landscape of the era.*

*The term **"Shinpo-to Party"** refers to a political faction that existed during the Meiji era in Okinawa, Japan. "Shinpo-to" can be written in Japanese as "進歩党," where "進歩" (shinpo) means "progress" or "advancement," and "党" (tō) means "party" or "faction." The Shinpo-to Party was known for its progressive stance and advocacy for modernization and reforms in Okinawa. They supported closer integration with mainland Japan and the adoption of Western ideas, institutions, and technologies. The party sought to improve education, infrastructure, and social welfare in Okinawa, aiming to bring the region in line with the advancements seen in other parts of Japan. The Shinpo-to Party's influence grew as Okinawa underwent modernization and transitioned from a kingdom to a Japanese prefecture. They played a significant role in shaping the social, political, and economic development of Okinawa during that period. It's important to note that political parties and factions during the Meiji era in Okinawa were not as formally structured or organized as modern political parties. They represented various groups and individuals with common interests and goals, and their influence and activities varied over time.*

Kingdom to Prefecture: The Transition

Emperor Meiji
1852-1912

During the "*End of the Kingdom Period*," there was understandably much confusion and chaos in Okinawan society. Temporary resident merchants from other Japanese prefectures took advantage of the situation and attempted to monopolize key Ryūkyū industries, such as sugar production, lacquer ware, textiles, and awamori spirits. These industries had been taken away from the Ryūkyū Kingdom after losing its control in Shuri. This situation was reminiscent of the confusion experienced by Okinawa during its reversion to Japan in 1972, after decades of US military occupation, which left a blurred image of Okinawan society.

In July 1972, Tanaka Kakuei won the Liberal Democratic Party (LDP) presidency and published a book titled "*Japan Archipelago Remodeling Policy*" outlining his plans for addressing depopulation, overcrowding, and pollution issues through the development of transportation networks and infrastructure. This led to a rapid increase in land costs around potential industrial sites due to land acquisitions.

In Okinawa's unique case, Japan took over administration after 27 years of US occupation, adding to the existing confusion. Establishing the new Okinawa prefectural government, police headquarters, self-defense forces, public utilities, and transitioning from US military to Japanese civil administration posed significant challenges. Changes in vehicle traffic lanes and currency added to the confusion experienced by the people of Okinawa.

The reversion to Japan created turmoil for local industries, similar to the challenges faced during the "Start of the Prefecture" under the Meiji era. Mainland Japanese businessmen exploited resources that rightfully belonged to the local Okinawan people, buying real estate at low prices, while the US forces occupied and leased properties without purchasing them. Japanese real estate brokers quickly acquired local lands, causing a surge in prices and soaring land costs, referred to as "the third Ryūkyū Disposition."

It is important to note that blame cannot be assigned solely for the exploitation of the Okinawan people during the "*End of the Kingdom*" and "*Start of Prefecture*" periods. The Meiji Revolution brought positive changes, such as the introduction of a new school system and rectifying inequalities in land ownership.

While the previous response mentioned the increase in the population of temporary resident merchants during that period, it is worth highlighting that this resulted in significant confusion in the Okinawan business world.

During Chōtoku's childhood and teenage years [i.e. 10 to 18 years old], there was a power struggle among merchants who came to Okinawa from other cities like Osaka, Fukuoka, and Kagoshima. These merchants were not permanent residents of Okinawa but were competing for leadership positions and influence in the region. The victorious Kagoshima merchant clan took over important positions in politics, economics, law enforcement and the educational system; This period is now referred to as "*The Lost Ten Years*"

Okinawa Sumo [aka Tegumi]

Chōtoku stated, "*I learned Sumo wrestling when I was ten years old*" in his memoirs. Okinawa Teacher's School was established when he was ten years old and the following year Kumoji, Tomari, Ginowan and Ishigaki Minami elementary schools were also founded. In April of 1881, the famous novelist Natsume Sōseki [夏目 漱石, 1867-1916] enrolled to Nishogakusha when he was only 14 years old; following year, Yoshida

The 1st Okinawan Prefectural Student Study Abroad Program
L-R: Ōta Chōfu (15 years old, 1865–1938), Yamaguchi Zenshu (aka Nakijin Chōhan, 18 years old), Kishimoto Gasho (15 years old), Jahana Noboru (18 years old, 1865–1908), Takamine Chōkyō (15 years old, 1869–1939) * Photo courtesy: Naha City History Museum [digital archives]

Kurazo, a nephew of Yoshida Shōin [吉田松陰, 1830-1859], enrolled in the same school. The first Okinawa Prefecture sponsored students, Ōta Chōfu [1865–1938], Jahana Noboru [1865–1908], Takamine Chōkyō [1869–1939], Nakijin Chōhan and Kishimoto Gasho went up to Tōkyō to study abroad at that time as a result of the revised Japanese education law which had spread to Okinawa. Chōtoku dared not enroll in any elementary school or teacher's school which was established by the Meiji Government.

Chōtoku received his education at home following the traditions of the Shuri Bushi. His father, Chōfu, taught him his first karate lesson when he was just 14 years old [eg 1874], after a special ceremony held to celebrate his coming of age. Usually, this ceremony took place at the age of 13, but Chōtoku's was delayed by a year.

Chōtoku mentioned, "*My father told my brother and me that we had to learn the fighting arts to become men, and he promised to teach us karate. The very next day after the ceremony, we started our karate lessons, just as my father said.*"

When Marquis Sho Tai, the former king of the Ryūkyū Kingdom, was permitted to return to Okinawa after a five-year absence, Chōtoku was 14 years old. Chōfu performed Chōtoku's coming-of-age ceremony during this visit. The ceremony involved exchanging drinks in front of the family altar, with the father fully dressed and the son with his top knot tied. Afterwards, a feast would be held with invited guests, including friends and family.

During Marquis Sho Tai's visit, Kagoshima people held important positions in Okinawa's politics, economy, police, and education. Kagoshima merchants, *as temporary residents*, were monopolizing Okinawa's products and businesses, causing disadvantages for the local people.

Chōfu had moved to Tōkyō with Sho Tai in 1879 and returned to Okinawa after five years, when Chōtoku was 14 years old. He had to return every year due to the growing influence of temporary resident merchants, as mentioned before.

Marquis Sho Tai, no longer a king, was deeply upset and angered by the state of his former retainers and the manipulation of the judicial, administrative, police, education, and economic systems in Ryūkyū by former Satsuma and Kagoshima people. In response, he set about to establish a commercial enterprise he would call *Maruichi Shoten*.

In 1883, one year before his return to Okinawa, Marquis Sho Tai established the trading company Maruichi-shōten [丸一商店], with the help of *Goeku Chōi* and other lineaged families who still received income. Kyan Chōfu served as the executive accountant, managing the Sho family's property, as they were former royalty of the Ryūkyū Kingdom.

* Trans. Note: Goeku Chōi, aka Gushikawa Chōi, had a close association with Sho Tai, and served as a trusted advisor and supporter, during the challenging times of kingdom's decline and the transition to Japanese rule. He played a significant role in negotiating with Japanese officials on behalf of the king and the people of Okinawa. Goeku's influence and connections helped protect the interests of Okinawa and its people during this period of political and social change. He was known for his loyalty to the former king and his dedication to preserving the heritage and culture of the Ryūkyū Kingdom.

Matsumura's Teachings

At the age of 16, Chōtoku began learning Karate from Matsumura Sokon, a highly respected practitioner of the martial art. Despite Sokon being 77 years old, Chōtoku mistakenly believed him to be in his 80s. Further strengthening his fighting arts spirit, Sokon taught Chōtoku the kata *gojushiho*. Chōtoku cherished his time with Sokon and said;

"*Matsumura Sokon taught me karate with great enthusiasm and emphasized that the fighting arts were not only about combat but also a path to peace. I greatly respected him as a pioneer ahead of his time, and his important teachings deeply motivated me to continue my karate practice.*"

At 18 years of age, and after learning from Matsumura Sokon, Chōtoku enrolled in Nishogakusha College, a school for Chinese Studies. Matsumura recognized Chōtoku as a person of strong determination and commitment, evident through his karate training, study of Chinese language and culture from a young age. He saw immense potential in Chōtoku, and not just because of his physical prowess but primarily due to his strong mental attitude.

Nishogakusha was a renowned institution specialized in the study of ancient Japanese and Chinese studies, although it is less known in Okinawa. The school referred to its head teacher as "*Sacho*" [校長, School Head], rather than the more common "*Gakucho*" [学長, Principal], used today. Notable figures who served as presidents of the school included *Shibusawa Eichi* [渋沢栄一, 1840-1931], considered the father of capitalism in Japan, Kaneko Kentaro [金子堅太郎, 1853-1942], one of the framers of the Constitution of the Empire of Japan, and Yoshida Shigeru [吉田茂, 1878-1967], a former prime minister after World War II.

Former Nishogakusha head *Shibusawa Eichi* is the face of Japan's new ¥10,000 note

The founding of Nishogakusha by Mishima Chūshū [三島中洲, 1830-1906], was apparently a response to compete with Fukuzawa Yukichi's [福沢 諭吉, 1835-1901], Keio University. Mishima Chūshū, a scholar of Chinese studies, established the school due to concerns about the encroachment of Western ideals and civilization. He believed that studying Oriental culture was crucial during that time to guide Japan toward its desired future. Mishima aimed to promote Oriental studies and develop individuals who would shape the new era. This led to the establishment of the specialized school for Chinese Studies.

Chōtoku recalled his connection to Nishogakusha in his memoir, stating, "*My father, who was an aide to Marquis Sho Tai, had to move to Tōkyō. As a result, my brothers and I accompanied him, and we were given a house on Sho Tai's premises. I attended Nishogakusha in Fujimi-cho to study Chinese studies under Mishima Chūshū.*" While Chōtoku had no choice but to enroll in Nishogakusha, the courses he took there would play a significant role in shaping his future.

Chōtoku's father, Chōfu, who served under King Sho Tai, believed that his children should learn Chinese studies. Chōtoku, along with his brothers *Asaho* and *Chōhitsu*, received an education in Chinese studies from a young age. Matsumura Sokon recognized Chōtoku's potential and guided him towards the path of martial arts, emphasizing that martial arts were a means of achieving and maintaining peace. This ultimately led Chōtoku to join Nishogakusha, where he enthusiastically studied martial arts theory.

Confucian Scholar Sato Issai

Sato's highly influential and widely studied *Shoheiko* (小平考) provided a detailed analysis and interpretation of the "*Daxue;*" Exploring its principles and moral teachings, the work contributed significantly to the spread of Confucianism in Japan and applying it to the social and intellectual challenges of his time.

Having received instruction in Chinese studies directly from Mishima Chūshū, the school's first president, Chōtoku's education primarily focused on Confucian studies; The main principles emphasized in Confucian teachings were "*governing someone after living a virtuous life*" and "*saving the suffering of common people through proper governance of society.*"

Mishima Chūshū's academic background began with the study of Wang Yangming Doctrine from the Confucianist Yamada Houkoku at the age of 14. He further pursued his studies with Saito Setsudo and delved into Neo-Confucianism. Additionally, he learned Confucian principles from Sato Issai at the Shoheiko School. Issai's work "*Genshi Shiroku*" was highly regarded, even by influential figures like Saigo Takamori, and it is considered a significant text for today's leaders. In May 2001, then Prime Minister *Koizumi Junichiro* quoted Saito Issai during a Diet deliberation on education, further popularizing his teachings.

Chōtoku was deeply influenced by both Matsumura Sokon and Mishima Chūshū during his time at Nishogakusha. The importance of ethical and moral education, as well as the ideal of governing for the well-being of society, resonated strongly with Chōtoku. Having observed his father's statesmanship, Chōtoku naturally inclined towards these doctrines.

In summary, Chōtoku's journey included learning karate from the esteemed practitioner Matsumura Sokon, enrolling in Nishogakusha under Mishima Chūshū to study Chinese studies, martial arts theory, and being inspired by the principles of Confucian teachings. These experiences and influences played a significant role in shaping Chōtoku's path and instilling in him a strong sense of duty, both in martial arts and in contributing to society.

A Spiritual Pillar

There's an intriguing notion, that Chōtoku may have glimpsed the essence of Karate during his time at Nishogakusha. It is certainly something that bears further exploration. The essence of Karate-do lies in the idea that if one devotes their entire life to training in karate but never finds themselves in a situation where they need to use those skills, then they have truly achieved the goal of their practice. This concept echoes the enigmatic truths and falsehoods often associated with Daoism.

To illustrate the significance of such a philosophy, let us turn to the story of Sakamoto Ryoma, a prominent figure in Japanese history. In Shiba Ryotaro's historical novel, "*Ryoma ga Iku*" [*a work which revolves around the life and adventures of Sakamoto Ryoma*], it recounts Ryoma having received permission to study in Tosa and traveling to *Edo* [i.e.

Tōkyō] to practice *swordsmanship* at Chiba Shusaku's dojo. Displaying exceptional talent, he achieved remarkable results in his training. However, during this time, the black ships of Commodore Perry arrived at Uraga, marking the opening of Japan to the outside world. It was at this moment that Ryoma realized the limitations of swordplay in facing such formidable foreign forces.

Promptly returning to his hometown, Ryoma made the daring decision to leave Tosa and return to Edo. As an advocate against foreign influence, he harbored negative sentiments towards figures like Katsu Kaishu [勝海舟, 1823-1899], in Edo Castle, who sought to open Japan to the world. Ryoma even went so far as to visit Katsu's residence with the intention of killing him. However, in a twist of fate, Katsu saw through Ryoma's intentions and offered a whimsical remark, questioning the ability of one man wielding "a knife" to bring about significant change in their nation.

His words and way of thinking profoundly impacted Ryoma, leaving him in awe of Katsu's insight and wisdom. After considerable thought, and gaining his trust, Ryoma asked and became a bodyguard for Katsu Kaishu; Hence, began his ascent in Japanese history. It is a common desire amidst young people to aspire to become masters of the fighting arts. The longing to excel in sports and competition transcends age and and culture. However, as the saying goes, *"sometimes we become so fixated on minor details that we end up losing sight of what truly matters."*

Chōtoku, in his reflections, emphasized the importance of not confusing the technique and the spirit of Karate. Simply boasting about physical strength often overlooks the training of the spirit and mind. In a forced fight between a man and a lion, it becomes a spectacle akin to a Roman holiday. In everyday life, if a lion were to approach a person closely, a wise individual would choose to retreat and avoid unnecessary confrontation. The secret and essence of Karate lie in the ability to face unexpected or unavoidable situations with spiritual training. This is precisely what Ryūkyū Karate aims to preserve as a legacy, passing down knowledge from master to student across generations.

Some practitioners of Karate mistakenly believe that the secret lies in the ability to deliver a single deadly strike. However, this perception is incorrect. The true secret of Karate lies in avoiding conflict altogether. Karate teaches us that if we can go through life without ever needing to utilize our martial arts skills, despite dedicating extensive time to training, then we have achieved the ultimate goal of our practice. It is important to contemplate these profound words left by Chōtoku, as he clearly stated in his memoirs.

Maruichi Shoten & Ryūkyū Shimpo

During Chōtoku's time at Nishogakusha, his father Chōfu was fully occupied with the management of the trading company "*Maruichi Shoten.*" This company had been established by Marquis Sho Tai and Goeku Choi, one of the few aristocrat families that still maintained a source of income. Among their branches, the Ishigaki Branch of Maruichi Shoten enjoyed particular success. It was common for children from lower status families [i.e. social rank within the aristocracy] to aspire to attend Shuri High School, which is now known as Shuri Senior High School. The behavior of the students in the classroom during that era, is depicted in "*Okinawan Social History in the Era of Meiji, Taisho & Showa,*" by Yamashiro Zenzo [山城善三], which describes how "*students, who were sons of samurai between the ages of 17 and 25, often carried cigarette cases in their waist and twirled their mustaches while attending class.*"

Prince Shō Jun [1873-1945], the fourth son of the last Ryūkyūan King, founded the Ryūkyū Shimpo [琉球新報] in 1893 with Ōta Chōfu [1865-1938].

At the age of 23, Chōtoku witnessed the establishment of "*Ryūkyū Shimpo*," a newspaper company, established by *Prince Matsuyama* [*Shō Jun*/尚 純, 1874-1957], the fourth son of Marquis Sho Tai [尚泰, 1843-1901]. *Shō Jun*, who was only 20 years old at the time, assumed the role of president. The founding members included *Goeku Choi* [*the groom of Sho Tai's first daughter, Mazurugani*], *Ōta Chōfu* [太田 長輔, 1865-1938 was the first foreign exchange student sent from the Ryūkyū Kingdom), *Tomigusuku Seiwa* [富城 精和], and *Takamine Chōkoh* [高嶺 朝光, 1854-1924].

One of the hidden keys to understanding Chōtoku's quest for the truth of Karate lies in the events surrounding the establishment of Ryūkyū Shimpo. It becomes evident when we consider that Chōtoku did not join the founding members in their newspaper venture.

Chōtoku's father, Chōfu, had previously managed the accounts of the former king, Sho Tai. Therefore, it is reasonable to assume that Shō Jun, the son of Sho Tai, utilized the funds associated with the Sho family as the initial capital for the conception of "Ryūkyū Shimpo." Being the guardian of the Sho family's resources, Chōfu was well aware of the formation of Ryūkyū Shimpo from its early stages. Given Chōtoku's completion of the highest level of education among his brothers, it would have been natural for Chōfu to nominate him as a founding member.

Natsumi Sōseki, also of Nishogakusha, is the face of Japan's ¥1,000 note

However, Chōtoku was not nominated, and the reason for this becomes clear and will be revealed later. In addition to the story, it could have been possible for Chōtoku to become a founding member of the import company "*Maruichi Shoten*" [丸一商店], which was established in 1883, when Chōtoku was 20 years old. He could have chosen to be employed there, but he did not. The question arises: Why didn't he engage in a fight against resident merchants and attempt to eliminate them from Okinawa as a member of Maruichi Shoten? The reason behind his decision, aligns with Chōtoku's Bushi spirit, and will be revealed shortly.

It is worth noting that many graduates of Nishogakusha pursued careers in education, such as *Kanō Jigorō* , *Natsume Sōseki*, and *Yoshida Kurazo* (the nephew of Yoshida Shoin). Why didn't Chōtoku follow suit and enter the field of education? The explanation will not be provided at this point, but one thing is clear: Chōtoku could not find a compelling reason to become an economist, journalist, or educator in the rapidly developing modern and capitalist society he witnessed. The Tokaido Train Line, enabling direct travel from Tōkyō to Kobe City, was opened when Chōtoku was 19 years old. It had been only 17 years since his father, Chōfu, attended the opening ceremony for the first locomotive between Shinbashi and Yokohama. In a span of just 17 years, the Japanese railroad network extended all the way from Tōkyō to Kobe. This remarkable achievement occurred only ten years after the introduction of the new prefecture system.

Let us compare the swift modernization of Japan with the outdated Okinawan system after the transition. According to *Yamashiro Zenzo*, Okinawa lagged behind in terms of modernization. It was slow to implement student uniforms and caps, collect tuition in middle schools, establish the Nago police station, adopt modern hairstyles for public workers, introduce uniforms for public workers and teachers, worship the picture of the Emperor and Empress in middle schools, enroll girls in elementary schools in Nakagami, develop copper mines in Haneji Kunigami, and transition Okinawa Hospital into a prefectural hospital.

Compared to the enthusiastic promotion of new industries in mainland Japan, Okinawa seemed like a small, tranquil stream in comparison to the resounding beat of progress.

Returning to the story of Tōkyō Station, it is a short walk from Sho Tai's Mansion in Kojimachi Fujimi-cho to Tōkyō Station. Along the way, if you pass through Ginza, you will come across the Imperial Hotel, designed by Frank Lloyd Wright and completed in 1890, located near the Rokumeikan building. Did Chōtoku appear near the Imperial Hotel or Tōkyō Station with his traditional Ryūkyūan hairstyle known as "Katakashira"? It is worth noting that during that time, individuals in Okinawa who chose to adopt modern hairstyles were often labeled as traitors by the Ganko-to party; Chōtoku was one Okinawan who had already cut his hair in the modern Western style.

Even Marquis Sho Tai had adopted the modern hairstyle, influenced further by the implementation of the Hair Cut Act in 1888, around the time Chōtoku enrolled in Nishogakusha College. Baron Shō Jun, the fourth son of Marquis Sho Tai, was only seven years old when he was taken to Tōkyō. When he returned to Okinawa for the opening ceremony of Ryūkyū Shimpo newspaper, he sported a modern, short haircut. According to previous accounts of Okinawan history, many Ganko-to party members were disappointed to see him with this modern hairstyle.

These incidents illustrate that the Ryūkyū Bushi residing in Sho Tai's Mansion in Tōkyō embraced the modernization of Japan and abandoned the traditional Okinawan and Ryūkyūan hairstyles. However, Chōtoku did not agree with this new idea. Western rationalistic concepts did not resonate with him, and he consciously chose not to embrace them.

Although he could understand these ideas intellectually, his heart did not yield to forgiveness or acceptance. Those who stayed with Marquis Sho Tai were expected to conform to the changes in his mansion, including the adoption of modern hairstyles. Chōtoku followed suit, and this became one of the reasons for his delayed return home. He empathized with the unpaid Bushi class in Okinawa and feared being labeled a betrayer or traitor by them. Despite having graduated from Nishogakusha and having numerous job opportunities, he never took advantage of such employment prospects.

* Trans. Note: Efforts are still ongoing to locate the confirmation details of Chōtoku's graduation.

The establishment of the Ryūkyū Shimpo newspaper might lead one to assume that it was created by conservatives aiming to foster dual dependence on China and Japan in Ryūkyū. However, this is not the case. The newspaper was actually founded with the intention of dismantling pro-China sentiments associated with the *Ganko-to Party*. The pro-Japan *Kaika-to Party* directly confronted the pro-Chinese faction, recognizing the changing times. Prince Shō Jun, who had resided in Tōkyō from a young age with his father King Sho Tai, held pro-Japanese views and had a deep understanding of the shifting currents of the era. The Kaika-to Party supported the establishment of the Okinawa Prefecture system in place of the Ryūkyū Clan under the Meiji Government, and sought to rectify the injustices of old Okinawa. Founding members of the Ryūkyū Shimpo, such as Ota Chōfu and Takamine Chokyo, switched their allegiances from the conservative *Gakushuin* to the progressive *Keio Gijuku*, highlighting the growing influence of Western ideas within the public consciousness.

In 1894, the Japanese-Sino War erupted. After a significant victory in the war, even members of the *Ganko-to* Party embraced modern hairstyles, cutting their hair in the latest fashion. *Two years after the Japanese-Sino War, Chōtoku returned home, and only a few unpaid Bushi accused him of being a traitor or criticized him for his modern haircut.* Chōtoku paid great attention to these minor details. Now, let's discuss the *Rokumeikan*, which served as a catalyst for adopting Western lifestyle. Traditional Japanese women's hairstyles shifted to modern styles, and kimonos were replaced by Western dresses. The Rokumeikan became a venue where people showcased their Westernized identity through events, dancing, and attire. Chōtoku likely had the opportunity to witness such modern gatherings.

In 1890, at the age of 20, Chōtoku studied classical Confucian studies directly under Principal Mishima at Nishogakusha. Years later, he reminisced saying, "*I trained in Karate with my father, who was incredibly strict and made me train even in severe weather conditions. He allowed me to have breakfast only after training in the snow. Thanks to the training my father provided, I never caught a cold, became strong, and enjoyed my youth during my nine years in Tōkyō.*"

Using DALL-E software I created this AI-generated image to illustrate how Chōtoku's training might have looked during the Tōkyō winters with his father

Trans Note: Yamashiro Zenzo's book, "Okinawan Social History in the Era of Meiji [1868-1912], Taisho [1912-1926] and Showa [from 1926]," focuses on the social history of cultural, political, and economic development in Okinawan society during those time frames; It explores topics such as the impact of modernization on Okinawa, changes in social structures and class dynamics, educational reforms, historical events, and the experiences of the Okinawan people and provides valuable insights into the transformation and challenges faced as it transitioned from the Ryūkyū Kingdom to becoming a part of modern Japan.

Trans. Note: The Ryūkyū Kingdom had not been free of perpetual and sometimes aggravated class conflict, and the annexation did not change this. Former Ryūkyūan aristocrats were quite conscious of their class interests and identity, and often prioritized them over the interests of Okinawans in general. One early example of this was local officials' resistance to the Miyako Peasants' Movement; Another was the protracted conflict between conservatives and progressives over land reform, taxation, and the terms of Okinawan self-governance. In 1898, for example, the question arose in the course of land reform of whether Okinawans who met tax qualifications should be allowed to vote in nationwide elections. Despite the Ryukyu Shimpō's frequent cries for increased Okinawan self-governance (jichi 自治), the former nobility lobbied against suffrage at this point, arguing that extant land tenure systems would make assessing individual tax qualifications problematic. As critics noted at the time, the former nobility's sole actual motivation was fear of disenfranchisement: their tax-exempt status, protected under the Preservation of Old Customs policy, would have rendered them ineligible to vote. We can deduce from this that when Okinawan elites spoke of jichi, they did not mean self-governance in the contemporary liberal sense of the term. Rather, they meant the maintenance of a semi-autonomous infra-political field within the structure of the state, in which they could continue to monopolize power and resources.

This exemplifies a persistent contradiction between Okinawan elites' political desire to be incorporated as equals into a homogenous national community and their class interest in maintaining the separate customs and institutions that sustained their privilege.

Elites such as Ōta Chōfu and the Shō family realized that they would not receive stipends in perpetuity, and that maintaining their local hegemony would require leveraging status power into economic power. Accordingly, they consolidated their stipends and used them as starting capital in various business ventures. In 1887, backed with capital by the Shō family, the former aristocrat who had managed the Ryūkyū Kingdom's shipping concerns founded a joint stock shipping company (Okinawa kōun kabushiki-gaisha 沖縄広運株式会社). Around the same time, the Shō family began mining operations near Haneji-mura and founded the first major Okinawan trading house in Naha (named Maruichi-shōten 丸一商店).

The Shō family's businesses almost exclusively hired former royal retainers, and reportedly used semi-coercive methods to obtain goods and labour from commoners at below market prices. Despite such "feudalistic business practices," these ventures provided economic and psychological stimulus, inspiring the formation of a number of

Okinawan-owned trading houses in Osaka during the following few decades. In 1899, the Shō family and other stipended former aristocrats moved to further increase their economic presence by founding the Okinawa Agricultural Bank and the Bank of Okinawa.

Their professed aim was to offer loans at lower rates than mainland banks, thereby increasing Okinawan capitalists' competitiveness. Wendy Matsumura describes the Bank of Okinawa clique's ideology as a type of "economic nationalism, that would enable the most benevolent type of exploitation – that of Okinawans by other Okinawans." With the Ryūkyū Shimpō as their mouthpiece, elites advocated insulating the local economy against mainland Japanese incursions by establishing complex capitalistic relations of production directly between Okinawans. In a 1901 article, for example, Ōta Chōfu laments the fact that "there is no clear division between capital owner and worker, and tomorrow's worker is today's capital owner, and vice versa."

More on Shō Jun & Ōta Chōfu, et al
https://en.wikipedia.org/wiki/Shō_Jun_(1873–1945)
https://en.wikipedia.org/wiki/Ōta_Chōfu

The portrait measurements, date and name of the private owner of this photo; i.e. Ikegusuku Anki, who is included in the photo with 4 others, are cited on the back side. L-R: Kin Pēchin, Arasaki Pēchin, Ikegusuku Uēkata, Gushiken Pēchin Unjou & Yamashiro Yamato. Ikegusuku Anki [1829-1877, seated centre], was born in Shuri and went by the Chinese name of Mou Yuhi. Until just before the Ryūkyū Kingdom was abolished, he served as Sanshikan [i.e. one of the three chief officials of the Royal Family], and negotiated on its behalf with Satsuma, the Ryūkyū Islands, and the new Meiji government. He traveled to Tokyo twice and conducted negotiations to ensure the survival of the Ryūkyū Kingdom, but died in Tokyo on, 30 Apr 1877. As he was appointed to the position of Sanshikan in 1874. As the photo is dated, 20 Sep 1871, it was obviously taken before his official appointment.

Translation & photo editing: Patrick McCarthy 2021
Photo courtesy of Hokama Tetsuhiro

Gichin's Impatience

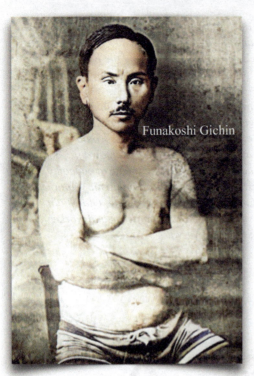
Funakoshi Gichin

Funakoshi Gichin [船越 義珍, 1868-1957], a renowned figure in karate, began his career as a teacher in 1890. Born in 1868 in Shuri Yamakawa village, he was the first son of *Funakoshi Gisue*. In his childhood, he was known as *Umikami*, and his Chinese name was *Yo Gijin*. Funakoshi's family belonged to the *Yo clan* and were *Tomari Bushi*, a branch of the *Yamada* family. They served the Ryūkyū Kingdom as lower-ranked Bushi for generations.

Gichin's grandfather, *Gifuku*, held an important position as a secretary to the *Kikoe-ōgimi [聞得大君], the highest female attendant to the King. However, Gichin's father, Gisue, faced personal challenges, including alcoholism, which led the family to experience a decline in their fortunes.

Trans. Note:
* *Kikoe-ōgimi* [聞得大君/きこゑ大きみ, Okinawan: チフィジン, romanized: Chifi-ufujin) was the highest ranking Noro priestess of the Ryūkyūan religion during the period of the Ryūkyū Kingdom. The position of kikoe-ōgimi was formally established during the reign of King Shō Shin (r. 1477–1526) in order to centralize the religious order. Only a royal woman could be appointed to the position of kikoe-ōgimi. After Ryūkyū's annexation by Japan in 1879, this position was formally abolished, but the last kikoe-ōgimi continued her role until her death in 1944. According to records, Asato Ōshu (安里翁主) was the *Kikoe-ōgimi* at the time of Funakoshi's grandfather; Her Okinawan name was Moushigani (真牛金, 1825-1909) and she was a daughter of King Shō Kō. Source: https://en.wikipedia.org/wiki/Kikoe-%C5%8Dgimi

Due to his premature birth and delicate health, Funakoshi was raised by his maternal grandparents, the *Oyadomari* family. Initially, he aspired to attend medical school but abandoned the idea as it would require him to cut his traditional Bushi hairstyle. Instead, he enrolled in a teacher's school and pursued a career in education. After completing a one-year course at *Okinawa Shihan Gakko*, he passed the certification test to become an assistant teacher and began working as a substitute instructor. He eventually advanced to become a certified teacher.

At the age of 16, Funakoshi studied karate under *Kojo Taitei* [湖城大禎,1837-1917], a prominent karate-ka in Naha, for a period of three months. The reasons behind such a short duration of this training remain unknown, but might be because of Kojo's travel to China. Subsequently, Funakoshi became a student of *Asato Ankoh* [安里 安恒, 1827-c.1906], a respected figure in karate from Shuri. Despite Funakoshi's lineage as a descendant of the Tomari Bushi and Asato's noble background in Shuri, the two actually became acquainted through the friendship of their sons.

The exact duration of Funakoshi's training under Asato remains uncertain, *and the subject of some curiosity*. Asato served under Marquis Sho Tai in Tōkyō for 13 years, starting from 1879, before returning to Okinawa in 1892. It is likely that Funakoshi received instruction from Asato between the ages of 22 and 24. It is worth noting that one of the two monuments erected at the Enkakuji Temple, in Kita-Kamakura, bears a statement that Funakoshi studied karate under Asato Ankoh and Itosu Ankoh from the age of 11, according to *Ōhama Nobumoto* [大濱信泉, 1891–1976], the former President of Waseda University. However, the claim raises questions as we know that Asato was in Tōkyō during the same period. Notwithstanding, Funakoshi excelled in the practicing of Kusanku Kata that he learned under MasterAsato.

Trans. Note: The other stone monument erected at the Enkakuji Temple and dedicated to Funakoshi Gichin bears the inscription; "Karate ni Sente Nishi" [空手に先手無] *"There is no first attack in Karate."*

Inconsistencies in Okinawan karate historical records, are considered a significant weakness. With the global popularity and widespread practice of karate, estimated to be around 50 million or more practitioners, the absence of concrete supporting documents, certainly pose a challenge. Neglecting these *inconsistencies may invite scrutiny and criticism from other countries. Any easily spotted mistakes could undermine the credibility of Ryūkyū karate history, potentially leading to changes in karate rules or the establishment of a world championship tournament under Western influence.

Western countries often tend to exert significant influence and take initiative in various fields. Judo, once a Japanese specialty, has undergone numerous rule changes, making it challenging to differentiate between traditional Japanese judo and Western-style wrestling. This exemplifies how Western countries, with their majority voting power, have revised Asian sport rules to the disadvantage of Asian countries. This not only applies to sports but also extends to economic matters. After the burst of Japan's economic bubble, Moody's Investors Service from the United States rated Japanese banks lower than those of Brazil, which resulted in a slowdown of the Japanese economy.

Stepping aside from this topic, it is important to note that I am not attempting to disrespect Funakoshi Gichin, as Chōtoku, another influential figure, highly praised Gichin for his efforts in promoting karate from the Ryūkyū Islands to Japan. With the passing of time, however, we have witnessed a shift from the individual study of the fighting art, as was embraced by Chōtoku, to a collective practice aimed at reaching the entire nation. *"Funakoshi's contribution of spreading karate, based on the principles of our peaceful culture without arms, has helped karate to flourish throughout the nation."* Chōtoku expressed his gratitude to Gichin as an important Okinawan figure, ensuring the preservation of and dignity of Okinawa as karate's birthplace. Together with karate leaders and their students, Chōtoku emphasized the ongoing dedication to karate and its values in Okinawa.

In conclusion, Funakoshi Gichin's journey as a teacher and karate practitioner, his association with influential figures like Kojo Taitei and Asato Ankoh, and the challenges faced by Okinawan karate in maintaining historical records and credibility, all contribute to the rich and evolving history of karate as a fighting art.

Trans. Note: Considerable advancement has been made in the research and documentation of historical records since Irei Hiroshi's investigation; e.g. "Okinawan Karate Kobudo Jiten," by Kashiwa Shobô, "Karate, It's History & Practice," by Nippon Budokan, "Karate 1.0" by Andreas Quast, and Motobu Naoki's blog at https://medium.com/@motobu715 and/or website Motobu-ryu.org along with many excellent Japanese-to-English translations of the pioneer's original works, etc..

Nine Years in Tōkyō
A Tale of Seasons, Exploration & Growth

In 1892, Chōtoku, a young man of 22, found himself in Tōkyō, marking four years since his arrival in the bustling city. The stark contrast between the endless summer of his native Okinawa and the distinct four seasons of Japan left a lasting impression on him.

A modern look out across the *Chidorigafuchi-pond at Kudanshita with the Tōkyō Budokan in the background*

The grandeur of Marquis Sho Tai's compound, sprawling over 2000 tsubo, resembled the residence of a feudal lord. Located in Kojimachi Fujimi-cho (*now known as Kudan Chiyoda Ward*), it stood in close proximity to Yasukuni Shrine. Chōtoku often traversed the shrine grounds en route to Nishogakusya College. Just a short distance away, he could catch a glimpse of the Statue of *Omura Masujiro* at Yasukuni Shrine by walking about 100 meters along *Chidorigafuchi*, perhaps donning wooden clogs. The picturesque Chidorigafuchi pond, adorned with beautiful cherry blossom trees, remained unchanged even after the passage of a century. Chōtoku likely experienced the ethereal beauty of cherry blossoms, their petals cascading like a gentle shower during sudden spring storms, multiple times during his Tōkyō sojourn.

The memories of Tōkyō for Chōtoku surpassed anything he could have imagined in Okinawa. One vivid recollection was his first encounter with snow at the age of 18, a sight that left an indelible impression. Even four years later, at 22, snow continued to evoke a strong sense of wonder within him. As white snowflakes floated gently from the cloudy winter sky, resembling soft cotton carried by the wind, Chōtoku couldn't help but feel a profound emotional response welling up from deep within his heart.

The Iwasaki Mansion

The Rokumeikan

It was in that winter, four years after his arrival in Tōkyō, that Chōtoku saw frost crystals for the first time and experienced the biting cold of the season. This sensation, unfathomable to those who had never encountered true winter, stirred nostalgic memories of his child-hood in Okinawa. He recalled his mother, *Mamatsu*, making *Mūchi* (rice cake covered with ginger leaves) for him—a heartwarming connection to his past.

Spring arrived, followed by summer, and Chōtoku found solace in the cyclical nature of the seasons, recognizing their vital role in preserving and protecting both nature and the country. The concept of self-defense became fundamental to his understanding of the state's responsibilities. As he witnessed the passing of his sixth winter, Chōtoku's appreciation for the interplay between nature and life deepened.

Mūchi

A mere 20-minute walk down from Kudanshita in Tōkyō, one would arrive at *Kanda Jimbocho*, a lively town frequented by students and renowned for its abundance of second-hand bookstores. A five-minute stroll from Jimbocho would lead to Ochanomizu, where construction on the *Nikorai-dō* (ニコライ堂), *Holy Resurrection Cathedral*, had begun in 1891 when Chōtoku was 21. The cathedral, belonging to the Church of Greece, took seven years to complete under the guidance of architect *Josiah Conder,* known for his involvement in other notable structures like the *Rokumeikan* and *Iwasaki's mansion*. During his walks in the area, Chōtoku observed these foreign residences, finding himself drawn to the contrasting architectural styles—wooden structures reminiscent of Shuri Castle, where his father Chōfu once served, and the sturdy masonry buildings that stood before him.

Heading east from Sho Tai's residence, a short walk of less than ten minutes would lead to *Iidabashi* Station. From there, if one were to head north for about five minutes, they would arrive at Hosei University in *Fujimicho*, Chiyoda Ward. During Chōtoku's time at Nishogakusha, Tōkyō Futsu Gakkou underwent a name change to Hosei University in accordance with the University Act of 1920. The university, founded in the early Meiji era, aimed to educate high-level legal professionals.

Taking a straight path from Sho Tai's mansion to Nishogakusha and continuing further, one would eventually reach Hanzomon. By continuing straight, Chōtoku could venture into Akasaka, catching a glimpse of the Crown Prince's Residence on the right, before eventually reaching the vibrant neighborhoods of Aoyama and Shibuya. On the other hand, turning right at Hanzomon would lead to the Yotsuya area. By continuing onward, Chōtoku would encounter Shinjuku, with the picturesque Shinjuku Gyoen Park located on the right.

These areas were easily accessible on foot, and Chōtoku likely took walks to Akasaka, Yotsuya, and Shinjuku for various purposes. Not only did he engage in his karate training, but he also indulged in his passion for collecting antiques. In the rapidly changing Meiji Era, valuable artifacts from older eras could be found, and Chōtoku found joy in preserving these remnants of the past. This period marked the youth of Chōtoku, who had journeyed to Tōkyō at the age of 18 alongside his father Chōfu and his older brother *Chōhitsu*.

During his nine years in Tōkyō, Chōtoku experienced the beauty of the seasons, marveled at the architecture and cultural landmarks, and expanded his horizons through education and exploration. His time in the capital city left an indelible mark on his growth as a martial artist and his appreciation for the intersection of tradition and modernity.

Chōtoku's Decision

In 1893, at the age of 23, Chōtoku faced a pivotal moment. The *Asahi Shinbun* reported that, "*Kimigayo*" would become the official national anthem of Japan. During this time, Chōfu, Chōtoku's father, had been absent from the Marquis' residence for several months.

Living in the Sho Family mansion were not only the Kyan family but also many former Ryūkyū Bushi who had relocated to Tōkyō after the implementation of the new social system in Okinawa. It was likely that Chōtoku heard about the upcoming establishment of the Ryūkyū Shimpo [newspaper] in Okinawa from *Hiyagon Ankoh*, who said, "*Hey Chōtoku, father told me yesterday, as he had just returned from Okinawa, that Prince Shō Jun will soon establish the Ryūkyū Shimpo in Okinawa.*"

Baron *Shō Jun* In Western attire

Chōtoku had prior knowledge of the Ryūkyū Shimpo several months in advance. His father, Chōfu, had discussed the purpose and the how and why of the newspaper with him. Goeku Choi, whose wife, *Mazurugani,* the daughter of Marquis Sho Tai, would be involved with the newspaper company.

Chōfu, having an idea in mind, casually asked Chōtoku, a recent graduate of Nishogakusha, about taking a job with the newspaper. Chōtoku's unexpected response was, "*I won't work with Ryūkyū Shimpo.*" Chōfu realized that he couldn't force Chōtoku to work for Ryūkyū Shimpo if he clearly didn't want to. As mentioned before, *the purpose of publishing Ryūkyū Shimpo was to counter the influence of the Ganko-to Party (Pro-Qing Dynasty) and propagate the pro-Japanese perspective; He knew this and that reporting would be biased and lack independence.* Chōtoku was not the type to calculate advantages and simply support the winning side. During his time in Tōkyō, he had gained an understanding of society through his studies and future occupation. He knew he needed to prepare himself mentally to face society through his chosen career path. *The notion of "Japanese spirit with western talent" had resonated with Chōtoku, but he found it challenging to satisfy himself, and it troubled him deeply.*

Prince Shō Jun, born on 2 May, 1873, was the fourth son of King Sho Tai and three years younger than Chōtoku. His mother was *Matsugawa Anji*, and he was also known as *Prince Matsuyama* or *Matsuyama Udon*. His pseudonym was *Rosen*. He married *Shinko*, the first daughter of *Izena Choboku*. When he was seven years old, he accompanied his father to Tōkyō and returned to Okinawa at the age of 20 in 1892 with his elder brother *Sho Inn*. In 1893, he co-founded *Ryūkyū Shimpo* with *Ōta Chōfu*, *Goeku Choi*, *Tomigusuku Seiwa*, and *Takamine Choko*. In 1899, he established *Okinawa Ginko* [bank]. *Shō Jun* also founded an import company and established a farm along with introducing pineapples and other plants to Okinawa. *Shō Jun* had six sons and ten daughters but tragically lost his life, along with his wife, first, third, and fourth sons, and his grandsons *Sho Chusho* and *Sho Chusei*, during World War II when he was 72 years old.

Baron Shō Jun arrived in Tōkyō at the age of seven, accompanying his father. He was deeply influenced by Western thought and embraced the ideals of a modernized Japan. As a child raised in a civilized society, he held disdain for the traditional Ryūkyū Bushi and the Ganko to Party, rejecting the remnants of the old ways. The publication of Ryūkyū Shimpo aimed to civilize and modernize Okinawa while criticizing the defenders of established interests.

King Sho Tai, recognizing the changing world trends during his visit to Tōkyō, underwent a shift in his mindset regarding the "*dominion rule*" policy and ultimately relinquished his royal status. Having resided in Tōkyō since 1879, he witnessed the rise of powerful Western nations and their encroachment into Asia. He was also aware of the fall of the Qing Dynasty and the increasing colonization by Western powers.

During that time, there was a profound cultural divide, and the flow of information between Sho Tai in Tōkyō and Kamegawa Uekata of the Ganko to Party in Okinawa was severely limited. Kamegawa Uekata was faced with the challenge of resolving issues related to unpaid Bushi resulting from the social upheavals in Okinawa. While it is true that Sho Tai had the advantage of being on the winning side, Kamegawa Uekata lacked such luxury. Chōtoku, however, did not possess practical ideas due to his limited life experience.

Baron *Shō Jun* 尚 順 age 45

Chōtoku firmly believed in the principle that Bushi lived by duty while merchants pursued profit, an ideology deeply ingrained in him. Chōfu, understanding his son's perspective, did not pressure Chōtoku to seek employment. It was when Chōtoku turned 24 years old that the war between Japan and the Qing Dynasty, known as the Japanese-Sino War, erupted. Foreign Minister Mutsu Munemitsu, who led the war, recalled that the main cause of the conflict was the power struggle between Japan and the Qing Dynasty over control of the Korean Peninsula.

Imperial Japan invaded China, while China held *suzerainty* over the Korean Peninsula during that period, in its pursuit of expanding Japanese territory. The motivations behind Japan's aggression towards the Ryūkyū Islands and the Korean Peninsula stemmed from its ambitions to build a modern state and empire, as well as its aspirations to analyze and adopt Western trends and establish a partition of Asia. Japan aimed to exert dual control over the ancient regime alongside China, but ultimately, Japan emerged as the dominant power in the Asian countries. The Qing Dynasty in China had already experienced significant divisions and weakening due to Western interventions following the Opium War. In a similar vein, Korea, out of respect for the declining Qing Dynasty, followed suit and aligned itself with Japan's increasing dominance in the region.

The Japan-Sino war had a deeper underlying truth: it served as a counter policy against Russia's "*Go southward*" strategy and the expansionist agendas of other Western countries. During the winter, Vladivostok, a Russian port, became immobilized by freezing waters, limiting their naval capabilities. Russia aimed to colonize Korea and gain access to the Yellow Sea, intending to establish a military port there for year-round maneuvers.

The importance of having an "*unfrozen*" military port for the Russian Navy cannot be understated. This invasion of the Yellow Sea raised concerns for both China and Japan. China found it troublesome that Russia was encroaching on its territory, while Japan worried about potential invasions by either China or Russia into the Korean Peninsula.

The Leaders of the Okinawa Middle School Strike Incident

Korea, a Confucian state, lagged behind in modernizing its country. In this Confucian society, force was seen as despicable, and civilians maintained control over the military. Both the Korean Dynasty and the Ryūkyū Kingdom were considered vassal states of the Qing Dynasty, with both countries acknowledging Qing's authority as a colonial power.

The new Meiji government in Japan focused on centralizing power, promoting cultural enlightenment, and bolstering military strength within its borders. It challenged existing treaties, tested its borders with neighboring countries, and established modern diplomatic relations with the Qing Dynasty under international law in international affairs.
As a result of Japan's modern diplomacy, the Japan-Sino war erupted, leading to the dissolution of the vassal relationships between the Ryūkyūs and Qing Dynasty and between Korea and the Qing Dynasty.

In the Ryūkyūs, the Ganko-to Party pinned its hopes on China for salvation and fiercely resisted the New Meiji government. They staunchly refused to cut their traditional hairstyles and resisted integration into the modern school system. Sabotaging official duties was another form of revolt. Surprisingly, a report at the time stated that 80% of Okinawans still maintained the traditional "*katakashira*" hairstyle. However, Japan's victory in the Japan-Sino war weakened the Ganko-to Party, despite their bravado. In the subsequent phase, they eventually adopted modern hairstyles and attire—an ironic demonstration of opportunism during that era.

An outbreak occurred in November of 1895 at Okinawa Middle School [aka "First Middle School" and currently, "Shuri High School"] to protest against Principal Kodama's abolishment of the English department; Caused by *Kanna Kenwa*, *Iha Fuyu*, and *Majikina Ankoh,* Kanna was expelled over the incident but later entered the Naval Academy, becoming the first student from Okinawa to do so. He achieved remarkable academic results, ranking fourth out of 123 admitted students. In the future, he would become the commander of the imperial battleship, "Katori," upon which the Crown Prince [Emperor Showa] would visit Okinawa [6 March 1921] while en route to Europe.

After a nine-year absence, Chōtoku returned to Okinawa the year following the strike at First Middle School and Kan-na Kenwa's enrollment in the Naval Academy. Chōtoku had settled down in Tōkyō, attending Nishogakusha and embracing the life of a city student with a modern hairstyle. However, the Ganko-to Party in Okinawa labeled a man with a modern hairstyle as a traitor. This may be one of the reasons why Chōtoku chose not to return to Okinawa and remained in the Sho Tai residence for eight years without employment.

In 1896, Chōtoku returned to Okinawa, two years after the conclusion of the Japan-Sino War. His modern hairstyle symbolized a departure from the traditions of the unpaid samurai in Okinawa. While he knew this was acceptable in Tōkyō, it was an act that was not forgiven in Okinawa.

Chōtoku's first teacher was Matsumura Sokon, and his studies led him to Nishogakusha, where he encountered his second teacher, Mishima Chūshū. Both teachers emphasized righteousness in their teachings, and Chōtoku's adherence to righteousness aligned with the spirit of the Okinawan Bushi. However, the Meiji modernization movement was bringing societal benefits at the time. Chōtoku grappled with an inner conflict between the benefits of civilization and the righteousness of the samurai spirit. Despite the potential opportunities such as working at Maruichi Company, Ryūkyū Shimpo, or becoming a school teacher, Chōtoku chose to return home. At 26 years old, he embarked on a new chapter filled with trials, discipline, and virtuous living in his birthplace of Okinawa.

"*At the age of 26, I returned home due to family matters and learned Karate from Matsumura Kosaku Sensei and Oyadomari Pēchin Sensei. The Karate masters of that time respected one another and taught their specialized skills and techniques. If I inquired about a Kata [i.e. skill] that was not his specialty, the Sensei would introduce me to the master of that particular skill. They sought a balanced approach, and I found it to be a beautiful thing.*"

Upon his return home, Chōtoku sought to learn from the foremost Karate-ka of that time, revealing his true thoughts and motivations. His determination was unstoppable. Although he could have pursued a career as a school teacher, a businessman, or a journalist, material wealth and conventional jobs held no appeal to him. His true desire was to explore the depths of Ryūkyū Karate. Immediately upon returning home after an eight-year absence, he devoted himself to this pursuit.

My deepest gratitude to the late Irei Hiroshi; historian, researcher, author and gracious host; RIP

Trans. Note: Leveraging AI-generated imagery alongside an extensive array of vintage photos subjected to restoration, enhancement, and colorization, the intention here was to cleverly craft a visual narrative featuring an assembly of Karate dignitaries seamlessly united within a reconstructed dojo. This collective pantheon of Karate luminaries provides a vivid and enthralling window into a bygone era of intrigue, research and creativity.

Masters of Shōrin-ryu; Kyan Chōtoku
by Graham Noble

Editor's note: This article has been edited and is reprinted with the permission of Graham Noble

The Life and Times of Kyan Chōtoku

Kyan Chōtoku was born into a high-ranking family in Shuri in 1870. His father Chōfu was a steward to [Sho] Tai, the last king of the Ryūkyūs. According to Nagamine Shōshin, Kyan Chōfu was such an able person that the king entrusted him with much of the business of the royal household.

In 1871 the Japanese government declared that the Ryūkyū Kingdom was to become part of Japanese territory and renamed Ryūkyū Han (fief). A few years later the islands were fully integrated into the Japanese local government system as Okinawa Prefecture. As a process of Japanisation began, the old Ryūkyū Kingdom was swept away.

King [Sho] Tai was deposed with the foundation of Ryūkyū Han. In 1879 he was removed to Japan and kept there for five years. He took with him over 90 retainers. Kyan Chōfu went with the king and took with him his young son, Chōtoku.

Located on the opposite side of the Hija River, left of the middle with the thatched-roof, is the Kyan Family home built in 1910. * Photo courtesy of Irei Hiroshi

Kyan Chōfu, a cultivated man with knowledge of both Chinese and Japanese literature, had been opposed to Japan's takeover of Okinawa. Ikeda Hoshu has in his possession a petition against the Japanese measures, and one of the seven signatories is Kyan. He was a traditionalist who did not want the old ways to die out, and it seems that it was he who kindled Kyan Chōtoku's enthusiasm for karate.

According to Funakoshi Gichin in *Karate-do Nyumon*, Kyan Chōfu himself had some knowledge of *te*, but although he trained his young son in wrestling (probably Okinawan *sumo*) to toughen him up, he entrusted the teaching of karate forms to others. Nagamine Shōshin believes that this was because he was too fond of Chōtoku to train him the correct, severe way. Anyway, at age 20, Kyan Chōtoku was put under the tutelage of famous experts: Oyadomari Kokan, Matsumora Kosaku, and Itosu Ankoh.

Kyan Chōtoku's biographers all state that he was small and weak as a child and this we can believe, because even when fully grown he was slightly built and frail looking. He looked more like a retiring scholar than a karate master, and as Tamae Hiroyasu (1906-1985) wrote, "*You were amazed that such a small man was so great a bujin.*"

Kyan had a strong personality that belied his small physique, and by the age of 30 he was recognised as an expert in both Shuri-te and Tomari-te. He was challenged often, and as he was not a person to back down, he had to fight frequently. As far as Okinawan karate historians are aware, he was never beaten in these fights. Because of Kyan's size he did not train to trade punches with bigger men but would practice stepping and other evasive techniques by the banks of the Hija River, over and over again. His method of fighting was to defend and then counterattack immediately. He was known to be an expert in kicking techniques, and altogether we can imagine him as a perfect example of the Shōrin-ryu stylist as described by Funakoshi Gichin: a smaller, lighter man whose karate was marked by quickness and mobility.

"*He excelled in practical fighting and had great confidence and power,*" wrote Tamae Hiroyasu. "*We all know of the famous incident when he threw the wrestler over the parapet of the bridge.*"

Well, as it happens... I don't know about that incident, unless it is another version of the tale told by Nagamine Shōshin. This happened when Kyan was about 40 years old and working as a wagon driver. He crossed the path of Matsuda, a big, strong fellow who was bullying the younger men of the village. When Kyan reproached him for his behaviour, Matsuda turned on him and challenged him to fight. He was aware that Kyan knew karate but felt that he would be too small and slight to make use of this in a real fight. When the two men met on the banks of the Hija River, Kyan took up a natural stance with his back to the water. As Matsuda went for him Kyan evaded the attack and countered with a kick that sent the big man into the river.

The abdication of the king and the establishment of Okinawa Prefecture led to the abolition of the old social ranking system and the loss of privileges and financial support for aristocrats. Kyan's family suffered in this way, and Kyan Chōtoku, whose father had been a retainer and friend of the king himself, found himself having to make ends meet by breeding silkworms and pulling a rickshaw. Yet throughout (or because of) all this, his enthusiasm for karate never diminished.

Kyan taught karate at the Okinawan College of Agriculture and the Kadena Police Station, and besides this he taught many other students directly. He and his students would demonstrate karate in the region around his home at Kadena. Apart from karate he would often teach his pupils the traditional dancing done at Okinawan festivals. Evidently he believed that these dances were related in some way to karate, and in this he was not alone. "*If you go into the Okinawan countryside you will often see men performing a traditional dance to the music of the shamisen [aka Sanshin]*," Funakoshi Gichin wrote in his first book, *Ryūkyū Kempo Karate* (1922). "*This dancing resembles karate and is different from the usual maikata dancing. I think it is related to traditional Okinawa te.*"

Kyan Sensei had many students but according to Murakami Katsumi his two favourites were Arakaki Ankichi and Shimabuku Taro. Murakami's section on Kyan in his book *Karate-do to Ryūkyū Kobudo* throws light on another side of the man's character. It is entitled "*Sensei Kyan Chōtoku: absorbing virtues as well as sins*," meaning that here was someone who lived life to the full.

According to Murakami, Kyan not only taught Arakaki and Shimabuku karate but also encouraged them to do many other things, including drinking and visiting the local brothel, on the grounds that an experience of everything is important for martial arts development. So it was that at times he would train these two students in the brothel.

Well, Funakoshi Gichin too had as one of his precepts, "*Do not think karate is only in the dojo*," but I don't think this was what he had in mind. Nevertheless, there was something behind Kyan's method. He stressed to his students that whatever they did they should keep in their minds the idea of *busai*, or correct martial way. I am not sure exactly what this involves. Perhaps it means that to some extent you should remain unattached to whatever you are doing and keep a clear mind and a strong spirit, whether drinking, visiting a brothel -- or even pulling a rickshaw.

Both Arakaki Ankichi and Shimabuku Taro would visit Kyan Sensei's home for training at night. They carried lanterns to light their way but Kyan told them to stop using the lanterns so that they could develop their night vision. When they trained at night he chose uneven terrain and sometimes even threw water on the ground to make a foothold difficult. In this way they developed their kata.

Kyan Chōtoku was fond of cockfighting and would often carry a fighting cock around with him. On one such occasion Arakaki and Shimabuku, wanting to test their teacher's ability, started a quarrel with a gang of young men and then ran off, leaving Kyan to face the group alone. The men attacked Kyan who quickly proceeded to beat them, still holding the bird under one arm. Even Arakaki and Shimabuku, who watched from a distance, were surprised at how he fought using only his feet and one free arm.

Toku Sanpo
徳三宝 1887-1945

Kyan's wife had to work hard as a dyer of cloth and pig breeder, but whenever a pig was ready for sale Kyan himself always insisted on taking it to the market. Murakami writes that Kyan would often cheat his wife of the money he received and use it to pay for women and travel. He liked to travel and on one occasion took Arakaki and Shimabuku to Hokkaido where they demonstrated karate in a large tent. When a local fighter named *Toku Sanpo* challenged them Kyan counseled Arakaki to step back carefully to the walls of the tent, then knock the challenger down if he moved on him. Unfortunately, Murakami does not tell us if a fight actually ensued or, if it did, what was the result.

It's too bad we don't have more information on this incident, but the story of another challenge match was given in a Japanese magazine. It occurred in Taiwan in c.1930, when Kyan's demonstration of karate somehow resulted in a challenge from *Ishida Shinzô*, judo instructor of Taipei Police Headquarters.

Kyan would have been 60 years old at the time but he agreed to the match straightaway. The only thing that concerned him a little was that the judoka might be able to take a firm grip to apply his throwing techniques. Because of this Kyan wore a vest on his upper body rather than a judo jacket.

Ishida himself was wary of karate's striking techniques and when the two men faced each other they kept their distance for some time, sizing each other up. Then suddenly Kyan closed in, thrusting his thumb into the side of Ishida's mouth and fiercely gripping his cheek. With a kick to the knee he knocked Ishida to the ground and followed him down. Kneeling astride the judoka he delivered a *tsuki* (thrust) to the solar plexus, just stopping short of full contact. Ishida immediately conceded the match.

Murakami Katsumi

All in all Kyan Chōtoku comes across to us as one of the most attractive karate masters, an interesting mixture of vices and virtues. No doubt he had his faults but he also had personal qualities which earned him the loyalty of his students and the respect of other experts and he remains one of the most important figures in Okinawan karate history. Even Murakami Katsumi, who tells us of Kyan visiting brothels and cheating his wife out of money, does not do so out of any desire to put him down. In fact he describes Kyan as one of the greatest karate experts.

Like Chibana Choshin, Kyan Sensei stressed that the way to success in karate was found through constant practice. He continued to train and teach throughout his life. Tamae Hiroyasu remembered him giving a demonstration when he was in his late sixties:

"In Showa 13 (1938) there was a demonstration of karate in which many famous experts were invited to display their kata. I was there, and many of the experts did not perform themselves -- they let their students do it. Only Kyan Sensei, in spite of the fact that he was nearly 70 years old, performed his own kata. At that time people over 60 were considered to be old and infirm but Kyan Sensei performed the kata at full power without displaying any infirmity. Only when he stepped down from the platform did he stumble slightly. The audience was impressed."

When Nagamine Shōshin opened his karate dojo in 1942 Kyan Chōtoku gave a demonstration of *passai* and a *bo* [staff] kata.[1] "*His beautiful performance at the age of 73 could still exalt his audience to the quintessence of karate-do,*" Nagamine recalled.

In April 1945 the Americans invaded Okinawa and during the next two months of heavy fighting at least 60,000 Okinawan civilians died. Master Kyan survived all this but at 75 his body was too weak to withstand the following privations and he died in September 1945.

Kyan's Kata

Kyan concentrated his teaching on seven (or perhaps eight) kata. These kata and the teachers from whom he is believed to have learned them are as follows [2]

Kata	Teacher
Ananku	Developed by Kyan Chōtoku
Wanshu	Maeda Pēchin
Chintō	Matsumora Kosaku
Passai	Oyadomari Kokan
Kusanku	Yara of Chatan
Seisan	Matsumura Sōkon
Gojushiho	Matsumura Sōkon

* Note: The chart has been edited by myself [P. McCarthy] based upon subsequent research and conversations with Dan Smith & Shimabukuro Zenpo; Ananku seems to have actually been developed by Kyan when bringing pieces of Seisan & Passai together for the purpose of teaching beginners; An idea originally pioneered by Itosu Ankoh [e.g. Pinan-gata] and, believed to have been brought to fruition by Kyan while in Taiwan. Upon his return, Ananku became the introductory practice taught to beginners and in particular, after he started teaching at the Agricultural School.

Clearly, if these attributions are correct, Kyan studied with a variety of masters, most of them famous during their day. I have no information on Maeda, but since *Wanshu* is always regarded as a Tomari kata we can be fairly sure that he was an expert in *Tomari-te*. The most famous Tomari-*te* master was Matsumora Kosaku, and he was one of Kyan's teachers. Oyadomari Kokan is less well known but in the opinion of Ikeda Hoshu he was equally as great as Matsumora. He was an officer on the staff of the Ryūkyū Royal Family and was often called Oyadomari *Pēchin*.

Chatan Yara [DOB 1816-?], was a teacher of what would become known as Shuri-te; Matsumura Sōkon I have written about elsewhere. Both these masters would have been in their seventies or eighties when Kyan began studying karate, and we cannot be sure they were even teaching at that time. Rather than learning direct, Kyan may have learned from their senior students.

There are two accounts of how Kyan learned *Ananku*. I have never felt particularly happy about the story that he learned it from a Taiwanese expert in Chinese boxing, mainly because the kata does not look Chinese. Still, in February 1941 the *Japan Times* published a photo of some men doing what looked like karate above this caption: "*A new form of defense has been worked out by Sai Chōkō* [蔡長庚 *aka Tsai Chōkō*], *of Formosa, combining points of judo and a kind of boxing perfected in the Loochoo Islands.*" So perhaps Kyan learned the kata from some Okinawan who lived in Taiwan. An alternative version is that his father taught him the kata. Another possibility, of course, is that Kyan developed the kata himself.

Kyan also may have taught *Naihanchin*, and if he did he would have learned it from Ankoh Itosu. Kyan is usually given in karate genealogies as a student of Itosu but generally his kata are quite different from the Itosu versions so I don't think the teaching here can have been very extensive. It is notable that Chibana Choshin, in listing Itosu's students, did not name Kyan. Instead Chibana referred to Kyan as a student of Oyadomari.

Kyan's favourite kata, which he often performed at demonstrations, were *Chintō*, *Passai*, and *Kusanku*. They are distinctive kata with significant variations in technique from the more widely practiced forms such as those of the Japanese Shotokan, Wado, or Shito schools. For instance, rather than the sequence of forearm blocks at the beginning of *Passai*, the Kyan (Oyadomari) *Passai* has a quite different sequence of sharper, open handed techniques. In *Chintō* (*Gankaku* in Shotokan), the two turns at the start of the kata are done in the opposite direction to those in the Itosu version. In the kicking techniques, rather than bringing the foot to the knee before kicking from a one-legged stance, it is brought behind the other foot into a *kosa-dachi* (crossed stance) and the kick is launched from this position. Ikeda Hoshu refers to these forms as *koryu*, or old style, and although Kyan may have made his own changes to the kata, much of the old style must have remained.

In his short memoir of Kyan Chōtoku, Tamae Hiroyasu mentioned an interesting thing. He wrote that other Shuri karate experts referred to Kyan's kata as *inaka-de*, or primitive; *In his translation Prof Karasawa explained that the words have something of a "country yokel" implication.* As I said, his kata do have their own character, but there are several reasons why such a view could have arisen.

First, to anyone who was used to the more widespread Itosu versions of the kata, Kyan's forms may well have looked a little strange; but this was mainly a question of unfamiliarity.

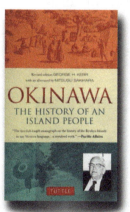

Second, Kyan's kata showed strong Tomari-*te* influences and Shuri Karate-ka tended to look down on Tomari kata as in some way inelegant or unrefined. Apart from any technical considerations this may have been part of a general feeling on the part of Shuri people that their culture was superior to that of the rest of Okinawa. *George Kerr*, an authority on Okinawan history, wrote: "*The pre-eminence of Shuri families and the privileges and advantages conferred automatically through residence at the king's capital, created a tradition of prestige which has persisted into the 20th century, for wherever Okinawans assemble for the first time, in Ryūkyū, in Japan, or in overseas communities, it is quickly but tactfully established if a man has been born in Shuri, educated in Shuri, or has married a woman of Shuri, in that order of precedence.*"

Third, it seemed that *Kyan did make his own changes to the kata*. As Tamae noted: "*Even when the kata was a well known one Kyan Sensei's version had strange additions and gestures. So an expert, even if he only glimpsed part of the kata could identify it as one of Kyan's.*"

Well, if some other experts did refer to Kyan's kata in a rather negative way I think it was mainly a question of style prejudice -- a case of his kata differing from the prevailing form. Personally I can't see that his kata are in any way inferior to other forms. In fact, in the case of *passai* and *Chintō* I prefer his kata to more widely practiced versions. The opening defensive sequences in Kyan's *passai* for example seem less cumbersome than the series of forearm blocks in the Itosu *Passai dai* and his *Chintō* in particular is light, sharp, and full of vitality. I guess it all boils down to personal tastes.

Endnotes
EN1. The staff kata would have been *Tokumine no kun*, which Kyan viewed as useful for preserving traditional Ryūkyūan culture and improving physical development.

EN2. According to an interview with Chibana Choshin conducted on 16 October, 1966 by the Okinawa Karate Do Association, Kyan's *Chintō* and *passai* kata were distinctive, and based on extensive personal knowledge of *te*. His *Kusanku* kata was learned from a direct descendent of Chatan Yara, and is today called *Yara Kusanku*. Kyan brought *Ananku* to Okinawa from Taiwan during the early 1930s, and then taught it at the College of Agriculture and Forestry. Nakazato Joen was a student at the College of Agriculture and Forestry at the time, and is one of the few modern teachers to have learned this kata directly from Kyan.

Chanmī - Kyan Chōtoku
by Graham Noble

Editor's note: This article has been edited and is reprinted with the permission of Graham Noble

Chibana Choshin

Chibana Choshin recalled that *"Kyan Chōtoku Sensei, nicknamed Chanmī was born in Shuri, moved to Kadena, and died after the last war at the age of seventy-five. He was the same age as Funakoshi Gichin and fifteen years older than me. He received his karate tuition from a sensei called Oyadomari who lived in Tomari. As we both used to give demonstrations together I came to know him very well. He used to demonstrate Chintō, Passai and Kusanku kata. He was a great man."*

Kyan Chōtoku was born into a high ranking family in 1870 in Gibo village, Shuri, one of twelve children, apparently (six boys and six girls, according to Nakazato Joen). He was the third son of Kyan Chōfu, a steward to King Shō Tai, the last king of the Ryūkyūs. Nagamine Shōshin wrote that Kyan Chōfu was a capable administrator and King Shō Tai entrusted him with much of the business of the royal household. Chōfu, apparently, was part of the *Ishin Keigashi*, the Meiji Restoration congratulatory delegation which went from the Ryūkyūs to Tōkyō in 1872. It was during this visit that the Japanese government announced that the Ryūkyū Kingdom was to be abolished. From then on the Ryūkyūs were no longer an independent kingdom, but became Ryūkyū Han, a part of Japanese territory, and Shō Tai was effectively deposed as King, becoming a Japanese Marquis [*i.e. Japan's Kazoku System* 華族; *"Magnificent or Exalted Lineage" was the hereditary peerage of the new Empire, existing between 1869 and 1947*].

This was a bitter pill for the Ryūkyū ruling classes, and then in 1879 the islands were fully integrated into the Japanese local government system as Okinawa-ken, Okinawa prefecture. In 1879 too, Shō Tai was removed to Japan and he remained there until his death in 1901, only returning to Okinawa once, in 1884, to pay respects to his ancestors. He took over ninety retainers with him to Tōkyō and one of them was Kyan Chōfu.

According to one account Chōfu relocated to Tōkyō in 1881, and Nakamoto Masahiro wrote that he stayed with the Sho family in Tōkyō as the house steward, *"and had great prestige among all the people in the house."* Nakamoto added that Kyan Chōfu's stay in Tōkyō is confirmed until 1892 but some time after that he returned to Okinawa and retired to Kume village. Nagamine Shōshin thought that after Kyan Chōfu's assignment in Tōkyō was completed, the Kyan family returned to Okinawa and lived between Shuri and Mawashi in Naha's Takaraguchi district.

Nakazato Joen, in his book *"Kyudo,"* stated that Kyan Chōtoku began to take lessons in martial arts from his father at the age of six, which would give a date of 1876, and joined his father in Japan at the age of about twelve, so in 1882 or thereabouts. Nagamine also believed that Chōtoku went to Tōkyō to be with his father at the age of twelve and was there up to the age of sixteen (1886), while Nakazato suggested that he stayed much longer. Nakazato thought though, that he would often travel between Tōkyō and Okinawa on matters relating to the ex-King.

Nakamoto Masahiro wrote that Kyan Chōtoku returned to Okinawa when he was around twenty years old (1890), and Nagamine gives twenty as the age at which he began studying karate under famous experts Matsumura Sōkon, Ankoh Itosu and Oyadomari Kokan. Nakazato simply stated that, as Kyan Chōtoku grew up he trained under experts Matsumura Sōkon, Matsumora Kosaku and Oyadomari Kokan. *"Sensei indeed became a true expert in Shuri."*

In a 1942 article published in the *"Okinawa Shinpo"* (*"My memories of Karate,"* 7 May, 1942) Kyan himself wrote that he had been small and weak as a child and that from being a boy his father had made him wrestle with his older brother *Chōhitsu*. At the age of fifteen his father had begun to teach him *Te* [手] and then at sixteen had taken him to the famous Matsumura Sōkon. Chōtoku studied with Matsumura for two years and learned Gojushiho kata from him. After that he moved to Tōkyō and stayed there nine years. He wrote that he returned to Okinawa when he was twenty six and then continued his study of karate with Matsumora

Kosaku and others. That gives dates of around 1888 to 1896 for Kyan Chōtoku's time in Japan, which contradicts the dates given by Nagamine and the others, but there is a problem here too.

If Kyan Chōfu began teaching Chōtoku Te [手] when he was fifteen, (1885) and took him to see Matsumura when he was sixteen (1886), that suggests that he, Chōfu, must have been in Okinawa during that time period, and that is at odds with the idea that he was resident in Tōkyō with the deposed king from 1881. But really, who knows what the history was?

It is all confusing and contradictory, and in the usual complete absence of any documentary evidence, we can't be sure of anything about Kyan Chōtoku's early years, the time he spent in Japan, who his teachers were, and when he studied with them.

In one of his blogs, ("*Snippet on Kyan Chōfu,*" blog 13 Mar 2016), Andreas Quast quoted from a 1915 book "*Characters at the Time of the Abolition of the Feudal System,*" which stated that Kyan Chōfu "*distinguished himself in the bugei (martial arts) and owned an extraordinary physique. After he had moved to Tōkyō in 1881 as a vice-steward to Shō Tai, the last king of Ryūkyū, he never neglected the practice of the bugei. Even on chilling cold winter daybreaks, with the cold wind blowing down from Mount Tsukuba he would go out to the courtyard to practice thrusting the straw post (makiwara), karate, kenjutsu, as well as other martial arts. Only after finishing practice would he go back inside to have breakfast, during which he easily consumed the extreme quantity of 10 bowls of food, or five pound of pork during one meal, which is indeed astonishing.*"

Interestingly, Kyan Chōtoku is not mentioned in that passage, but the tradition is that Chōfu was a stern taskmaster and that when they were in Japan he trained Chōtoku in all conditions. In his book on Okinawan karate masters Nagamine Shōshin recalled "*Sometime around the year 1932 I was working at the Kadena police station. The head of that station in those days was a man named Hiyagon Ankoh. I remember Mr. Hiyagon once telling me a story about when Kyan and his father lived in Tōkyō. The father of Hiyagon Ankoh, like Kyan's father, had once been employed by the Sho family and was a former Peichin [aka Pēchin].*

When it got cold in Tōkyō, Hiyagon Ankoh and his brother often snuggled together under the kotatsu (a table covered by a quilt to contain the heat source from underneath) to keep warm. Whenever he did this, Hiyagon's father would scold them by saying 'You are the sons of a Peichin, don't be such cowards! Did you know that Chōtoku and his father always train outside on such miserable days!'

What that training consisted of we can't be sure. The translation of Nagamine's technical book ("*The Essence of Okinawan Karate Do*") says that it was in "*sumo and karate wrestling*," but it's not clear what "*karate wrestling*" could have been. In fact, it's not really clear how much karate Kyan Chōfu knew: apart from that old 1915 reference there seems to be almost no evidence on this. In his section on Chōfu, in his 2006 book "Kobudo", Nakamoto Masahiro wrote quite a bit on his lineage and his career in the Sho administration, but had virtually nothing to say about his experience in karate beyond that "*he excelled in martial arts*." All we can say is that Kyan Chōfu seems to have known some karate, and that may have stirred Chōtoku's interest in the art. Not surprisingly, Chōfu had been against the Japanese takeover of the Ryūkyūs. Ikeda Hoshu, in his book "*Karate Do Shugi*," refers to a petition asking for the postponement of the Ryūkyū Shobun, and one of the seven signatories is Kyan Peichin, who Ikeda assumes to be Kyan Chōtoku's father. Chōfu, then, was a traditionalist who did not want the old ways to die out and it is often said that it was he who encouraged young Kyan Chōtoku's study of karate, although the young Chōtoku probably didn't need much encouragement in that direction anyway: he seemed to have been one of those people who have a natural attraction to, and talent for, karate.

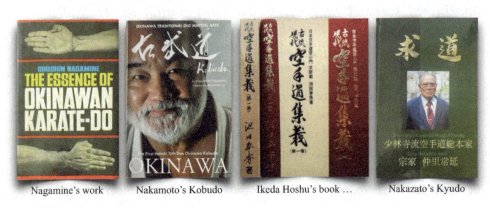

Nagamine's work   Nakamoto's Kobudo   Ikeda Hoshu's book …   Nakazato's Kyudo

Nakazato Joen, in his book "*Kyudo,*" wrote, '*Once when Kyan Chōtoku and his father were in Tōkyō, a man came to the former King's residence in Koji-machi to try and extort or defraud money from Shō Tai. This man claimed that the money was to support expenditure on the Sino-Japanese war. Chōtoku and his father both felt this was suspicious, and when the man got angry, drew out a gun and began shooting randomly, they were able to subdue him and hold him down before turning him over to the police.*' Nakamoto dates this incident to 1895, probably because the tale is linked to the 1894/5 war between China and Japan.

Kyan Chōtoku's biographers all state that he was small and weak as a child, and Mark Bishop (1989) wrote that he was also asthmatic and often bedridden, so really, he had a mountain to climb in becoming a karate expert. Even in maturity he was slightly built and frail looking, but he must have had a strong character because by the time he was thirty years old he was well known in and around Shuri and Naha by the name *Chanmī* (*Small Eyed Kyan*). "*During Master Kyan's era,*" wrote Nagamine, "*kake-dameshi was a popular practice among confident men of karate. Chanmī rarely if ever refused any challenge from hot-blooded young men, and never lost a single match.*"

Nagamine thought that, because of Kyan's size he did not train to trade punches with bigger men but would practice stepping and evasion techniques over and over again by the banks of the Hija River, or with his back to the railings of the bridge. His method of fighting was to defend and then counterattack immediately. He was known to be an expert in kicking techniques and altogether we can imagine him as a perfect example of the Shōrin Ryu stylist described by Funakoshi Gichin in his 1922 "*Ryūkyū Kempo Karate,*" a smaller, lighter man whose karate was characterised by quickness and mobility.

Chibana Choshin told Pat Nakata that Kyan's technique "*was quick and elusive*" and that he had "*powerful punches and strikes, belying his size.*" Pat also recalled that, "*Chibana Sensei told me a story of Motobu Sensei and Kyan sensei having a makiwara punching contest that was judged by Itosu Sensei. Each participant hit the makiwara fifty times with each hand. At the conclusion Itosu declared the contest a draw.*"

Tamae Hiroyasu & his book "Karate-Do"

Although Itosu may have called it a draw, not wanting to favour one or the other, that outcome could perhaps be seen as a moral victory for Kyan, who was the smaller and lighter man.

In his short memoirs of the old Okinawan masters, (included in the 1977 compilation "Karate Do"), Tamae Hiroyasu wrote;

"Sensei Kyan was a very small man and you would have been surprised to learn that such a small man was so great a Bushi. He excelled in practical fighting and had great confidence and power. We all know of the famous incident when he threw the wrestler over the parapet of the bridge."

He had only one eye so was called *Chanmī*

The name Chanmī or small eyed Kyan, was said to arise because he had narrow eyes, or a permanent squint. Ikeda Hoshu, in his book "*Karate Do Shugi,*" had a more exotic explanation: "*His method of training was never to wear a gi top. This was to allow the air to temper the skin and allowed detailed observation of the muscles. This was considered to be a sophisticated attitude to training at that time. This half-naked method allowed him to make detailed observations of the movement and tension of the students' muscles, and his habit of fixing his eyes rigidly on the student to see if he was using his muscles correctly earned him the name "Chanmī ."*

Ikeda may have been speculating on the basis of statements made in Miki and Takada's 1930 book "*Kempo Gaisetsu.*" The main reason for Kyan's nickname though probably had to do with his sight. It can't have been too good as in almost every photograph we have of him he is wearing glasses. Tamae's statement that Kyan only had one eye doesn't seem to be repeated elsewhere, except in an article by Charles Goodin on Sunabe Shozen, an old Okinawan living in Hawai'i, who said he had been a private student of Kyan for twelve years from the age of six, from 1925 to 1937.

According to Sunabe, "*Many years ago Kyan Sensei was sitting and drinking sake with a friend next to a hibachi (charcoal burner). The friend was stirring the coals with saibashi [菜箸, long chopsticks] and, for some unknown reason, and without warning, the friend poked Kyan Sensei in the eye with the hot end of them.*"

Charles thought that this incident and the resulting loss of his sight in one eye made Kyan very cautious and very aware of those around him. Of course, karate experts were expected to be aware at all times of possible attacks, but Charles believed that this was particularly the case with Kyan: "*He felt that he had to always be ready to defend himself.*" When sitting he would always be in a position to deliver a kick, and if he was offered a cup of tea he would always take the cup with one thumb pressed firmly against it to prevent the hot liquid being thrown in his face. He would be careful going through doors and round corners and when eating with chopsticks he would hold them sideways so they couldn't be knocked into his face or throat.

In his short memoir Tamae mentioned the tale of Kyan throwing a wrestler over a bridge but unfortunately he didn't elaborate on that. But there was a story, told originally I think in one of the old American Shōrin Ryu newsletters, which may be it, or a form of it. In this account Kyan was sitting one day on the rail of the bridge over the Hija River while a group of labourers was at work loading sugar. They were a rough crew and one of them picked on Kyan and went to push him over the bridge but instead found himself going over and into the water. As the man pushed, Kyan had moved slightly and pulled him forward, so the attacker was carried over the bridge by his own momentum. Another man came forward and was thrown, and then another, until in all thirteen labourers had been thrown into the river. After that Kyan was left alone.

And maybe this too is just another version of the story told by Nagamine Shōshin in which Kyan, now around forty years old and making a living hauling carts, crossed the path of Matsuda, a big, loud fellow who was bullying the younger men of the village. When Kyan reproached him for his behaviour, Matsuda turned on him and challenged him to a fight. Matsuda was aware that Kyan knew karate but felt that his knowledge of kata would be useless in a real fight and he would be too small anyway. When the two men met on the banks of the Hija River before a crowd of villagers, Kyan took up a natural stance with his back to the water. As Matsuda came forward to strike, Kyan evaded the attack and countered with a kick that sent the big man into the water.

Kyan seemed to have had a few run-ins when he was hauling carts. In a 2011 magazine interview with Shimabukuro Zenpo, another story from this time was told: *"Because Kyan Sensei was small and appeared fragile, when he travelled from Kadena to Shuri and back with loads of sugar cane, rice, or firewood in his cart, bullies would pick on him. Blocking the passage of people and vehicles, and often the worse for drink, these thugs would terrorise travelers. Not realising that he was a famous karate master, one grabbed him roughly one day to be rewarded for his rudeness with a vice-like grip on his hand that allowed Kyan Sensei to lead the bully around at will and humiliate him. In the best tradition of Okinawan karate, he solved the problem without fighting, and taught the bullies a lesson."*

Shimabukuro also believed that although Kyan was small he had unusual strength. *"For example"* he told the magazine, *"one day at the port, workers were loading a ship with barrels of sugar cane. It was hard and heavy work, and as each man was struggling to transfer the cargo, barrel by barrel, onto the ship, they were amazed to see the tiny Kyan, a barrel suspended from each end of the bo perched across his shoulders, striding up the gangplank and onto the ship with a double load of sugar cane."*

The abdication of the king and the disappearance of the old Ryūkyū kingdom were harsh facts of life for many Okinawans. *"The entire Ryūkyūan population fell into great disarray,"* and in a way it may have been harder for those of higher birth because they had further to fall; The government reforms led to the abolition of the old social ranking system and the loss of their privileges and financial support. The period covering the abolition of the Han system, and the establishment of the Prefecture, was called the *Haihanchiken* and Nagamine Shōshin quoted a poem of the time which refers to the changed status of the aristocratic families (*kemochi*) at this time:

"Before the Haihanchiken, Ryūkyū aristocracy would strut about. Now, however, after losing their position and stipend, they have been reduced to hiding their faces under their hats as coachmen pulling carts. It's pitiful to see them."

Undated pre-war local Naha-based rickshaw driver in front of *Sogenji*
* Photo courtesy of the Naha City Museum Digital Archives

The Kyan family lost its position too and Kyan Chōtoku, whose father had been a royal retainer and friend of the king himself, knew only hard times after that. He tried to make ends meet by breeding silkworms, hauling carts and pulling a rickshaw. Yet throughout all this his enthusiasm for karate never seemed to diminish.

In his book *"Weaponless Warriors"* Richard Kim referred to an old newspaper article in the *"Asahi Shinbun"* by columnist *Sugiyama Heisuke*; which concerned a bully in the Naha area who was always starting and winning fights in the Tsuji district. One night this man picked on a rickshaw driver who threw him into the harbour. The article had gone on to say that, *"At that time, according to this particular observation, visitors arriving at Naha harbour were greeted with the sight of rickshaw men with noble appearance, waiting for their customers. Most of these rickshaw men were from Tomari-machi, two kilometres from Naha-shi. They were from the Bushi-class, which had fallen onto hard times, forcing them into the rickshaw trade to earn enough to eat. Most of them worked into the evenings when the entertainment quarters opened and continued until the wee hours of the morning."*

The newspaper article focussed attention to the fact that these men were or had been students of Matsumora Kosaku, a karate master who lived in Tomari. The braggart had been thrown into the harbour by one of these men.

Nakazato Joen believed that Kyan moved to Yomitan, by the River Hija, around 1910, when he was forty years old. Nagamine Shōshin doesn't give a date but stated that *"finally for financial reasons"* Kyan Sensei had to relocate to Yomitan village. The family still had a small inheritance and had the use of a small plot of land there handed down by the Sho family.

At Yomitan, Kyan cultivated silkworms and pulled a cart, and was able to carve out a meagre existence. He taught karate to a number of young villagers in his yard and then began to teach at the College of Agriculture and Forestry and the Kadena police station. That must have helped him financially, although the modern memorial stone set up in his memory states that his material circumstances forced him *"to live very modestly"*.

He and his students would demonstrate karate in the region around his home. According to Ikeda Hoshu, *"He also trained the young men in the traditional karate like dancing called 'Mēkata [舞方],' which is demonstrated at festivals. In country districts (Inaka) people display Mēkata-gwā [舞方小] and many people believe that techniques of Ryūkyū martial arts were passed down secretly through these dance movements. We should keep this in mind when watching these traditional dances."* On the same subject, by the way, Funakoshi Gichin wrote in his first book, the 1922 *"Ryūkyū Kempo Karate:"* *"If you go into the Okinawan countryside you will often see men performing a traditional dance to the music of the shamisen. This dancing resembles karate and is different from the usual maikata dancing. I think it is related to traditional Okinawa-te."*

Miki Nisaburo, a Tōkyō University student, spent several months in Okinawa in 1929 researching karate. Shortly afterwards, with Takada [aka Mutsu] Mizuho, he wrote a book, *"Kempo Gaisetsu"*, about the karate he had studied in Okinawa. *"Kempo Gaisetsu"* noted that Kyan was then the karate instructor at Kadena-cho Agriculture school as well as *Hijabashi Toudi Kenkyu-jo* (Hijabashi Karate Research Club), and Miki wrote that *"Sensei practises karate naked"* (presumably wearing the fundoshi-style underwear). I asked him about this as I had a rather strange impression of the demonstration. Sensei said that it had been his habit since he was young. He stated that he had been making his students do the same as well. He explained the reasons for not wearing clothes were to toughen the skin and to clearly feel the distribution of power in the muscles. When wearing clothes, it is difficult to see the action of the muscles clearly and this might allow students to cheat or practice incorrect technique.

"*Chanmī*" is a well-known nickname given to him and it is said that if a three year old child hears the name when he was crying they would stop immediately. "*He also gave me valuable advice on makiwara practice.*"

That his name was used to stop children crying . . . that's interesting; it means he had a reputation. "*One day in December of 1927*" wrote Nakazato Joen, "*He was relaxing at the public bath at Inami, Hijabashi. As it was in the early evening, it was very crowded. There were not even enough washtubs for all the people. There was a place in Hijabashi where people raised calves. Several young men from the southern area were there to purchase cows. They came into the bath in force. One of them tried forcefully to take the washtub away from Sensei. Sensei had the washtub in his left hand, and was drying his body with his right hand. The young man could not even move the washtub at all from Sensei's hand. It was as if it was nailed down onto the floor. The old man who was watching this closely had to come by and scolded the young man: 'Do you have any idea who this man is? He is Kyan Sensei!' The young man suddenly realized who he was dealing with. Looking pale, he apologized profusely. Everyone in Okinawa had heard about the famed name, 'Chanmī.'*"

During his stay in Okinawa Miki Nisaburo accompanied Kyan and *Oshiro Chojo* to karate demonstrations at Nishihara and Urasoe grade schools, and Kyan seemed to have been quite active in public demonstrations of the art. Although no one else mentions this, Nakazato Joen believed that Kyan took part in the 1921 demonstration before Crown Prince Hirohito when the prince stopped off at Okinawa on his way to Europe. Occasionally he travelled outside Okinawa to demonstrate or teach karate. Nakazato wrote that Kyan's daughter *Yasuko* (DOB 1911) accompanied her father to Osaka in 1925, "*living with relatives during her father's training,*" and that around 1927 he made demonstration tours to the "*Kansai area of Japan, Kyushu and Taiwan along with judoka and Russian boxers. He worked hard to spread the real karate.*" Nakazato thought that it was during this tour that Kyan learned Ananku kata from a Chinese in Taiwan. The dates here may be a bit hazy because Kyan's Taiwan challenge match with the judoka is supposed to have taken place in 1930. Who knows, really?

"In August of 1932" Nakazato wrote, *"the Japanese Empire Navy combined fleet gathered in Nakagusuku Bay. A public demonstration was held for the navy personnel. A young man failed at his tameshiwari demonstration. As Admiral Kanna Kenwa witnessed the young man's failed attempt, he asked Kyan Sensei to perform the tameshiwari. Sensei completed the breaking successfully at his first attempt. Admiral Kanna was delighted; he seemed to be close to tears, and shook Sensei's hand. Sensei was sixty two years old at the time."*

In his 2014 analysis of Tokumine no Kon, Andreas Quast referred to three newspaper articles from 1931 which mentioned Kyan's trip to Ishigaki in the Yaeyama Islands, the southernmost islands of Okinawa prefecture. Kyan was described as *"The Ryūkyū Karate Authority"* and again, even in his sixties he was energetic in his efforts to preserve the old art of karate and develop it as a modern budo. He was making that journey to Yaeyama "on the special occasion of the establishment of a 'training facility' for karate, which we later find described as the Southern Islands Butokuden."

Andreas noted that on 14 Sep, 1931, Kyan, then sixty one years old, gave a demonstration of karate "at the Yaeyama Hall in Ōkawa on Ishigaki Island, and another one at the same place was scheduled for the following day . . . . Instruction in karate by Chōtoku took place from 8 to 11 a.m. and from 7 to 11 p.m., with a membership fee of two yen. The admission fee was devoted to help cover the construction costs of the Southern Islands Butokuden.

"Newspaper companies of Ishigaki further sponsored a charity demonstration meeting in aid of the Southern Islands Butokuden, for the opening of which 'Kyan Chōtoku gathered the youth of the island for diligent instruction.' The charity demonstrations began on December 7th, 1931, and continued every day for the course of one week. The performances started at 7 p.m. at the 'Banzai Office'.

". . . . The admission fee was 15 *sen* (=1/100 yen) for adults, and 10 *sen* for children. Chōtoku himself promoted active participation by the islanders, saying that "Ishigaki Town is keenly aware that it does not yet have a facility for the practice of physical education. Because it recognized the need for a dōjō for the large number of their sons and daughters, I ask the distinguished attendees for their sympathy."

Incidentally, the demonstration of karate included the following: karate; karate kata; kumite; bo; bo no kumite; Tinbe; Sai and Nunchaku. Interesting: what form did the kumite and bo kumite take, for example?

Tokuda Anshu, a one-time student of both Kyan Chōtoku and Miyagi Chojun, wrote a memoir of his training for the 1950s, "*Gekkan Karate Do*" magazine. He remembered that he had once been surrounded by bullies from another school but had been helped out of trouble by Kyan Chōtoku's wife, and that led to him becoming a student of Kyan himself when he was eleven years old, (around 1930?). "*I first learned Seisan from him,*" Tokuda wrote. "*I found this kata to be monotonous, lacking interesting moves . . . However, I did my best to learn it. The next kata was Wanshu, and I was not too excited by this kata either. Then I moved on to Passai. I was delighted by its more flashy movements. The training consisted of practice on such kata as Chintō. Gojushiho, Ananko and Kosokun (Kusanku). It appeared to my eyes that the purpose of Sensei's training was to develop graceful kata.*"

"*One evening under the moonlight I accompanied Sensei along with other Agricultural College students and travelled by horse wagon to Nakadomari Village to put on a demonstration. The small branch school where we were to demonstrate was located at the outskirts of the fishing village facing the East China Sea. We received extraordinary treatment by the people of the village. We were invited to dinner by the alderman and the committee members, and we were treated with raw octopus sashimi that were as big as a grown man's wrist. When the people were slightly intoxicated by drink our demonstration began. Nakadomari Village was located in the centre of the long and narrow island of Okinawa. It was at the narrowest part of the island: the distance between the Pacific Coast and the East China Sea Coast was just three miles.*

We did our demonstration on the playground. Light stands were placed on several desks. As the youngest member of the group I was told to go up first. I performed Seisan. It was my very first time doing kata in front of people and I was very nervous. The grass on the playground was wet with the night dew, and you could see fishing lights on the coast. The people were laughing and saying 'That young kid really does karate? That's very unusual." "*I was eleven years old. My knees were shaking. Out of desperation I made my bow, tightened my headband and began Seisan kata. As soon as I began my kata demonstration my mind was focussed on kata and nothing else.*"

"Under the moonlight, as young as I was, I continued my kata to the best of my ability. As I finished my demonstration with my last uke I heard loud applause from the crowd. Then the more senior Agricultural College students performed kata and some kumite."

"Kyan Sensei then stood up, walked to the centre of the playground and said 'Can anyone come up and try to straighten my bent arm?' The alderman wearing formal attire came up and pulled Sensei's arm trying to straighten it. However, his arm did not move at all. Then a couple of strong muscular young men tried, but Sensei's arm stayed as steady as a rock. Sensei's arm remained in the same position even when a couple of people together tried to pull it straight. To my young mind, it was like a miracle: how could small, thin Sensei possess so much strength? The crowd were just as astonished as I was."

"We headed back home on the horse wagon. My grandfather had stayed up waiting for my return. After hearing my story, he told me to do the kata I had done in Nakadomari. He was extremely pleased with my kata. To show his appreciation for Sensei, my grandfather purchased a pair of paulownia wood geta as a gift."

Murakami Katsumi's 1974 book on Karate and Ryūkyu Kobudo

Murakami Katsumi wrote about Kyan Chōtoku in his 1974 book, "*Karate Do to Ryūkyū Kobudo,*" describing him as one of the greatest karate experts. The relevant section in the book is entitled "*Sensei Kyan Chōtoku: absorbing virtues as well as vices.*"

Murakami wrote that Kyan Sensei's two favourite students were Arakaki Ankichi (1899 – 1929) and Shimabuku Taro (1906 – 1980). According to Murakami, Kyan not only taught Arakaki and Shimabuku karate but also encouraged them to do many other things, including drinking and visiting the local brothels – on the grounds that an experience of different areas of life was an important part of martial arts development. So it was that at times he would train these two students in the brothel.

Well, Funakoshi Gichin wrote as one of his precepts *"Do not think karate is only in the dojo,"* and Kyan stressed to his students that whatever they did they should keep in mind the idea of *busai*[1], or correct martial way. I am not sure what this involves exactly but perhaps it means that to some extent you should remain unattached to whatever you are doing, stay alert and keep a clear mind and strong spirit, whether drinking, visiting a brothel - or just pulling a rickshaw.

Both Arakaki and Shimabuku would visit Kyan sensei's home for training at night. They carried lanterns to light their way but Kyan told them to stop using the lanterns so that they could develop their night vision. When they trained at night he chose uneven terrain and sometimes even threw water on the ground to make a foothold difficult. In this way they developed their kata.

Kyan Chōtoku was fond of cock fighting and would often carry a fighting cock about with him. On one such occasion Arakaki and Shimabuku, wanting to test their sensei's ability, started a fight with a gang of young men and then ran off, leaving Kyan to face the group alone. The men attacked Kyan who then proceeded to beat them, still holding the bird under one arm. Even Arakaki and Shimabuku, who watched from a distance, were surprised at how he fought using his feet and only one free arm. This may be another version of the story told by Eizo Shimabuku about Kyan clearing the Shuri-Naha roadway of thieves.

I can't imagine how, but Nakazato Joen dates this incident to July of 1926. In Nakazato's account, Kyan was on his way to visit his oldest brother, Chōho, who lived in Shuri. He was bringing a 'game cock (for cock fighting)' as a gift to his brother during the sixteen-day-old moon. When he arrived at *Oojana*, it was already past midnight and for some reason the game-cock began to crow. That alerted a group of young men, about ten or more who took Kyan for a thief and began to attack him. Holding the game cock on his left-side, Kyan avoided and deflected all their punches and kicks before continuing on to Shuri. Later, it was learned that this had actually been a planned attack arranged by Arakaki and Shimabukuro to test their teacher's skill in karate. Nakazato added that, *"Motonaga Choyu*, Sensei's grandchild, talked about this incident in recent years. Motonaga heard about it from one of the people in Shimabukuro's group! His words were as follows;

---

[1] *"Busai?"* Not 100% sure but possibly 武才 [i.e. Martial Age] and seemingly referring to competency, both technical and social. ~ Patrick McCarthy

"Just as the old saying goes, *Neo shimete kazeni makasuru yanagikana* [*Willow branches do not resist against the strong wind, they bend with the wind. Therefore neither the branches nor the roots ever break*], Sensei moved effortlessly to avoid the young men's attacks as if he was playing with them. Those young men were astonished by Sensei's incredible skills."

Kyan Chōtoku's wife worked hard as a dyer of cloth and pig breeder but whenever a pig was ready for sale at the market Kyan himself always insisted on taking it. Murakami wrote that Kyan would often cheat his wife of the money he received and use it to pay for women and travel. He liked to travel and on one occasion took Arakaki and Shimabuku to Hokkaido where they demonstrated karate in a large tent. When a fighter called *Toku Sanpo* challenged them, Kyan counseled Arakaki to step back carefully to the walls of the tent, then knock the challenger down if he moved on him. We don't know what happened thereafter as unfortunately Murakami just leaves the story there.

In 1975, Nagamine Shōshin recalled, he was told a story by his friend Kudaka Kori, who in 1930 had accompanied Kyan and Kuwae Ryosei to Taiwan where they gave a demonstration of karate. Before the demonstration began, *Ishida Shinzo*, a judo 6th dan and judo teacher at the Taipei Police Station, came up to the group and said he would like to test the strength of karate by fighting one of the group. Concerned about the loss of face if they refused the challenge, the sixty year old Kyan accepted. He took off his gi and stripped to his underwear to face Ishida, looking small and thin compared to his opponent. Kyan stood in a natural stance awaiting for Ishida, and as the judo-man reached for a grip Kyan thrust a thumb into his mouth as if to pull his cheek away while stamping on his foot (or knee) and pulling him down. As Ishida hit the ground Kyan delivered a strike which he stopped just short of contact, just to show what he could do. Ishida immediately submitted, "as defeat was obvious." After the challenge fight Kyan, Kuwae and Kudaka went on to give their demonstration. Kudaka thought that Kyan had stripped down to his underwear to eliminate any advantage the judoka might have had by grabbing his gi.

Nagamine tried that mouth-grabbing technique (fish-hooking as it's sometimes called) against some of his students and found it surprisingly effective, especially when you are seized. He thought that Kyan's *"knowledge of such things clearly demonstrated his understanding of techniques no longer practiced in modern karate."*

Nagamine told Cezar Borkowski that Kyan was *"the most well-rounded teacher I have ever met,"* adding that "The younger Kyan was small, very muscular, and quick. He enjoyed the Chinese classics. He was also a firm believer in the daily practice of kata and was, by many accounts, a fighter without equal. Although frequently challenged, even when he was in his sixties, to my knowledge, he never yielded and was never defeated."

However . . . as Joe Swift wrote in an email to the KSL forum (*IRKRS' Karate Study List on 8 June 2002*): *"Lest we inadvertently place the old master on an unnecessary pedestal,"* and *"if only to show that even the old masters were only human, so to speak,"* there is another Kyan story which Joe picked up in the literature: The story comes through Kinjo Hiroshi, who heard it from his uncle Kinjo Koboku, who was actually there when the incident happened. This event apparently took place in Osaka, Japan, before WW2.

"Kyan Chōtoku came to me saying that he would like to try his hand at a bout between karate and boxing. I took him to a gym, where he decided to exchange a few friendly blows with one of the students there. However, right off the bat he took a punch and lost his legs. There was no way that he could beat a boxer."

This story sounds believable, to me anyway. If Kyan Chōtoku had got involved in a boxing-type match then he would have been unaccustomed to the variety, timing, angle and distance of boxing punches and could well have been hit had he, for example, simply tried to defend. Unlike a trained boxer he would not have been able to absorb or ride the punches and from photographs he had a thin neck, which wouldn't have helped his punch resistance. And also, if this took place sometime in the 1920s or 1930s, (*which ties in with the history of western boxing in Japan*) then again, he would have been into his fifties or sixties at the time of the match.

Nagamine, the founder of Matsubayashi Shōrin-ryu, originally learned karate from *Iha Kotatsu* (1873-1928) an expert in Tomari-te who taught at the Tomari Student Association. He was also able to learn the kata Passai, Kusanku and Chintō from Kyan students Arakaki Ankichi and Shimabuku Taro, and then in late 1931 he was transferred to the Kadena Police Station and had the opportunity to learn from Kyan Chōtoku himself. As Nagamine later told Chibana Choshin in their discussion for the "Ryūkyū Shimpo" newspaper, he *"was most impressed with the kata of Kyan,"* so this was a wonderful opportunity to study with the master himself.

Nagamine thought that, *"Because he was so small, Kyan Sensei had always trained much harder than anyone else,"* and he recalled how the master would talk about the importance of consistent training, on the makiwara, for example, which should be struck every day to maintain the conditioning of the fist.

Nagamine was awarded the Renshi rank by the Butokukai in 1940 and in 1942 he opened his own karate dojo in Naha. He had several important guests at the formal opening of the dojo, including Admiral Kanna Kenwa, but to Nagamine the most important guest was Kyan Chōtoku who had come from Yomitan to be there. And one thing about Kyan, he must have kept training through all his later years because at sixty eight he had given that powerful demonstration referred to by Tamae Hiroyasu, and now at over seventy years old he gave a demonstration too at Nagamine's dojo opening, performing Passai and bo.

"The greatest guest of them all was Kyan Chōtoku Sensei," Nagamine remembered. "He came all the way from Yomitan village, with his assistant Arakaki Ansei (*the brother of Arakaki Ankichi*), and demonstrated both kata and the bo. Kyan Sensei was then seventy three years old. Watching the old master perform filled my eyes with tears because I was so deeply moved by his obvious mastery of budo, his determination to support me regardless of the great distance and his age, and his life-long dedication to karate.

"Even at his advanced age the other guests were in awe, not only of Kyan's sharp and powerful movements but also the master's indomitable spirit. Sensei really looked great at that time. It was, nonetheless, the last official demonstration of his life."

Although Nagamine may have believed that this was Kyan's last official demonstration, (whatever "*official*" might mean), Nakazato Joen recalled a couple of demonstrations taking place after this. In August 1943, accompanied by Nakazato, *Okuhara Bunei, Yonamine Shinko* and *Jintoku Takayoshi*, Kyan put on demonstrations for the bereaved families of front line troops at Nakijin and Motobu grade schools. *"He put on the demonstration along with us, young men,"* Nakazato wrote. *"Sensei was then seventy four years old, and he broke four cedar boards. I could never forget Sensei's ability even in his old age."* There was another demonstration in January 1944 at the Yomitan airfield construction site, where Kyan demonstrated Chintō and Tokumine no Kun kata.

Soon after that, of course, the war truly came to Okinawa when the bombing raids began and then American forces attacked the island In April 1945. The ensuing action, *"The Typhoon of Steel,"* was the bloodiest fight of the Pacific War. There were 50,000 American casualties and perhaps over 100,000 Japanese troops were killed. Estimates of civilian casualties vary from around 40,000 to 100,000 killed, but in any case these were staggering figures for a pre-war Okinawan population of something over 300,000. It was only after almost three months of desperate, terrible fighting that the island was taken, leaving widespread destruction and shortages of food and supplies. Kyan Sensei had been forced to move from his home in Kadena to Ishikawa during the fighting. He survived the end of the war but died not long after in the Ishikawa refugee camp on 20 September 1945. The causes of death were said to be fatigue and starvation. *"He was indeed missed by people around him."*

Kata

Kyan Chōtoku is said to have taught eight empty hand kata and one bo kata, (Tokumine no kon). The eight empty hand forms, and the teachers he is supposed to have learned them from, are:

Naihanchi – Ankoh Itosu, or Matsumura Sōkon
Seisan and Gojushiho – Matsumura Sōkon
Passai – Oyadomari Kokan
Kusanku – Chatan Yara
Chintō – Matsumora Kosaku
Wanshu – Maeda
Ananku – A Taiwanese expert

This is an interesting set of kata, and the various attributions seem to tie everything up neatly . . . . but it's problematic. The links between the kata and the different teachers seem to come from Nakazato Joen, who studied with Kyan at the Agricultural College and his home for six years or so, from 1937 to 1943. Whether Nakazato got this information from Kyan himself, or just speculated on the transmission, we don't know, but in the complete absence of any contemporary evidence, it's hard to be certain about anything.

Nakazato actually lists Naihanchi as coming from Matsumura, but the Naihanchi shown by Kyan's various students (Naihanchi Shodan) is the orthodox Ankoh Itosu form, and most people consider this kata to have come from Itosu. Kyan is usually listed as a student of Ankoh Itosu, and Chibana Choshin, in his 1957 newspaper discussion with Nagamine Shōshin lists Kyan as one of his seniors under Itosu.

But then, quoted in Murakami Katsumi's 1974 book "*Karate Do to Ryūkyū Kobudo,*" Chibana does not refer to Kyan as an Itosu pupil; rather, he describes him as a student of Oyadomari. And even though Kyan's students seem to teach Naihanchi, it's not certain that Kyan himself taught the kata. Apparently Nakazato Joen was asked this question directly by an American student in 2003 and replied that Kyan did not teach the kata – thus, by the way, contradicting his own list of Kyan Chōtoku forms. It may, or may not, be significant that Naihanchi is the only one of the kata that Nakazato did not show himself in his book "*Kyudo.*" And the Okinawan Karate Encyclopedia entry on Shimabukuro Zenryō, one of Kyan's senior students, states that "*Shimabukuro dedicated himself to learning the seven Kyan kata*" - and Naihanchi is not included in the listing of those seven kata. *Apparently Naihanchi came into Shimabukuro's Seibukan school much later from his son Zenpo, who learned the kata from Nakama Chōzō.* According to Dan Smith, Naihanchi and the other forms which Shimabukuro Zenpo learned from Nakama, were not brought into the Seibukan curriculum till as late as 1975 ("*so many of the earlier students of Seibukan did not learn these kata*").

In 1918 a karate study group was set up in Shuri which included Funakoshi Gichin, Chibana Choshin, Oshiro Chojo, Tokuda Anbun, Mabuni Kenwa, Gusukuma [Shiroma] Shimpan, Tokumura Seicho, and Ishikawa Hoko. Tokumura and Ishikawa I don't know about, but the others were all former students of Itosu Ankoh, and so this group may have come together to preserve and develop Itosu's teaching. So it may be significant that Kyan Chōtoku is not listed as a member, although later he did join another informal, more multi-style group which included Choyu and Motobu Choki, Miyagi Chojun, Gusukuma and Mabuni.

But then, having said all this, according to Nakaya Takao's "*Karate-do. History and Philosophy,*" Kyan himself told Nakama Chōzō (Nakaya's teacher) *that he had learned from Itosu*. Nakaya concedes however, that this may only have been for a short time as Kyan did not teach Itosu's forms.

That seems reasonable. The main point is that, apart from the possible exception of Naihanchi, Kyan Chōtoku's karate does not include any of the Itosu kata, even where there are well known Itosu versions of the forms, such as Passai, Kushanku, and Chintō. What is clear, in fact, is how different Kyan's versions of the kata are from Itosu's. Rather than follow Itosu's forms he preferred to practise and teach versions of the kata that seem to have been related to Tomari. It may be telling, too, that unlike many other instructors, Kyan never adopted Itosu's Pinan kata as training forms.

The transmission direct from Matsumura Sōkon is also problematical for reasons of age. Matsumura's dates are uncertain but there seems to be a consensus that he was born in 1809, so if Nagamine and Nakamoto were right in saying that Kyan Chōtoku started serious karate training at the age of twenty (1890), then Matsumura would have been over eighty and there must be a question of just how much active teaching he was doing at that time. The old 1942 "Ryūkyū Shimpo" article stated that Kyan started learning from Matsumura at the age of sixteen, which would have been in 1886, when the old master would have been in his late seventies. That's a little more plausible, but you still wonder. Also, if the chronology in that article is correct, then any instruction would have been cut short when Kyan went to Tōkyō with his father. Still, that would have been enough time to learn a couple of kata.

1923 Commemorating the departure of Tokuyama Chōkun [渡久山 朝勲, seated 2nd from left] to San Francisco; Seated to the far left is village mayor Kyan Chōtoku
* Photo courtesy of the Naha City Museum Digital Archives

One slightly puzzling thing about Nakazato's listing of Kyan Chōtoku's teachers is that it shows no input from his father, who was supposedly a karate expert himself, a direct student of Matsumura Sōkon, and who, in some accounts, taught his son karate from the age of six. It's possible, I suppose, that Chōtoku could have learned some Matsumura karate from his father and that influence is there in some way in the forms that have been passed down to the modern day.

For the other kata – Oyadomari Kokan (1831-1905) and Matsumora Kosaku (1829-1898) were possibly the best known Tomari Karate-ka in the late 19th century. It's important to note though that although Kyan's Chintō has been attributed to Matsumora, neither Chibana or Nagamine refer to Kyan as a Matsumora student. Hokama Tetsuhiro, ("100 Masters of Okinawan Karate") in listing Matsumora's students does not include Kyan. Overall, I don't think we have any real proof that Kyan ever learned from Matsumora Kosaku. And we simply have no idea who Maeda Pēchin, *the supposed teacher of Wanshu*, was, except that he is said to have been a Matsumora student.

Kyan's unique version of Kusanku is said to come from Chatan Yara, though this cannot be the well-known Chatan Yara of history because his dates are given variously as 1740 to 1812, or 1816 to 1884. The story is that Kyan came by this kata when he moved to Yomitan at around the age of forty, and learned it from a descendant of the Yara family who had been managing the riding stables there. That long period though, from the early 1800s to the early 1900s, takes us further away from the original Chatan Yara and so we know nothing, really, about the distant origins of this form of the kata.   Kyan later told Arakaki Ankichi that the Yara he had learned from had had great power in his legs in his youth but was old and infirm at the time he learned from him.

At the time this is supposed to have happened, Kyan was a well-known expert and it seems a little odd that he would have learned Kushanku [aka Kusanku] at the age of forty or so: Kushanku was one of the best known karate kata and it seems likely that he would have already known a form of the kata by the time he moved to Yomitan. However, he could then have learned a different version of Kushanku which appealed to him more and which he retained in his teaching.

As for *Ananku* . . . This kata does not appear in any other karate style. It is said to be associated in some way with Taiwan and the usual version of events is that Kyan learned this from a Chinese expert when he was on the island (c.1927? ...1930?). However, Ananku does not look like a Chinese form at all, either Northern or Southern, and in the versions shown by Nakazato and Shimabukuro Zenpo, it seems to simply be a combination of movements from other kata – Seisan, Passai and Gojushiho mainly, with many karate-style forearm and knife hand blocks. There seems to be no mystery about this form; *the most likely history is that it was put together by Kyan himself.*

The supposed wide variety of sources for Kyan's kata seems a little unusual by the standards of today's traditionalists, where the idea is that karate and its kata are so profound that you need to stay with a single style or teacher for many years to learn and perfect the techniques. So from that perspective, if Kyan did go from one teacher to another, learning maybe just one or two kata from each, that could demonstrate a certain shallowness of approach. Personally, I don't get that impression, and in those days anyway, when it was said that a well-known expert might only know a couple of kata, an enthusiastic student like Kyan would have to study from several teachers to build up a wider knowledge of the art. Or perhaps he actually learned most of his kata from one teacher, possibly Oyadomari – we simply don't know.

Also, despite the lingering tradition of secrecy and the practical difficulties of learning karate back then, maybe sometimes things were a little easier and more informal in the old days. The fact that Kyan may have gone to several different teachers only demonstrates his eagerness to learn and his love of karate at a time when knowledge of the art was limited and difficult to acquire, except by personal transmission. It is quite possible that Kyan actually knew more kata than he taught but decided that practice of seven or eight forms was quite sufficient and chose those versions for his teaching. The end point of all this speculation is that we don't have any clear idea of where Kyan Chōtoku's karate came from, except that it was pulled together from that mysterious, late 19th century, unorganised but fruitful environment of different teachers and kata that came into being with the gradual disappearance of the old tradition of secrecy. I imagine he felt too that he was preserving a treasured art of old Okinawa: in his essay on karate included in "*Kempo Gaisetsu*" he wrote that its origins went back over four hundred years, to the Oei (1394 – 1428) and Eikyo (1429 - 1441) periods, and that it was an art unique to Okinawa, a fighting art which used no weapons.

In his short memoir of Kyan, Tamae Hiroyasu mentioned that some other Shuri karate experts referred to Kyan's karate as *'Inaka-de'* or *"primitive."* The translation of Tamae's section in the 1977 book, *"Karate-Do"* was carried out for me by Professor N. Karasawa, working with Ian McLaren, and in his translation Professor Karasawa told Ian that the words *"Inaka-de"* had something of a, *"country bumpkin"* implication. Kyan's kata do have their own unique character but there are several other reasons why such a view could have arisen.

To anyone who was used to the more widespread and accepted Itosu versions of the kata, Kyan's forms may well have looked a little strange or unorthodox, but that was mainly a question of unfamiliarity and of what was then the accepted orthodoxy. Also, Kyan's kata probably showed strong Tomari influences and some Shuri Karate-ka may have looked down on Tomari kata as in some ways inelegant or unrefined. Apart from any technical considerations that may have been part of a general feeling on the part of Shuri people that their culture was superior to the rest of Okinawa. George Kerr, in his authoritative *"Okinawa. The History of an Island People,"* wrote that *"The pre-eminence of Shuri families and the privileges and advantages conferred automatically through residence at the King's capital, created a tradition of prestige which has persisted into the 20th century, for whenever Okinawans assemble for the first time, in Ryūkyū, in Japan, or overseas communities, it is quickly but tactfully established if a man has been born in Shuri, educated in Shuri, or has married a woman of Shuri, in that order of precedence."*

Nakamoto Masahiro, in *"Kobudo,"* mentions an old story that had been told to him by Nakama Chōzō: *"In 1924 at the Matsuyama udun, Tokumura Seiki, a student of Nakamoto Seicho, who was an expert in sai-jutsu, ridiculed Sōkon Hohan, saying 'Show me if you can use a sai,' but Sōkon at first ignored the provocation, answering back 'You silly old man.' However, when Chanmī spoke out and said 'This person here is an expert in sai-jutsu,' Sōkon reconsidered and performed sai. Asked by Tokumura where he was from, he said 'I am from the countryside.' He then was praised with the reply, 'You're good for someone from the countryside.'"* The main point is that, as a matter of course, anyone from outside the main centre *was regarded as of inferior skill.*

It's also possible that Kyan made his own changes to the kata. Tamae noted that *"Even when the kata was a well known one, Kyan Sensei's version had strange additions and gestures. So an expert, even if he only glimpsed part of the kata, could identify it as one of Kyan's."*

As an incidental technical point on changes, which often occur in kata, in the Passai taught by Kyan students Shimabukuro Zenryō and Nakazato Joen, the first movement stepping forward into kosa-dachi is done with the hands in an augmented block position with the left hand held in a fist by the right elbow. The double punches later in the kata are done at middle and high level. However, in the 1930 "*Kempo Gaisetsu*", assuming that Miki Nisaburo represented the kata correctly, the first movement in *Kyan no Passai* shows the *open* left hand supporting the right fist, and in the double punches both fists are directed at lower-middle level. Clearly, a change was made somewhere along the line, though interestingly the Chito Ryu version of the kata, taught by Chitose Tsuyoshi, another one time student of Kyan, has these two techniques as shown in the 1930 book.

Much of kata performance, of course, boils down to personal taste; as Nagamine Shōshin explained, he "*was most impressed by the kata of Kyan,*" and there are attractive features to these forms. The Kusanku, for example, has a little more technical content than the Itosu kata and the Passai has a sharp series of open hand opening movements compared to the Itosu Passai which starts with a series of forearm blocks. The Kyan Chintō is light and quick and although there are several points in the kata where the feet are crossed – in Western combat sports they tell you never to cross your feet – it avoids the rather fanciful one legged stances and difficult- to-control 180 degree final spin of the Itosu form.

The important thing is that Kyan preserved a whole line of kata which may represent older versions of the forms and which could otherwise have been lost. And in fact these kata are often valued in modern day competition because of their distinctive appearance and content: for example, the Chatan Yara Kusanku became popular in kata tournaments a few years ago, albeit in super-polished competition form, for this reason.

Of Kyan's supposed two favourite students, Arakaki Ankichi died young and Shimabuku Taro didn't seem to have set up his own school, so that line of transmission faltered. However, there were other students who carried his karate, or elements of it, down to modern times. They included Shimabukuro Zenryō, Nakazato Joen, Nagamine Shōshin, Chitose Tsuyoshi, (founder of Chito Ryu), and Isshin Ryu founder Shimabuku Tatsuo. Shimabukuro Zenryō moved to Chatan in 1931 to set up a bakery business and in 1933 he began training with Kyan Chōtoku, continuing up to 1944. In 1952 Shimabukuro began teaching karate at his home and then in 1962 at his newly constructed Seibukan dojo. He died in 1969 at the age of 60 and was succeeded by his son Zenpo.

Nakazato Joen, who was born in 1922, studied with Kyan at the Agricultural College and at his home between the ages of seventeen to twenty one, (so 1939 to 1943). He went off to the war in 1943 and returned to Okinawa in 1947, but he didn't begin teaching till 1954. According to Shimabukuro Zenryō's student, Dan Smith, Nakazato didn't know the kata Chintō or Kusanku and learned them from Shimabukuro. In turn, Shimabukuro had forgotten, or had never learned, the staff kata Tokumine no Kon and Nakazato shared that with him. Dan Smith observed that Nakazato had been a bayonet instructor in the Japanese army and that may have affected the form he taught. Such are the problems of trying to establish the lines of karate transmission.

Dan Smith was an American serviceman on Okinawa when he began training at the Seibukan dojo. The regular classes were taken by Shimabukuro Zenpo, but after a while he was asked if he also wanted to attend the morning classes held by Zenpo's father Zenryō, the founder of the school and a student of Kyan Chōtoku. That was in April 1968 and Dan attended those classes for a year and a half until Shimabukuro's sudden death on a visit to mainland Japan. I corresponded with Dan and interviewed him by email in 2002. His recollection of those morning classes gives a nice insight into an older way of training:

"I attended the morning session and Zenryō did not say anything to me other than 'Seisan di,' which was his way of asking me to perform Seisan. I got about one third of the way through the kata and he started me over, giving me corrections on the first movements. We stayed on those first movements for well over a month before he let me move on.

". . . I went to the morning class that Zenryō taught up until his death in October 1969. He only taught kata in the morning class, and the only people who came to the class were older, senior students of not only the Jagaru (Seibukan) dojo, but men who had their own dojo. I was the only person who came daily as most would only come once or twice a week to get instruction from Zenryō Sensei. He taught in the old Okinawan method of learning each kata movement with an explanation of what the movement could be for, and how if you did not execute the movement correctly then you would not have the proper balance and strength. He stressed the exact movement of the kata and expected you to make the strength, speed and power through your own training.

"These morning sessions with Zenryō Sensei were also centred around individual training. No group exercises or kata. We never practiced the entire kata we were working on all the way through. He took sections of the kata and worked you on them or had you work by yourself as he watched. Most days he would not say or do anything. He would just watch the students who came for training perform their kata. This is where I learned the value of training alone and thinking that Sensei was always watching."

So the transmission was through the study and practice of kata. What about the kumite techniques that Kyan may have developed through his various experiences in fighting, such as the fish-hooking technique he was said to have used against Ishida, the judoka? Despite some speculation that Kyan's ideas have worked their way down to modern styles it seems that not much of that has come down to us. The books by Nagamine Shōshin and Nakazato Joen, for example, consist almost solely of kata, although in Nakazato's book (*"Kyudo"*) there a few photos from 1941 of him and *Okuhara Bunei* practicing a couple of kumite techniques: an open *kamae* that seems to come from Passai, a counter punch going off to the side, (as in Kusanku), and an open-handed counterattack to the face as the kicking leg is grabbed - in the photograph the foot is about to be twisted using the final technique of Seisan kata. These techniques may reflect a part of Kyan Chōtoku's teaching, or the photographs may just be of a couple of younger guys working out practical fighting moves . . . . but intriguingly that second technique, the counter against the foot grab is also shown in photographs of Kyan students Shimabuku Tatsuo and *Shinjo Heitaro*. Presumably that represents some common origin in Kyan's teaching.

Nakazato Joen, quoted in Mark Bishop's book, stated that sparring was carried out at Kyan's dojo, sometimes with protectors and sometimes without. Sometimes, *"the students would dip their fingers in soot and touch rather than strike their opponents, later assessing their success or failure by examining the soot marks on their opponents' bodies."* But such "touch" practice wouldn't reflect the depth and penetration of attacks in a real fight. We don't have a clear idea of where kumite stood in Kyan's teaching.

Modern *jiyū kumite* and competition techniques develop from constant practice and experience in those areas, but of course Kyan Chōtoku was practising and teaching karate in a pre-jiyū kumite and pre-competition era, and he would have conceived of kumite in a different way. And although he may have taught some movements and principles, such kumite techniques as he may have had would have been individual to him.

Nagamine Shōshin didn't seem to care much for jiyū kumite or competition, but Mark Bishop, who trained in Okinawa in the 1970s, noted the hard sparring in Shimabukuro Zenpo's dojo, and that Nakazato Joen's *Shōrinji Ryu* was "*a style to be reckoned with at the various high school sports competitions in which full protectors are compulsory.*" And back in the early 1960s Shimabukuro Zenryō's was one of those Okinawan schools that competed with bogu, protective gear. That experiment only lasted till the early to mid 1970s, but it does demonstrate an awareness of the need for practical fighting experience, though interestingly it never seemed to encroach into the core teaching of kata.

As Dan Smith recalled, the bogu "*was cumbersome and limited the techniques you could use. It favoured the larger opponents and those who could drive forward with a strong punch or side kick. There was no preparatory training for fighting with the bogu. Some nights Zenpo Sensei would direct us to put it on and fight. These were nights that most of us did not look forward to because even though the bogu protected your vital body parts you would definitely go home with bruised arms and shins, along with a neck ache if someone punched you or kicked you in the head.*"

In his 1930 "*Kempo Gaisetsu,*" Miki Nisaburo mentioned that Kyan Chōtoku was writing a book about karate training and "*shiai knowledge and attitude. . . . As Sensei is extremely knowledgeable about the art, it is our sincere wish that not only is his book published as soon as possible but also that he continue his research on the art. It is indeed a great contribution to the art.*"

Whatever happened to that book? Apart from Miki, no one makes any reference to Kyan Chōtoku and a book, and all knowledge of it is now lost. We do, though, have some written guidance from Kyan in Miki and Takada's 1930 "*Kempo Gaisetsu.*" This book had two editions, a 183 page version, with hand written text, and a slightly later printed edition with additional material. Kyan's advice appears in this later edition.

Whether this is part of the manuscript of Kyan's lost book, or the text is taken from notes that Miki made in his few months on Okinawa isn't clear, but hopefully it is an accurate reflection of Kyan's teaching. In a short introduction to this section, Miki wrote that *"Mr. Kyan is sixty one years old this year. He surely puts young men in shame with his spirit. Mr. Kyan is a karate shihan and currently teaches at both the Agriculture School and Hijabashi Tode Research Centre. He is providing valuable training and education to young people.*

Notes

Kyan in Kadena - Shimabuku Eizo, in his 1964 book on the old karate masters, noted that Kyan's *"house was in Kadena, which, before the war, was the third largest city in Okinawa, bustling with people. The Hija bridge area was the sister port of the port of Naha, and with the boats of numerous merchants coming and going, it prospered as the main part of the central district. At that time the master's residence was near Hija bridge and there he built a dojo."*

Kyan and the name Shōrin Ryu – Although Kyan karate is almost always referred to as Shōrin Ryu (or Shōrinji Ryu), according to Nakaya Takao (*"Karate Do. History and Philosophy"*), during his lifetime, Kyan never actually named his style.

Kyan in Hokkaido and Sanpu Toku - Nakaya Takao had doubts about the story of Kyan going to Hokkaido with Arakaki and Shimabukuro. Among other things Nakaya mentioned that his own teacher, Nakama Chōzō, had been a close friend of Arakaki Ankichi since they were young and the two had practiced karate together. However, Nakama had never heard of the Hokkaido story.

"Kempo Gaisetsu" by Miki Nisaburo and Takada [aka Mutsu] Mizuho (Mutsu) – This a very rare book. I am very grateful to Ohgami Shingo for supplying me with photocopies of both editions. The translation into English of Kyan's advice is by Brian Sekiya. *"Kempo Gaisetsu"* was reprinted by Yoju Shōrin in 2002.

Kyan and Naihanchi kata – This is a puzzle since Kyan's well-known students, such as Shimabukuro Zenryō, Nakazato Joen, Nagamine Shōshin and Shimabuku Tatsuo, seem to have pretty much all taught the kata.

According to Dan Smith, a student of Shimabukuro Zenryō/Zenpo: "The Naihanchi kata that we practice comes from Nakama Chōzō, a student of Chibana Choshin and Motobu Choki. Master Shimabukuro Zenryō and Nakama sensei were very good friends and Nakama sensei stayed at the Shimabukuro dojo and home often. He worked at the Camp Kuwae hospital, which was located next to Jagaru village, but his home was at Shuri so he would spend the night often with the Shimabukuro's to avoid the long drive to Shuri. It was during this time that Nakama sensei taught Shimabukuro Zenpo the Naihanchi kata. I was privileged to be able to observe and learn these kata on Sunday afternoons with Master Shimabukuro Zenpo looking on. Since I had learned the Tekki kata version while a student of Shotokan before coming to Okinawa I was able to learn the kata by watching and then asking Zenpo sensei for instruction after class during the week. The Naihanchi kata were not taught as part of the Seibukan curriculum until after 1975 so many of the earlier students of Seibukan did not learn these kata. This is also true with Jion and Passai Gwā." (From a post on the website of the American Black Belt Academy, Colorado Springs, consulted 2008.) Still, it's interesting that pretty much all of Kyan's successors chose to teach Naihanchi.

Re the Pinan kata - Kyan did not teach the Pinan, although they were widely practiced during his lifetime. Some of his students or grand-students though, such as Nagamine Shōshin and Shimabukuro Zenpo, subsequently brought the Pinan into their teaching. Others such as Nakazato Joen and Shimabuku Tatsuo did not teach Pinan.

Again, according to Dan Smith it was Nakama Chōzō who taught Shimabukuro Zenpo Pinan and Naihanchi, as well as Passai Gwā and Jion: *"These kata were not part of Kyan's training... Zenryō Sensei never practiced these kata but had Zenpo Sensei learn them and incorporate them into the Seibukan dojo syllabus."* Shimabukuro Zenpo told "Dragon Times" no. 16 (2000) the same thing: *"I learned the kata Pinan, Naifanchi, Jion and Passai Gwā from Nakama Sensei and he learned these kata from Chibana Sensei."*

Sunabe Shozen – He was featured in an article by Charles Goodin in "Classical Fighting Arts" magazine, Nos 45 and 46, (2012). Sunabe (1919 – 2008) told Charles that he had been raised in Yomitan, began karate with Kyan at age six and trained with him for twelve years at his (Kyan's) home. He recalled that Kyan taught Seisan as the first kata. Sunabe did Seisan for three years, working on a set of three movements at a time, although the other kata were learned fairly quickly. After Seisan he learned Naihanchi Shodan to Sandan (?), Ananku (two kata, dai and sho) (?), Passai, Gojushiho, Chintō, and Kushanku. Kicks were done with the toes, and Kyan could walk around the house on his toes.

Tokumine no Kon – It's generally agreed that Kyan also taught the bo kata Tokumine bo (kun) kata, which came from the bo expert Tokumine Shitsunen. According to the article on Motobu Choki in "*Aoi Umi*" magazine, (Number 70, Feb. 1978, by Jahana Seiji), one day Tokumine was very drunk and disorderly in Tsujimachi and had a fight with several police. He was arrested and exiled to a remote island in Yaeyama (Ishigaki island) where he died later. Kyan Chōtoku visited Yaeyama to learn the bo kata of Tokumine, only to find that he was dead. Kyan did learn, though, that the owner of a small inn where Tokumine once stayed had learned the bo kata directly from him, and he passed the kata Tokumine no kon on to Kyan. Jahana wrote that *"In Yaeyama today there still remains the kata of Tokumine No Kun."* Nakamoto Masahiro wrote that it was Kedabana Gisuke (1843-1943) who had received training in Bōjutsu from Tokumine and passed the kata on to Kyan.

In an email discussing differences between the kata of Kyan students Shimabukuro Zenryō (Dan's teacher) and Nakazato Joen, 18 August 2006, Dan Smith told me: *"Nakazato told me that he did not have Chintō or Kusanku and that Zenryō Sensei taught him the kata. Zenryō Sensei had forgotten Tokumine no Kun and Nakazato shared that with him but it had a different flavour as Nakazato had been a bayonet instructor and it appeared many of the movements were influenced by this."*

Shimabuku Tatsuo also taught a Tokumine no kon but according to Andreas Quast this is quite a different form. It appears then, that the modern form of Tokumine no Kon comes from Nakazato Joen.

There is footage of Nakazato performing the kata on You Tube, and he shows it in his book ("Kyudo") where he also mentions this in his section on Kyan Chōtoku: "During the War January of Showa 19, (1944) Kyan Sensei visited the airport construction site at Yomitan for a demonstration. At the age of 75 Sensei demonstrated Chintō kata and Tokumine no Kon. The labourers recruited from Okinawa at the event were impressed and encouraged by Sensei's performance." Possibly it was around this time that Nakazato learned the kata.

I know almost zero about the bo/kon or Kobudo (the practice of the traditional Okinawan weapons) but the "*Aoi Umi*" magazine story about Kyan going to Yaeyama to learn the kata from Tokumine sounded a little strange. To make such a trip specifically for the purpose of learning a bo kata would suggest that Kyan was a passionate practitioner of the bo. However, there is no indication that this was the case: in fact Tokumine no Kon is the only bo kata taught by his successors, and it seems to have been transmitted solely through Nakazato.

In his brilliant analysis of Tokumine no Kon's history, (April 21, 2014) Andreas Quast noted that "There seems to be no source that even gives an approximate year as regards when Kyan went to 'Yaeyama' to study the bōjutsu of Tokumine." However, Andreas did point to three newspaper articles from 1931 which reported on Kyan's visit to Ishigaki Island to demonstrate and teach karate "on the occasion of the establishment of a "training facility" for karate, which we later find described as the 'Southern Islands Butokuden' . . . . As the first of these articles is from September 1931, and the last one from early December 1931, Chōtoku either stayed in Ishigaki for about four months, or he visited Ishigaki at least twice within this timeframe, meaning of course that he might have returned to Okinawa in between." As Andreas points out then, this information "points to the year 1931 as the year that Kyan learned Tokumine bōjutsu on Ishigaki."

Acknowledgements
For material and help with this historical essay, thanks to: Nakazato Joen, Charles Goodin, Dan Smith, Ohgami Shingo, Patrick McCarthy, John Sells, Ian McLaren and N. Karasawa.

* Deeply grateful to my dear friend, Graham Noble

Karate for Milk
The story of Sunabe Shozen
By Charles Goodin

Editor's note: This article is reprinted with the permission of Charles Goodin.

One of my privileges and great joys as a Karate researcher is to find and meet with unknown Karate experts and their families. Okinawan immigration to Hawai'i formally began in 1900 (the first Okinawan person, Kawakami Kisaburo, may have actually come to Hawai'i in 1896). By the 1920s, there were over 20,000 Okinawans living in Hawai'i, including many young man who had learn karate back in Okinawa. Most Okinawans at that time came to Hawai'i to work on sugarcane plantations on the various islands. Because of the great distance involved and the lack of modern communications, Karate students in Hawai'i often lost touch with their teachers and fellow students in Okinawa. Some Hawai'i students had studied with prominent teachers, such as Matsumura Sōkon, Itosu Ankoh, Motobu Choki and Miyagi Chojun. Had they remained in Okinawa, they might have become well known instructors. But in Hawai'i, they literally disappeared from Karate history. This story of one such student who studied in Okinawa for 12 years with Kyan Chōtoku at his home in Kadena.

I first heard about this student in a very roundabout way. My wife and I went to high school together in Honolulu. One of her good friends was an Okinawan girl named Lori who was very active in Okinawan dance and culture. I remember seeing her perform a few times at school, including one occasion where she and her younger brother skillfully used the sai. At the time, I was a student of *Kenpo Karate* (under the *Mitose* line), and was very impressed by the precision and classical appearance of their kata. I remember Lori saying that her father had studied Karate on the Big Island and taught both herself and her brother.

Not long afterward, my wife's brother visited from the mainland where he was studying the Matsubayashi Ryu form of Shōrin Ryu while attending law school. He took me to meet Tommy Morita Sensei at the Nuuanu YMCA. Morita Sensei what is the senior instructor of Matsubayashi Ryu in Hawai'i [FN 1], and referred us to his student, Rodney Shimabukuro Sensei, who was teaching at Our Lady of the Mount Church in Kalihi. We both became students of Shimabukuro Sensei and I have practiced Shōrin Ryu ever since (now also under Shinzato Katsuhiko Sensei, Head of the Kishaba Juku of Shōrin Ryu). But it was because of seeing Lori and her brother perform at my high school that I really wanted to learn Okinawan Karate. Two years after graduation, Lori was the maid of honor at our own wedding.

Over 20 years later, I thought back about Lori's father, Teruya Tamotsu [1928-2008], and called him. We discussed many aspects of his training on the Big Island of Hawai'i. By that time, I had read quite a bit about Karate history, but still have no idea that there were Karate instructors in Hawai'i before World War II.

Tamotsu's father, Kamado, was a Karate instructor who had learned in Okinawa. He had planned to teach his son Karate when he reached a certain age, but unexpectedly passed away before that time. Tomotsu knew his father's Karate friends and other Karate experts living on the Big Island. He mentioned search names as, Gibo Sensei, Higa Sensei, Arakaki Sensei, and Urasaki Sensei. Eventually, he became a student of Urasaki Seiichi, who, like his father, had learn Karate and Okinawa.

But he also mentioned another name. He said that one sensei he had met on the Big Island had a son who had studied under a very "high class [FN 2] Okinawan teacher. That teacher was a certain "Kyan." My ears perked up. Could he be talking about the legendary Kyan Chōtoku [1870-1945], one of the pioneers of my own style of Shōrin Ryu? I discovered that this Sensei was a Mr. Sunabe, whose son now lived on the Island of Oahu, in Waianae. A quick check of the telephone directory revealed a Mildred Sunabe living in Waianae. I nervously called the number, spoke to Mrs. Sunabe, who handed the phone to her husband, Shozen. After identify myself, I mentioned my friend Laurie and her father, Tomotsu. As it turned out, Sunabe Sensei new Lori's paternal grandmother back in Okinawa. Next came the big question. Had he in fact studied with the legendary Kyan Chōtoku? There was no delay. *"Oh yes,"* he said, *"for 12 years at his house."*

Nevertheless, I sensed that there was some reluctance on his part to meet with me. Over the years, some people here in Hawai'i had tried to persuade Sunabe Sensei to teach them Karate, but he steadfastly refused. Although I was interested primarily in background information about Kyan sensei, I soon wondered whether Sunabe Sensei might consider teaching me.

Every few months I would call and request a meeting during such calls, ask him for more information about his years of training with Kyan Sensei. Finally, on six March 1998, a meeting was arranged at a local store where I picked up Sunabe Sensei and took him to my house. After a short visit, during which he demonstrated kata, Seisan, Sunabe Sensei invited me to his home in Waianae. There, we ate lunch with his wife and talked about Karate. My wife had picked up *bento* [boxed lunches] from a Japanese restaurant and made some mochi. Mrs. Sunabe had made some delicious salmon, shrimp tempura and other dishes.

Now Sunabe Sensei had been to my house, and I knew exactly where he lived. Most importantly, he told me that he wanted to describe and show me what he had learned it is 12 years of study at Kyan Sensei's house. This, he said, was his way of honoring the memory of his teacher.

Before I proceed, I should explain why I never identified or written extensively about Sunabe Sensei. The answer is very simple. While living, he did not want to be publicly known and I respected his wishes. Many of the early Okinawa Karate experts in Hawai'i were extremely private, and would even deny knowing Karate when asked. In addition, as will be shown later in this article, Sunabe Sensei served in the Japanese military during World War II. Japanese soldiers tended to keep a low profile in Hawai'i, particularly in the first few decades following the war. Sunabe Sensei passed away in 2008, and I feel that he would now feel comfortable with me publishing my notes. I will try to give us much detail as possible so that more research can be conducted about him.

c.1923 Shozen as a child...

According to his family record [*Koseki Tohon*], Sunabe Shozen was born on 8 October 1919, in *Owan*, Yomitan-son, Nakagami-gun, Okinawa. When I interviewed him, Sunabe Sensei told me that he was actually born on 23 March 1919. Discrepancies in such records are not unusual. His father, Sunabe Shoyei [or Shoei], was born on 1 April 1901 and died on 18 April 1999. His mother was named Kamado or possibly Tamako [died in the 1960s]. His grandfather, Sunabe Shoin, was born in 1878 [died in 1961]. His paternal grandmother, Sunabe Kamado, was born in Furugen in 1879 [died in 1937].

Shortly after Shozen was born, his father, mother, and grandfather immigrated to the Big Island [the Island of Hawai'i], in the van, territory of Hawai'i. Being the first son, Shozen was left in Okinawa to obtain a proper Japanese education. It might have also been to travel by ship with an infant at that time. Additionally, all immigrants were obliged by contract to work on the sugar cane plantations for a certain number of years. As a result, Shozen was raised at the family home in Yomitan by his grandmother, who was also named Sunabe Kamado [like his mother], add his paternal aunt.

In 1923, when Shozen was just four years old, his father returned to Okinawa to bring him to Hawai'i. Shozen steadfastly refused, however, stating that it was his responsibility to take care of his grandmother and aunt. Shozen would eventually immigrate to Hawai'i, but it would not be for another 35 years, in 1958.

Becoming the Student of Kyan Chōtoku

In 1925, Sunabe Shozen, age 6, was a student at the *Furugen* Elementary School. One day [a Saturday], the class had a very distinguished visitor, none other than Kyan Chōtoku. At that time, Kyan was about 56. According to Sunabe Sensei, after examining the class Kyan Sensei recognized Shozen as the little boy he had often seen at the nearby dairy asking the dairy woman for milk. Then and there he decided that Shozen would become his student. "*Come to my house,*" he said, "*and I will make sure that you get a big glass of fresh milk each day.*" In those days, a glass of milk was a luxury few could afford. Malnutrition was common in Okinawa, which explains why so many Okinawans sought work on mainland Japan, or immigrated to Hawai'i, the US mainland, or South America for work. Shozen agreed to go to Kyan's house the next day.

When he returned home, Shozen recounted the events earlier that day to his grandmother, Sunabe Kamado. "*How unbecoming of a Bushi to beg for milk*! "She scolded the child. "*You will not go to that man's house!*"

On Sunday, Kyan sought out Shozen I've asked him why he had not come as promised. Shozen explained what his grandmother had said and added that as a Bushi it was his duty to protect his grandmother and aunt. "*Are you a Bushi?*" Asked Kyan. "*Well, so am I!*" He told Shozen that by studying with him he would learn how to protect his family and would also get a precious glass of milk.

Even at that age, Shozen was very assertive. "*Why did you pick me out of all the children?*" he boldly asked Kyan. "*I had to pick someone,*" answered Kyan.

I asked Sunabe Sensei if he could think of any reason why Kyan I picked him. When I pressed, he mentioned that his father, *Shoyei*, had previously learned Karate from Kyan at the Agricultural School. I suspect that this was the main reason for his selection. Knowing that his former student had moved to Hawai'i, Kyan probably felt a sense of duty to teach the child Karate - an important aspect of a young "Bushi's" education. During the course of my research, I have found that most Karate students in Okinawa, at least before World War II, had a father, uncle, or grandfather who had also studied the art. It was very difficult to be excepted as a Karate student, but somewhat easier if I close relative had been a student.

1910 The thatched roof was the new house of Kyan Chōtoku along the Hija River on the other side of the Hija Bridge; The person in front of the home is could even be Kyan himself but we don't know for sure. Irei Hiroshi [RIP] launched a campaign around 2011 in hopes of having the house rebuilt on its original location; sadly, the project never came to fruition!

This was the case with my family friend, Teruya Tamotsu. It appears that Urasaki Seiichi excepted him as a stupid because Teruya's father had died before he could begin his son's Karate training. Otherwise Urasaki Sensei would probably have been unlikely to accept a student. In addition, he was referred by Sunabe Shoei [Shozen's father]. Back in Yomitan, the Sunabe family lived next to Tamotsu's mother's house. So there was a connection between the Teruya and Sunabe families.

In any event, the six year old Shozen agree to learn from Kyan sensei. During the next 12 years, he trained almost every day at Kyan Sensei's house at the Southern Bank of the Hija River [the Yomitan side]. Chatan [or Kadena] was on the Northern Bank of the river.

Kyan's House was downstream on the *Hijagawa* [Hija River] next to the *Hijabashi* [Hija Bridge], which at that time was made of stone and had but a single lane. Right below the house, on the riverbank, was a lumberyard. Wood from the surrounding area was brought to the lumberyard and loaded onboard boats which would come up the river at high tide, and returned downstream to the ocean on the next tide. With a lumberyard nearby, Kyan and his students had no trouble finding a replacement would whenever a makiwara would break.

Sunabe Sensei remembered spending many happy days swimming in the Hija River. He would usually ride his bicycle to Kyan's house [about a five minute ride from his house in Yomitan]. The Kadena police station was located on the other side of the bridge. Shozen did not have a permit for his bicycle and always worried that he would be caught by the policemen. But he never was.

There was a steep ravine on the Kadena side of the bridge. One day when passing over the bridge on the way to practice, the chain on his bicycle came off leaving a child with no way to stop. As the bicycle careened toward the ravine and crashed into some bushes, Shozen flew off and saved himself by grabbing onto some branches. He recovered the bicycle and replace the chain. Kyan had watched the incident from in front of his house. "*That was pretty good*," he would later say of his agile student.

During the 12 years that he trained with Kyan Sensei, he was the only student to regularly learn at Kyan's house. Kyan also taught at the Agricultural School and the Kadena police station, but there were certain things he would not teacher there, such as weapons [bo, sai, and nunchaku]. From time to time, students from the Agricultural School and police station would visit the house. When he was older, Shozen was asked to teach them. He could recognize that there were certain things that Kyan was not teaching the students which I will describe in the next part of this article.

During this time, Kyan earn his living by teaching what he called "Shuri-Ryu." At that time, the art was not generally referred to as Karate. The Karate curriculum in the public schools, based on the five Pinan Kata, was established by Itosu during the period from 1901 to 1907.

Prior to that time, new students in the Shuri system typically started by learning either Seisan or the three Naihanchi [Naifuanchi] kata.

There has been some question about whether Kyan was a student of Itosu. While he did not study with he Itosu, he was actually more of a contemporary of the elder teacher. They both had learned from Matsumura Sōkon. So while Kyan had learned from Itosu, and respected him as a senior, he did not consider him to be his Sensei.

March 1937 photo taken by the Ryūkyū Shimpo to commemorate both the establishment of the Okinawan Prefectural Karate-Do Promotional Society and the Kihon-gata of Karate-do. The photo first appeared in Nakasone Genwa's 1938 publication, "*Karate-do Taikan*" [The Encyclopedia of Karate-Do].
Top Row L-R: Gusukuma Shimpan, Maeshiro Choryo, Chibana Choshin & Nakasone Genwa.
Seated L-R: Kyan Chōtoku, Yabu Kentsu, Hanashiro Chomo & Miyagi Chojun.

The first three years of Sunabe Sensei's training were spent on a single Kata: Seisan. Kyan sensei Felt that Seisan what is the foundation for training. Students who learned at other locations might have focused on the Pinan or other kata. Thus, when "outside "students came to Kyan Sensei's house, Sunabe Sensei was often asked to show them Seisan.

Shozen did learn the Pinan kata when he went to Iccho Middle School, but by that time he was purely advanced in his training. The teacher there was Tokuda Anbun, a student of Itosu. At one time, Shozen asked Tokuda Sensei whether he could join the schools karate club. "*You are the student of Kyan Sensei,*" he was told. "*It's not necessary for you to join the club.*" Shozen also met Chibana Chōshin, another student of Itosu, who also taught at the school, and was also told that as a student of Kyan Sensei, it was not necessary for him to join any other clubs or learn karate elsewhere.

By the way, Shozen did get his glass of milk every day he train with Kiyan and Sensei. The dairy was immediately uphill and up river from Kiyan and Sensei's house. He also received a daily treat from Mrs. Kyan, a pastry [usually a *manju*] broke to the house by the Baker of Kadena.

Notes:

1. The Matsubayashi-Ryu form of Shorin Ryu was founded by Nagamine Shoshin, whose main instructors were Arakaki Ankichi, Kyan Chōtoku and Motobu Choki.
2. I did not understand the significance of the term "*high class*" at the time. In karate, "*high class*" generally means Karate from the Shuri area, where most Karate instructors and students were from the upper class of Ryukyu society. Shuri was the location of the Shuri Castle, where the king and his court resided before the abolition of the Ryukyu Kingdom, and it's annexation by Japan. Rank in Ryukyu society was based on one's relationship and position of service to the King. Kyan Chōtoku' father, Chōfu, was a member of the Ryukyu Kingdom's last *Sanshikan* [Council of Three], arguably the highest governmental body next to the King himself. He served King Shō Tai when he was exiled to Tokyo, and eventually became his chamberlain. Kyan Chōtoku actually grew up in Tokyo. See *Okinawan Karate, A Man Called Chanmie*; by Irei Hiroshi, 2011, trans. By Toma Shinsei.

Learning Seisan

A quick recap; At the age of 6, Sunabe Shozen became a student of Kyan Chōtoku. for the next 12 years, he learned from Kyan Sensei almost every day at his house next to the Hijagawa Bridge, in Kadena, Okinawa. Sunabe Sensei lived nearby in Yomitan, about five minutes away by bicycle. He was selected as a student after Kyan Sensei had visited his elementary school in Furugen and given a lecture and demonstration on Seisan kata. Sunabe Sensei's father, Shoyei, had also been a student of Kyan Sensei at the Agricultural School. In addition to the Agricultural School, Kyan Sensei also taught karate at the Kadena Police Station. Sunabe Sensei's parents and paternal grandfather, had emigrated to Hawai'i shortly after Shozen was born. He was raised by his maternal grandmother and aunt at the family residence in Yomitan.

Sunabe Sensei told me many times that Kyan Sensei would not teach a student Karate unless he liked him. By the time that, Sunabe Sensei became his student, Kyan Sensei made his living by teaching karate at the Agricultural School and the Kadena Police Station [which was just across the Hijagawa bridge]. He had no other job. He called his art, "Shuri-Ryu," rather than Karate.

Kyan Sensei actually taught two forms of Karate: a public version and private version. The public version was taught at the Agricultural School and the Police Station, where classes were generally open to the public. The private version was taught at his home to private students.

In accordance with tradition, Kyan Sensei would only teach one or two private students at a time. He would teach them from a young age until they reached a level of proficiency, usually about the age of adulthood. He would only teach a private student if, he "liked him," or in other words, was confident in his character based on such factors as his family background and social class, referrals from trusted friends and peers, and his own interaction with the student over time. The reason for the screening process was that Kyan Sensei felt personally responsible for the actions of his students. If a student fought, it was as if Kyan sensei had fought. If a student injured someone, it was as if Kyan sensei himself had done so.

Kyan Sensei had an internal conflict because he could not be selective of his public students, that is, the students at the Agricultural School and the Kadena Police Station. He made his living by teaching Karate and thus was financially dependent on having public students who paid tuition. He still felt personally responsible for them, but he did not have the long-term personal contact with them that he had with his private students, nor could he be as strict or physically demanding on them. This is the reason why he taught two forms of Karate, a private [complete] Version and a public [simplified] version. It might have looked like he was teaching the same thing in form, but the content and depth different greatly.

A stone monument erected by Nakazato Joen in honour of Kyan Chōtoku stands next to the Hija River, on the opposite side of the bridge not too far from his original home. The inscription reads; "Kensei Kyan Chōtoku Sensei, aka Chanmi-gwā." *Photo by P. McCarthy*

I will give you an example. In a short time, I can teach a student the movement of Naihanchi Shodan kata. That does not mean that he truly understands the kata - just the outer form. If I then spend many years, I might be able to teach the student the body mechanics of each movement of the kata, the relationship of each movement to the others, and the bunkai or applications applicable to each movement and combination of movements. Now the student is beginning to learn the inner meaning of the kata. The inner meaning of the kata, once grasped, unlocks the kata. Until then, the student is just going through the motions.

I am sure that Kyan Sensei talk different levels of kata to his students, depending on his trust in them, their years of training and level effort, and other factors. Some of the more advanced students from the Agricultural School and the Kadena Police Station were invited to his house, from time to time, for more advanced training. But his private students were taught the private form of a Karate from the beginning. They were more like apprentices or disciples. And during his 12 years of training [from 1925 until 1937], Sunabe Sensei believed that he was one of only a handful of private students. I should add that Sunabe Sensei said Kyan Sensei might teach the same kata differently to different students. This might explain why students who all learn from Kyan Sensei might perform the same kata differently.

There is another point about the private and public forms of Karate. Matsumura Sōkon, the teacher of both Itosu Ankoh and Kyan Chōtoku, among others, only taught privately. He did not have a large school or dojo. Students were selected by Matsumura Sensei, based on their references, character, add rank or status in the Ryūkyū Kingdom.

Itosu Ankoh was the leader in the introduction of Karate to the Okinawan secondary school system. He developed the five Pinan kata to be taught to these young students. They apparently learned the three Naihanchi kata first, followed by the Pinan kata. But unlike his private students, who learned the complete range of meanings and applications for each movement in the kata – including the grappling, joint manipulation, *Kyusho* [vulnerable points], and breaking and tearing techniques which are generally known as "*Ti*," the secondary school students learned only the outer form, with limited applications. This is when Karate became known as a system of punches, blocks, strikes and kicks, a tremendous reduction and simplification of a complete art talk by Matsumura Sensei and his predecessors.

Thus, public students of Itosu Sensei might have learned and been able to perform the Pinan Shodan kata, almost like a dance or exercise. His existing private students, such as Yabu Kentsu, Hanashiro Chomo, Tokuda Anbun, and Chibana Chōshin, would also know the Pinan kata [and the older kata] but could use the techniques of the kata in the complete, old ways, which included the *Ti* applications. Itosu Ankoh's "public school" form of karate spread throughout Okinawa, and generally formed the basis for the Karate that became popular on mainland Japan in the 1920s and 1930s.

Unlike Itosu Sensei, Kyan Sensei taught far fewer students in far fewer locations. And it appears that his "outside" or public students were adults rather than school children. He seems to have avoided the Pinan kata, which at the time of their introduction were considered to be for children only [and their teachers]. However, despite teaching adults at the Agricultural School and the Kadena Police Station, Kyan Sensei still felt the need to simplify his kata both in form add application, including the elimination or de-emphasis of the *Ti* applications.

Sunabe Learns Seisan
Sunabe Sensei learned Shuri-Ryu [Kyan Sensei did not call the art "Karate" at the time] by learning kata, and according to him, the most important kata to Kyan Sensei was Seisan [literally "Thirteen Hands "]. Seisan what is the key to understanding all other kata and techniques. It does not appear that Sunabe Sensei was taught an introductory set of basics [punches, strikes, blocks, kicks, etc.]. Instead, his first 3 1/2 years of training consisted entirely of learning and practicing the Seisan kata.

The first day of training, Sunabe Sensei what is taught the first three movements of Seisan kata. Kyan Sensei carefully showed him each movement and then have him practice them over and over again. Kyan Sensei would make corrections, and the process would be repeated until he was satisfied with Sunabe Sensei's performance of the first three movements. This might take many days. Only when Kyan Sensei was satisfied would the next three movements we taught. This continued until Sunabe Sensei had learned the entire kata, which he would perform under Kyan Sensei's watchful eye. The learning process took about half a year.

Sunabe Sensei did not have any time to feel a sense of accomplishment. As soon as he had learned and could perform the entire kata, Kyan Sensei handed him a set of stone dumbbells [round stone weights connected by a stone shaft]. For the next year of his training, Sunabe Sensei performed Seisan kata holding a stone dumbbell in each hand, grasping each dumbbell horizontally by the shaft. The second year of training, Sunabe Sensei performed the kata while grasping each dumbbell from the top [holding it hanging down vertically]. The third year, the dumbbells were replaced by stone jars [*kame*] with a smooth lip, making them very hard to grip. Sunabe Sensei what how to perform the kata wow grasping the jars. To make it even harder, Kyan Sensei would periodically add sand to the jars.

Thus it was the Sunabe Sensei spent his first 3 1/2 years with Kyan Sensei Learning and practicing the Seisan kata with stone dumbbells and stone jars. I had often heard the expression "one kata, three years," and asked Sunabe Sensei if he learned any other kata, and if so, how long he spent on each one. As it turned out, the "one kata, three years "expression only apply to the first kata [Seisan]. After that, he learned the other kata in Kyan Sensei's curriculum very quickly, usually spending only a couple of months on each. He learned the remaining kata in the following order:

Naihanchi Shodan, Nidan, and Sandan
Ananku Sho [made by Kyan]
Ananku Dai [made by Kyan]
Passai * Gojushiho * Chintō
Kusanku [Kyan Sensei's version]

Sunabe Sensei also learned the five Pinan kata while attending public school. He said that Kyan Sensei never taught him these kata at the house. It appears to me that Ananku what is something like Kyan Senseis version of a Pinan kata. The version I learned in Matsubayashi-Ryu is very simple add linear, moving in the four cardinal directions [no diagonals]. I used to joke that it was like Pinan six.

In addition, Sunabe Sensei learned bo, sai and nunchaku from Kyan Sensei. Two kata were tight for the bo, but none were taught for sai and nunchaku. For sai and nunchaku, Kyan Sensei taught him various striking ad blocking techniques. Sunabe Sensei stated that Kyan Sensei did not teach weapons at the Agricultural School or the Kadena Police Station. Weapons were only taught at his home.

Sunabe Sensei did not mention to me whether the kata he learned were of Shuri, Tomari or Naha origins. My understanding is that most of the kata taught by Kyan Sensei were of Tomari origin. Over the years, I have heard from various sources that Kyan Sensei modified his kata to suit his small stature and light weight. I suspect that he would have also modified his kata to suit the stature, weight, strengths, and weaknesses of his students.

1905 Okinawa Prefectural Junior High School Graduation Commemorative Photo; *Courtesy of Kochi Municipal Library Collection*; *Miyake Sango*, the person with the white mustache, standing 2nd from the left in the second row, had previously been mistakenly identified as *Itosu Ankoh*; However, it has since been determined that the person standing to the far right, in the second row, is actually *Itosu Ankoh*.

In spite of trying to repair, colorize, enhance and enlarge the 1905 photograph, in which Itosu appears, the quality of the image remained relatively poor; As such, I [Patrick McCarthy] worked together with Hemanth Kumar [India], Scot Mertz [Okinawa] and Neal Simpson [USA] to reproduce this likeness of Itosu Ankoh.

Sunabe Sensei did say that students from the Agricultural School and the Kadena Police Station would sometimes come to Kyan Sensei's house for training. When they did, Sunabe Sensei said that he noticed that, "*Something was missing*" in their kata - that is, the full range of applications of the movements [including *Ti*] and weapons training. Usually, even though he was much younger than the visitors, Kyan Sensei would ask him to work with the visiting student, almost always on the Seisan kata.

"Banya" Guardhouse at Shikina-en
The guard house is strategically located near the entry gates as well as the palace. It is essentially a small, well-appointed residence built in a traditional Ryūkyu style for palace guards. At one point after the annexation of Ryūkyu to Japan, Karate master, Bushi Matsumura Sokon, was a guard here. As such, it is said that he taught the fighting arts to his disciples, including Kyan Chōtoku, here on this sacred ground.

* Photo by Patrick McCarthy

Matsumura Seisan

I practice the Kishaba Juku form of Shōrin Ryu, but originally practiced a Matsubayashi-Ryu form, which was founded by Nagamine Shōshin, who trained under Kyan Sensei [as well as Arakaki Ankichi, Motobu Choki, and others]. Nagamine Sensei, who was a police man in his early years, learn from Kyan Sensei at the Kadena Police Station. I remember that when I first started to learn Matsubayashi-Ryu, the basic kata were the Fukyugata (2), Pinan (5) and Naihanchi (3) kata, in that order.

We did not practice the Seisan kata. Over the years, I heard various reasons for the exclusion of Seisan from the Matsubayashi-Ryu curriculum. These included the fact that Naihanchi was our basic kata [for body mechanics] and that the dynamic tension of Seisan was dangerous to the health. However, I also wondered about the exclusion of Seisan, particularly given Kyan Sensei's emphasis on the kata. Of course, it was up to Nagamine Sensei to choose the kata in his curriculum.

I asked my senior friend, Sensei Pat Nakata, who learned from Chibana Chōshin [a student of Itosu Ankoh], about Kyan Sensei's Seisan kata. I had originally thought that Seisan what is a Goju-Ryu kata. Nakata Sensei explain that while Seisan is generally consider to be a Naha-Te kata and is practiced in Goju-Ryu, the form that Kyan Sensei learned was from Matsumura Sōkon, who learn the kata in Beijing, China. Matsumura Sensei is generally considered to be the founder or pioneer of the *Shuri-Te* form of Karate. Since he learned the kata in China, it would not be correct to call it Naha-Te kata [which generally can be traced to Higashionna Kanryo, who also learn in China, but in Fuzhou, Fujian province]. I would actually call Matsumora Sensei's version, *Shuri-Te Seisan*, which differs quite a bit from the Goju-Ryu version.

Sunabe Sensei actually performed his Seisan kata at my house, twice. Here are my observations; Before he would perform the kata, Sunabe Sensei remove his shirt [leaving only a tank top style T-shirt], glasses, and partial denture. He said that he would not wear his glasses and partial (denture) because during kata you have to act and feel like you are in a real fight. In a real fight, glasses and a partial (denture) could be used against you as weapons. He demonstrated that an attacker could pull off your glasses and stab you with them [*particularly in the eyes or the temples*].

What amazed me most was Sunabe Sensei's posture. When he took the opening position of the kata, he lowered his shoulders more than I thought possible! He did not seem to exert much force to do so. It almost seemed that his shoulders were hinged and could be lowered at will.

Sunabe Sensei's Seisan was light and sticky. He did not rush from movement to movement. By "sticky "I mean that there was a feeling of *muchimi* in his movements. His movements were not staccato, rough, or forced. It seemed like he moved lightly, but with his body firm, and just punched or struck at the end of the movement. Let's take a standard punch, *chudan tsuki*. Some people exert force right from the beginning [where are the fish is chambered]. Sunabe Sensei's punch seem to extend out smoothly and quickly, but easily with the force [*kime*] exerted only at the very end of the punch, followed by a short recoil.

He did not *kiai* loudly for any moment. He exhaled for each movement, but quietly. His movements were very upright. He did not take any low stances.

Shimabukuro Tatsuo

I mentioned all of this to my friend Angel Lemus Sensei, who practices a form of Shōrin Ryu that traces [its origins] to Shimabukuro Zenryō [*another direct student of Kyan Sensei*]. He asked me to review footage online of various people performing the Seisan kata. Of all the examples, the one that reminded me the most of Sunabe Sensei's Seisan was an early film of *Shimabukuro Tatsuo* [another direct student of Kyan Sensei and founder of the *Isshin-Ryu* form of Shōrin-Ryu]. Like Sunabe Sensei, Shimabukuro Sensei stood upright. In addition, the recoil of Shimabukuro Sensei strikes and particularly his kicks were very much like the way that Sunabe Sensei moved.

In addition, Shimabukuro Sensei appear to move in a very nonchalant way. His movements were not forced. It almost seemed that he was just walking through the kata. Sunabe Sensei moved the same way.

I have to admit that when I was young, I thought that some of the footage of the early Karate masters looked like "*old man*" Karate. I thought that lowered shoulders and the walking pace of their movements were just due to old age. Was I ever wrong! Only recently have I come to appreciate the refinement of their movements. They move fast without looking fast. Their strikes and kicks almost look like they are stabbing.

Another important point: Sunabe Sensei's movements seem quicker on the recoil or return than on the outgoing movement. For example, the recoil of his kick appeared to be faster than the kick itself, much like the saying that the recoil of a strike should be twice as fast as the strike. As a young karate instructor, I was more impressed with the outgoing speed. Now I appreciate the recoil speed and control.

I have another friend who reminds me of Sunabe Sensei. Sensei Alan Lee learned from Arakawa Tomu Sensei who learned from Izumigawa Kanki who learn from Higa Seiko. Lee Sensei's Seisan, compared to some versions of Goju-Ryu, appears to be light, but powerful. It is this light touch with a heavy hit that reminds me of Sunabe Sensei. Interestingly, I understand that Higashionna Kanryo's movements and breathing may have been lighter than Miyagi Chojun's. Higashionna was a contemporary of Matsumura Sōkon, so it is possible that their Seisan may have been more similar than the present day Shōrin-Ryu and Goju-Ryu versions. Higa Seiko originally learned Higashionna Kanryo.

My friend, Lee Sensei, also mentioned an interesting thing to me about posture. He said that in Goju-Ryu, the student is taught proper posture through the Sanchin and Tensho kata. These teach the proper posture for all kata. I believe that Kyan Sensei used the Seisan kata for the same purpose. In Kishaba Juku, we often say that all kata should look like Naihanchi. I suspect that Kyan Sensei would have said that all his kata should look like Seisan.

Body Conditioning
Body conditioning was a large part of Sunabe Sensei's training regime. He said that Kyan Sensei would always say, "Make your fingers and toes like *Yari* [spears], your body like iron, and your arms like katana [swords]." For the fingers, Kyan Sensei gave Sunabe Sensei bags filled with sand. As a child, Sunabe Sensei would strike these with his fingertips. In time, the sand was replaced by pebbles.

Training was always done in the yard of Kyan Sensei's house or on the beach [on Sundays]. The yard itself was sandy. Kyan sensei said that one should train in the sand to develop kicks and stopping ability. It was not possible to train inside because the *tatami* mats and floor boards would be broken by the stopping movements and the various kata, particularly Naihanchi kata.

Conditioning of the fists and feet [among other parts of the body] was done on the *makiwara*. Sunabe Sensei had his own *makiwara* planted in Kyan Sensei's yard. He would practice on the *makiwara* every day. Today, students tend to make a big deal about breaking *makiwara*. However, if you train with your *makiwara*, you know that they do break from time to time.

Kyan Sensei's house was right above the lumberyard on the bank of the Hija River. Boats would go up river to get the lumber with the incoming tide and then take it out to sea with the outgoing tide. Kyan Sensei knew the lumberman, and always had a ready supply of free lumber for his *makiwara*. Thus, Sunabe Sensei did not have to worry about breaking his *makiwara,* something he did routinely.

Once, when Sunabe Sensei was about to begin striking his *makiwara,* he noticed a faint glint. He stopped, and carefully examined the rope wrapped around the wooden plank. Someone had embedded broken glass in it! If he had hit it, Sunabe Sensei would have been seriously injured. Even though he did not know the identity of the perpetrator, he said that it was undoubtedly the student of another Karate instructor. Other students, according to Sunabe Sensei, were jealous of his relationship with Kyan Sensei.

Front kicks were done with the tips of the toes [*tsumasaki geri*]. Sunabe Sensei said that Kyan Sensei's toes were so strong that he could walk around his house on the tips of his toes. Kyan Sensei also had Sunabe Sensei wear heavy *tetsugeta* [iron *geta*] at night [presumably saw that the *geta* would not be seen]. After wearing the *geta*, kicks became quick, easy, and powerful. The first two toes had become very strong by gripping the straps of the *geta* to hold them to the feet.

While Sunabe Sensei trained with Kyan Sensei, he also attended regular school. He was very active in track and field, and was the high jump champion of his school. He said that he practiced at Kyan Sensei's House to be able to jump straight up to his own shoulder height, something that Kyan Sensei could also do. In the high jump, Sunabe Sensei could jump higher than his own height.

Kyan Sensei also had Sunabe Sensei practice the, "*Duck walk*," something with which martial art students worldwide are very familiar. Sunabe Sensei's son mention to me that his father would practice Duck walking for 10 laps at the school track, 2.5 miles!

18 June 1939 Naha Butokuden opening; School students demonstrate Seiunchin Kata! Kyan Chōtoku also performed Chintō Kata on this very day along with other dignitaries; i.e. Go Kenki [Hakucho], Chibana Choshin [Chintō], Kyōda Juhatsu [Suparinpei], Miyagi Chojun [Tensho], Higa Seiko [Seisan], Nakama Chozo [Kusanku-dai], Iraha Choko [Nepai] and Nagamine Shōshin [Yara Kusanku], et al …

Through such rigorous training, kata [including with weights], physical exercises, and *makiwara* training, Sunabe Sensei's body literally became like "iron." He said that when someone hit him, he did not even feel it at all. Kyan Sensei literally shaped Sunabe sensei's body so that it was in peak condition when Sunabe Sensei graduated from high school. I cannot emphasize this enough, Kyan Sensei not only taught Sunabe Sensei, he forged his body to optimize it for the execution of Karate techniques.

Applications & Meanings
Kyan Sensei used to say that *"You should practice like you were going to fight, but not fight."* Sunabe Sensei's exact words were that *"Kyan Sensei always teaching fight kine [kind] and then no fight."* In training, you had to prepare for the real thing, both physically and mentally. But you had to avoid fighting. Karate was for self-defense only. Fighting was not allowed and I did not hear of any incidents in which Sunabe Sensei got into a fight.

I asked Sunabe Sensei how he learned the applications or meanings of the movements in the kata. His answer was very direct: Kyan Sensei demonstrated them on him all the time. That was part of each day's training. Kyan Sensei would identify a certain movement or technique and Sunabe Sensei attack him. Kyan Sensei would respond to the attack and demonstrate various applications. Sunabe Sensei was very clear about one point: every single technique ended up with him on the ground. Kyan Sensei would remain standing but Sunabe Sensei would be laid out on the ground.

Sunabe Sensei also study Judo while at school. His Sensei was Itokazu Sensei [who may have also been an instructor of *Shuri-Te*] and he rose to the rank of *ikkyu* [first *kyu*]. It did not appear that Kyan Sensei used standard type Judo throws. Instead, his takedowns were destructive; he slammed the attacker on the ground, a rock, wall, etc. He also demonstrated joint manipulations, seizing and tearing techniques, and techniques designed to inflict extreme pain. Such techniques would be applied prior to, or in connection with, the takedown. In other words, Sunabe Sensei would be hypothetically injured before he hit the ground.

On the topic of Judo, Sunabe Sensei said that he remembered Miyagi Chojun was also a Judo instructor, and that he may have assistant Itokazu Sensei. I have not read this about Miyagi Sensei. Sunabe Sensei actually remembered that Miyagi Sensei held a 5th Dan in Judo.

Sunabe Sensei also remembered Yabu Kentsu who he described as tall [5' 6"] and frightening! He had a stern demeanor, blackened knuckles, and fingertips with no fingernails [from striking and conditioning exercises]. Kyan Sensei said the blackened and knuckles were undesirable, particularly for members of the Okinawan Bushi class. He taught Sunabe Sensei that soaking the knuckles in salt water after striking the makiwara would keep them soft and free of unsightly calluses.

Sunabe Sensei said that Kyan Sensei have a unique way of "*catching*." By this, I understood that he would catch or receive a punch or strike in a unique way. I asked Sunabe Sensei if he ever saw Kyan Sensei in a fight or a challenge match. He indicated that he had done so. Whenever someone attacked Kyan Sensei, according to Sunabe Sensei, Kyan Sensei would catch the attackers arms with his hands and that was it, the attacker which scream from Mercy. Kyan Sensei's hands and fingers were incredibly strong, and he apparently knew which *kyusho*, or pressure points, to attack.

Kyan Chōtoku　喜屋武朝徳

In addition, Sunabe Sensei said that when Kyan Sensei grabs someone with his two hands, he could kick them in the throat or face with a piercing and devastating toe kick! In fact, Kyan Sensei could interlace his fingers kick through his arms. Thus, it was almost as if Kyan Sensei's legs were like additional arms.

He was also adept at jumping-somewhat like a fighting chicken with his kicking leg close to his stomach/chest. After seizing the attacker, a flurry of kicks was always ready. Kyan Sensei's defense strategy thus appears to have been to catch or seize the attacking arms, control them, and inflict incredible pain, and then kick if necessary!

Night
According to Sunabe Sensei, during his youth on Okinawa it was exceptionally dark at night! There were no street lights and generally no electricity. Except for the light provided by the moon and stars, it was jet black. Fighting had to account for this. That is why so many of Kyan Sensei's kata [and Tomari kata in general] have searching movements with the hands and feet. In a night fight, you have to be very quiet, locate the attacker, strike, and move. For the feet, the type of searching would differ depending on the terrain. On a smooth surface, the foot could slide on the ground but on a rough or rocky terrain, the foot would have to be lifted while it searched.

Some kata have movements that were used to shield the eyes from the moonlight and better identify the attacker. There were also some movements in which the defender dropped to the ground to silhouette the attacker against the sky. Sunabe Sensei said that breathing is important in all Karate techniques, but especially when they are executed at night. He said that there are times when he would have to fight for 30 minutes straight at night. I did not learn, however, how breathing differed during the day and night.

Using Weapons
When it came to weapons, Sunabe Sensei said that the traditional ones such as the bo, sai and nunchaku were impractical in Okinawa at the time he learned. Instead, the best weapon was a simple cloth, the kind that young men often wore on their heads to absorb sweat. According to Sunabe Sensei, Okinawa was very rich in one thing, rocks. People usually were barefoot, and they were rocks everywhere. It was very easy to haul the two ends of a coif and slip a rock into the center. Then the cloth, with

the rock, could be swung and used almost like a nunchaku. He added a wet cloth work better. If the authorities came, the rock could be easily dropped and the cough would not be incriminating.

Other Students

I have mentioned that Sunabe Sensei trained alone with Kyan Sensei. Kyan Sensei taught many other students at the Agricultural School and the Kadena Police Station. Some students would visit Sensei's house from time to time, but Sunabe Sensei said that he was one of the few students who trained there on a daily basis. This took place from about 1925 through 1937.

I asked Sunabe Sensei about the earlier students of Kyan Sensei. As a young student of Matsubayashi-Ryu, I was familiar with *Arakaki Ankichi* [1899-1929], who apparently was taught at Kyan Sensei's house like Sunabe Sensei. Photographs of Arakaki show his athletic physique, something rare in Okinawa at the time due to poverty and malnutrition.

c. 1932: Seated left is Kyōda Juhatsu with Kyan Chōtoku beside him in the middle and [possibly even] Chitose Tsuyoshi standing behind; The sign board reads 唐手道 指南所　師範 喜屋武朝徳
"Karate-do Shinanjo ~ Shihan Kyan Chōtoku" [*Karate Educational Centre; Instructor Kyan Chōtoku*]
* Photo courtesy of the Chitose family

Arakaki Ankichi

But Arakaki was from a wealthy family and devoted his youth to Karate training. There is an incident reported in various Karate history books, such as Nagamine Shōshin's, "*Tales of Okinawa's Great Masters*," about Arakaki losing a Sumo match to a much larger opponent. Later that night, at a tea house, Arakaki met up with the opponent, got into a fight, and inflicted a toe kick that eventually led to his death. What made this scandalous at the time was that Arakaki apparently, "*played dead*" at one point and inflicted the kick as a surprise tactic.

Sunabe Sensei was familiar with this story and added that Arakaki had not gone to the tea house and called out the opponent. It was not a chance meeting. He also told me that Kyan Sensei would not state Arakaki's name. At the time, a persons house had a name. Kyan Sensei would only refer to the name of Arakaki's house.

Sunabe Sensei also mentioned to me that Kyan Sensei had a former student who had gotten into a fight with another Karate student and was killed. Kyan Sensei felt so badly about the incident that he stopped teaching Karate for sometime. Sunabe Sensei did not tell me the name of the student.

As I mentioned earlier, Kyan Sensei felt personally responsible for the actions of his students. If his student killed someone, it was as if he had done so himself. I also mentioned that Kyan Sensei emphasized realistic training. You had to train as if you were in a real fight, but not fight. Other Karate instructors seemed to think that Kyan Sensei encouraged his students to fight. The incident with Arakaki would seem to confirm this, at least to some other Karate instructors. Obviously, it would be unforgivable for cure Sensei to encourage students to fight, and then for his students to unnecessarily fight and wrongfully killed someone. There is some speculation that shame and stigma of the earlier described event, led to the early death of Arakaki due to stress, ulcers, and depression.

By the time he selected Sunabe as his student, Kyan Sensei was adamant that fighting was not allowed. Training was realistic but the techniques of Karate could be used for self-defense only. Sunabe Sensei was very clear about this to me.

Kyan Sensei had another former student named Mr. Kina who was a resident of Kina about 2 miles from Kyan Sensei's house. After training for several years with Kyan Sensei, Mr. Kina went to China to further his martial arts studies. One day, after he returned to Okinawa, Kyan Sensei took Sunabe Sensei to Mr. Kina's house in Kina. There, Mr. Kina demonstrated some of the techniques he had learned in China. One demonstration involved holding two long bamboo stalks, one in each hand. The bamboo was about 2 inches in diameter. Walking forward, Mr. Kina would crush the bamboo stalks at each joint in his bare hands.

Mr. Kina had a *papaya* tree in his yard [*the plants in Okinawa are very similar to the ones we have here in Hawai'i*]. Mr. Kina thrust his spearhead into the trunk of the papaya tree and pulled out the fibrous meat. I thought it might have been a banana tree, which has softer trunk, but Sunabe Sensei confirmed that it was a papaya tree.

Sunabe Sensei commented at this point that Chinese "Karate" uses the open hand, while Okinawan Karate generally uses the fist. Mr. Kina's spearheading technique was typical of the Chinese method. Of course, many Okinawan Karate techniques use the open hand, particularly in the older kata.

Kyan Sensei did not say much during Mr. Kina's demonstration. On the way back to his house, however, he told Sunabe Sensei that he did not approve of Mr. Kina's training and demonstration. After that, he would not teach Mr. Kina. I have to admit that I do not know Mr. Kina's first name, and I do not know who he was. I am only repeating what Sunabe Sensei told me.

One day, after Sunabe Sensei had trained at Kyan Sensei's house, and was riding his bicycle to elementary school, he was stopped by an adult who challenged him to a match. This seemed pretty incredible to me - that an adult would challenge a child - but Sunabe Sensei excepted. Sunabe Sensei considered himself to be a *Bushi* and challenges were something to be faced with honour. He said that the man would attack and he would defend and encounter. This went on for sometime, when Sunabe Sensei asked to stop. "*I have to go to school*," he said. "Can we continue this later?" The adult agreed. Sunabe Sensei said that he suspected that the man was a former student of Kyan Sensei who wanted to see what Sunabe Sensei had been learning. The match was never resumed, and Sunabe Sensei did not know the man's name.

In the first part of this article, I mentioned that Sunabe Sensei would receive a glass of milk after each training. He also received a pastry, which came from the baker of Kadena. Students of Shōrin Ryu will have realized that this was most likely Shimabukuro Zenryō. My impression was that the pastries were given to Kyan Sensei or his wife by the baker.

Martial Awareness

Kyan Sensei did not just teach the techniques of Karate. He also taught martial awareness to an extreme extent. Sunabe Sensei told me that Kyan Sensei's nickname "*Chanmī*" or Small Eyed Kyan, was not quite correct. He said that Kyan Sensei, who always wore glasses, had only one eye. Many years ago, Kyan Sensei was sitting and drinking sake with a friend next to a *hibachi* [charcoal burner]. The friend was stirring the coals with his *saibashi* [菜箸, *long chopsticks used in cooking*] and, for some unknown reason, and without warning, the friend poked Kyan Sensei in the eye with a hot end of them. Beside affecting his vision, this event seems to have also made Kyan Sensei very cautious and suspicious. He felt that he had to always be ready to defend himself.

For example, when someone handed him a cup of tea, Kyan Sensei would always make sure to receive a cup with one thumb press firmly against it. This was to prevent the person from being able to throw the hot tea into Kyan Sensei's face. When eating with chopsticks, Kyan Sensei would always hold them sideways, never pointing toward his mouth. If the chopsticks were pointed toward his mouth, an attacker could hit their ends and stab them into Kyan Sensei's throat. When sitting crosslegged on the floor, Kyan Sensei would always make sure that he could stand up quickly. One of his feet would always be pre-positioned on the floor for this purpose. Doorways and corners were always treated as places where an attacker could be lurking. Kyan Sensei's jumping skills are well known, but I have never figured out how he could walk on the rail of a bridge, jump out over the water and land back on the rail. Perhaps we will never know. But Sunabe Sensei told his son that Kyan Sensei could jump backwards in his house and brace himself in the corner of the ceiling, like a ninja.

Kanzashi [i.e. *kami-sashi* & *jīfā*] were ornamental hairpins worn by men and women measuring up to 20cm in length; Not surprisingly, they also had a longstanding tradition as doubling as an accessory weapon used in self-protection.

There were two movements in a Kata that showed practical applications based on items used in the Ryūkyū Kingdom. There is a movement in Kyan Sensei's Yara Kusanku kata in which a left open block is made over the head, and ending behind the head [the right hand executes a *shuto* with the hand up]. It is sad that this catching and writing type block was done by Kyan Sensei because he was so short. Sunabe Sensei said that the hand brushed over the head in order to grab a hair pin [*kami-sashi* or *jīfā*]. Such pins were worn by those above the commoner class in the Ryūkyū Kingdom. With the pin in hand, the next moment in the Kata is to stab the lower side of the attacker.

There is a movement at the beginning of the Tomari Chintō kata in which the two open hands are together at the wrists at about chest height. They then rotate clockwise, the right hand catches a punch, and the left-hand punches. Sunabe Sensei set that this technique was used when their hands were bound. The ropes used in Okinawa were fibrous. By twisting the hands and wrists together, the rope could be loosened and the hands could escape.

As previously mentioned, many movements in kata reflected the fact that self-defense techniques would often have to be executed in pitch blackness. This can be seen in many searching and catching techniques with the hands, and searching techniques with the feet [as in Tomari Passai]. Once the attacker was located, a limb would be seized and a quick punch or strike would be executed.

It is important to be quiet at night so not to give away one's location. Thus, stepping was done quietly, unless the intention was a stump. Today, students often make a stomping sound when stepping even if the stomp is not intended.

Fist Variations

I will close this part of the article with an incident that took place at my house. Before Sunabe Sensei demonstrated Seisan for me, he came close to me and said, "*In Karate, we use many forms of fists.*" During that brief sentence, he placed his fist on various locations of my head and in each one used a different form of fist: Two knuckles, one knuckle, the first joint of the index finger, the first joints of four fingers, the side of the index knuckle ... It happened so fast that I could not even think! He explained that a specific form of fist or hand position was used for each target.

I have to admit at the time, I only knew about *seiken* [knuckle fist]. I used that for everything! I felt like a school child in the presence of a Karate surgeon and still due to this day when I think about Sunabe Sensei.

Notes: In the final part of this article, I will discuss Sunabe Sensei's experiences on mainland, Japan, during World War II, and here in Hawai'i.

According to Shimabukuro Zenpo Sensei, in the Okinawa language [Uchinaguchi], "gwa" can signify missing as in "ti gwa," a person, missing their hand or arm. He also pointed out that. "gwa" is a somewhat derogatory or impolite term. Chan Mi Gwa, therefore, would mean, in informal speech, the person called Chan [Kyan in Japanese] Mi [with an eye] Gwa [missing].

Shozen & Mildred

Meeting his Future Wife
The pier at Yokohama Harbor must have been crowded, but somehow Mildred Yamashiro, the *biwa* student from Kaneohe, Hawai'i, met Sunabe Shozen, the Karate student from Yomitan, Okinawa. Actually, both were there to meet their uncles, who happened to be staying at the same hotel. This made it convenient for the young and country Shozen to get to know the girl from Hawai'i better. He probably told her that his parents and grandfather lived in Hawai'i on the Big Island. She remembered that he was exceedingly handsome but also very fresh to speak to her so directly. He asked her to dinner. They would spend a lifetime together.

The first meeting took place in 1941, probably just months before the Japanese attack on Pearl Harbor, which formally began World War II for the United States. Actually, the war in the Pacific and Japanese aggression toward its neighbors had begun years earlier, as early as 1937. This helps to explain why visits of Karate experts to Hawai'i had stopped after Miyagi Chojun returned home to Okinawa in 1935. Before Miyagi, Hawai'i had been visited by Mutsu Mizuho and Higashionna Kamesuke [in 1933], Motobu Choki [in 1932] and Yabu Kentsū [in 1927].

Nevertheless, many Hawai'i residents studied on mainland Japan before the formal outbreak of World War II. For Japanese and Okinawa residence of Hawai'i, studying in universities or cultural schools on mainland Japan was an honor. You have to remember that many Okinawans who came to Hawai'i to work had every intention of returning to Okinawa after they had made their fortunes. For many, what had begun as a visit intended for perhaps a few years, grew instead to decades and lifetimes.

Mildred Yamashiro [an Okinawan] learned to play the *biwa*, a stringed instrument, from her neighbor in Kaneohe [on the Windward side of Oahu]. He recommended that she further her studies in Japan and become certified to teach the instrument. Her instructor in Japan was Tachibana Soke, a man, she told me, who was prone to throw things when he was displeased with her progress. With the outbreak of war, Mildred along with countless other Hawai'i residence, became trapped in Japan. Even though they were Japanese or Okinawa ancestry, they were treated as *gaijin*, or foreigners, in Japan - suspicious foreigners. It was very difficult for foreigners to live in Japan during the war, especially as food and medical care became increasingly scarce. Mildred probably had to rely on the support of relatives and friends.

It is not widely known but many Hawai'i residents were sent to Okinawa before the United States attack on the island chain near the end of the war [the Battle of Okinawa, code named Operation Iceberg]. The Japanese hoped that American forces would be less willing to attack Okinawa if American citizens were present. That made no difference as almost 18% of the Okinawans were killed in the fighting.

Studying at Waseda University
As I mentioned earlier, Sunabe Sensei studied at the Shuri First High School, the finest in Okinawa, and generally reserved for students whose families had been of the upper classes in the Ryūkyū Kingdom. Sunabe Sensei had trained daily with Kyan Chōtoku for 12 years at his house in Kadena. Upon graduation from high school, he traveled to mainland Japan and enrolled in Waseda University, where he studied both biochemistry and law. As an attorney myself, I am very impressed that Sunabe Sensei could have studied both science and law. He must have been an exceptional student.

Despite his demanding studies, he did find time to visit a gymnasium on campus where Funakoshi Gichin was teaching the Shotokan form of Karate. Several *makiwara* were lined up along the wall. One day, Sunabe Sensei stood at the last *makiwara* and lightly punched it. He might have done so before, but on this day, Funakoshi Sensei happened to visit the dojo. Funakoshi Sensei asked one of his students who is this young man punching the *makiwara* was and the student replied that he was a Karate student from Okinawa. According to Sunabe Sensei, Funakoshi Sensei then said something to the effect that he must not be a very good student because he was hitting the makiwara like a child or a girl. The student repeated this to Sunabe Sensei.

Funakoshi striking the makiwara in his geta

You have to remember that Sunabe Sensei regularly practice at Kyan Sensei's house on the *makiwara* and with various [*chishi, sashi,* etc.]. It was an integral part of his training. He explained to me that he was only striking the *makiwara* lightly at the Waseda class because he did not want to break them. There was an inexhaustible supply wood at the lumberyard immediately below Kyan Sensei's house, on the bank of the Hija river. It would be hard to replace the *makiwara* at Waseda.

Nevertheless, when the students reported Funakoshi Sensei's comment, Sunabe Sensei's blood began to boil and he proceeded to break three *makiwara* with three punches. The student was amazed and Funakoshi Sensei abruptly departed.

I asked Sunabe Sensei where is the *makiwara* broke - at the bottom or the top. He said that they broke at the tops. I understand that *makiwara* break at the bottom when they are essentially hit hard with a pushing type movement, but break at the top when they hit very fast with a snapping type movement. I would like to add a personal comment at this point. It is considered very rude to hit a *makiwara* at someone else's dojo unless you ask permission first. I suspect that Sunabe Sensei had been granted permission by a student.

Seated 6th from the left, sporting a trendy Fedora hat, Funakoshi Gichin poses with members of the Tōkyō University Karate Study Group

But it is considered to be a dojo challenge when you break someone else's makiwara in the way that Sunabe Sensei did. I understand that it is acceptable to break *makiwara* in your own dojo or style, but not to do so outside your dojo or style - unless you intend to challenge the dojo and it's instructor. Did Sunabe Sensei intend to challenge Funakoshi Sensei and his students?

Well, after this event, it appears that some of the students begin to receive instruction from Sunabe Sensei in *makiwara* techniques. This was reported to Funakoshi Sensei, who apparently observed Sunabe Sensei a second time. On this occasion, he asked to see Sunabe Sensei's stances. Sunabe Sensei told me that the Shotokan stances were far too low and slow. I imagine that Funakoshi Sensei and his students thought that Sunabe Sensei's stances were too high - but this is exactly how the Karate experts in Okinawa at the time taught.

I mentioned that Sunabe Sensei felt that the Shotokan stances were too low and slow. I was interested in the "slow" part of his comment. After this event, Funakoshi Sensei invited Sunabe Sensei to meet him at an *ofuro* [public bathhouse]. One thing led to another, and Sunabe Sensei was invited to perform *kumite* with several of the students, including Funakoshi Sensei's son [I don't know which one].

Sunabe Sensei told me that it was impossible to spar with the students because they were too slow. He said that none of them could touch him. Sunabe Sensei emphasized to me that they were all far too slow, and I took this to mean that at least part of the reason for this was there low and long stances. At this point, I would like to explain to readers that I take no pleasure in reporting these events. I have respect for all styles of Karate and particularly for Funakoshi Sensei. But I have no reason to disbelieve Sunabe Sensei. If I may offer my own conjecture … Sunabe Sensei had not been trained to spar - he had been trying to fight. In Okinawa at that time, when someone challenged Karate student, it was to engage in *shobu*, or a match - to fight! Okinawan fighting was not limited by formal rules, and sometimes resulted in serious injury or even death.

I can imagine that when Funakoshi Sensei's students began a Kumite match with Sunabe Sensei, he stepped back into some sort of a long, fixed stance. Sunabe Sensei most likely did just the opposite - he probably stepped right up to the opponent at very close range. Close range fighting defined Kyan Sensei's system of Karate - the closer the better!

And when it comes to speed, I remember a friend explaining speed to me. He stood a few feet away from me and waved his hands. Then he moved just a few inches away from me and waved his hands right in front of my eyes. He explained that his hands moved at the same speed in both instances, but look faster to me when they were so close. They certainly did.

Up close, with long stances and fixed positions, the Shotokan students probably had a difficult time executing techniques. Sunabe Sensei probably crowded them and executed techniques that seemed unorthodox and were probably illegal in their system of *kumite*. In short, the students and Sunabe Sensei were not playing by the same rules. And, this is important, or university students almost certainly have not been practicing Karate every day for the past 12 years, let alone one-on-one basis with an expert of Kyan Sensei's caliber.

In any event, after the unsuccessful *kumite* matches, Funakoshi Sensei informed Sunabe Sensei there was no need for him to come to his dojo at Waseda or anywhere else for that matter. This was fine with Sunabe Sensei.

While attending the University, Sunabe Sensei return to Okinawa every summer and visited and train with Kyan Sensei. On his next visit home, he recounted his experience with Funakoshi Sensei and his students. Kyan Sensei told Sunabe Sensei that he, *"couldn't learn anything from Funakoshi Sensei."* Once again, I am just reporting this ad mean no disrespect. My own interpretation is that Kyan Sensei felt that Sunabe Sensei should not learn modern Karate [as being taught on mainland Japan] add instead should concentrate on the old style, Shuri-Ryu.

Sunabe Sensei did not meet Funakoshi Sensei again, but he did begin to teach some of his students and some other students. He told me that he taught a group of about 50 students. And it appeared to me that this group was left alone by other instructors.

Upon graduation from Waseda University, Sunabe Sensei immediately entered the Japanese military. He was assigned to Manchuria [in China] and served there as a pilot throughout the war. During this time, Sunabe Sensei told me that he observed and learned some Chinese martial arts. However, this was more for comparison. He continued to practice Kyan Sensei's art.

Sunabe Shozen as a pilot in Manchuria

On 22 January 1944, in Tōkyō, Sunabe Sensei married Mildred Yamashiro. The war end it the next year, and in 1952, a couple had a son, Shoryu. Mildred and Shoryu moved to Hawai'i in 1954. As a former member of the Japanese military, it was more difficult for Sunabe Sensei to immigrate to Hawai'i. He was not able to join his wife and son until 1958.

Kyan Sensei had died in 1945. Without his Sensei, it appeared that Sunabe Sensei stop practicing Karate. He did not learn from any other instructor or teach any students. After the war, he had to take odd jobs. One of them was building sets for samurai movies. His son told me that many years later while watching a samurai movie with his father, Sunabe Sensei said, *"I built that set!"*

In Hawai'i

When Sunabe Sensei immigrated to Hawai'i in 1958 and was reunited with his wife and son, he was almost 40 years old. He told me that he was too old to teach Karate. I am sure that he was also preoccupied with making a living in his new home. Initially, he worked as a biochemist. Eventually, the company you work for closed, and he started to make fertilizer. He then purchase land in Waianae [on the island of Oahu] and started a Vanda orchid farm. After a few years, however, the orchids were hit by a disease that killed them all. Shoryu told me that he gave his father the idea to plant Plumeria trees [which produce a flower widely used in Hawai'i for *lei*]. Soon the farm was filled with Plumeria trees.

By the time I met Sunabe Sensei [and Mildred], in 1996, the Plumeria trees were all dead. Only the dried outer shells of their trunks and branches remain. I did ask Sunabe Sensei if he ever taught Karate to anyone in Hawai'i. He said that he did not, but Shoryu told me that his father had taught him and a friend when they were young. Shoryu said that his father continued to practice on the *makiwara* at the farm. At first, all the *makiwara* would break, so he planted a 4 x 4 in the ground. That worked. Sunabe Sensei told me of a single instance when he had to use Karate in Hawai'i. He was drinking at an inn one night with a friend. When the friend left and walked out to the parking lot, he was jumped by three men. Sunabe Sensei went out and dropped the three men with three punches; he made it sound very easy, and it probably was for him.

He added that a Japanese Karate instructor who taught in Hawai'i at the same time was also in the in and had observed the event. The instructor asked Sunabe Sensei if he would tutor him in his form of Karate. Sunabe Sensei declined. He told me that he would not teach other instructors in Hawai'i. But he did initially agreed to teach me. Why? I believe that it was because I have been referred to him by my family friend, Teruya Tamotsu. You might recall from the first part of this article, lived on the Big Island of Hawai'i and grew up knowing Sunabe Sensei's father. After the death of Teruya's father, Sunabe's father [who had also been a student Kyan Sensei but did not want to teach Karate] referred Tamotsu to Urasaki Seiichi. In addition, Mr. Teruya's wife's mother lived next to the Sunabe family in Yomitan. I believe this is why Sunabe Sensei agreed to teach me, which he did, but only a very little, and share his stories, and his respect, for his Sensei, Kyan Chōtoku. I had met him when his wife's health was declining and his did too not long there after. He died in November 2008, at the age of 89. Mildred died the next year.

Final Thoughts

One of my missions is to learn about the early Karate experts in Hawai'i. Sunabe Shozen did not come to Hawai'i until 1958, but he is connected to other early Karate students and experts who lived here. I will always remember Mr. Teruya telling me that he knew of a man who learned from a "high class" teacher in Okinawa. He was speaking about Sunabe Sensei, whose teacher, Kyan Chōtoku, was the son Kyan Chōfu, a member of the last *Sanshikan* [Council of Three] in the Ryūkyū kingdom and a close adviser to the last King of The Ryūkyū Kingdom. Like Kyan Sensei, Sunabe Sensei came from a "Bushi" family - generally families in the Pēchin and Uekata classes in the Ryūkyū Kingdom.

I have practice karate since the mid 1970s, and I thought I knew something about the art when I first met Sunabe Sensei. But I found out that he was describing an art that seemed somehow foreign. He had never been part of a formal or large dojo - he trained one-on-one with Kyan Sensei every day. He never paid for a lesson - in fact, Kyan Sensei gave him milk and pastries. He had no right or title - just skill and conditioning. My goodness, what a concept!

I know and have met many instructors. Sunabe Sensei was like no one I ever met. He was highly skilled but very shy and evasive about his training, until I got to know him better. Then he was very direct and down to earth about it. If you saw him on the street he would never know that he was a Karate expert. He was completely hidden.

Sometimes things happen for a reason. I have been holding off on finalizing this last part of the story about Sunabe Sensei. Partly this was because I still feel bad that he is gone, but it was also because it is very difficult for me to express the feeling of his teaching and the approach he had to learn from Kyan Sensei. Then just a couple of weeks ago, I received a donation from Mario McKenna of his recent translation of, "*The Study of China Hand Techniques*" by Itoman Morinobu, which was originally published in 1934. Mario visited Hawai'i last week and I had the privilege of having lunch with him and discussing his excellent translation.

To make a long story short, Itoman's book, which was published doing the same time that Sunabe Sensei trained with Kyan Sensei, captures much of the feel and spirit of the training that Sunabe Sensei received.

The book does not show any kata. Instead, it concentrates on practical techniques, which Mario describes in his introduction as, *"Not only kicking and striking techniques, but also locking, throwing, and choking techniques; techniques which in other books on Karate-do during that time were only alluded to but never shown or explained."* In addition, it discusses what we today would call situational awareness, being aware of your environment and being able to use things around you. This was the corner stone of Kyan's teaching.

I recently read a discussion online [*with my name mentioned*] about whether or not a certain teacher had train with Kyan Chōtoku. Sunabe Shozen never identified other students who trained with him at Kyan Sensei's house. At the same time, he never said that any person did not train with Kyan Sensei; Kyan Sensei certainly taught students outside of his house [at the Agricultural School and the Kadena Police Station, for example]. My intention in writing this article was to preserve what's Sunabe Sensei told and shared with me. He wanted to honor the memory of his teacher, and I also want to honor both Sunabe Sensei and Kyan Sensei. Sunabe Sensei did not want to be known while he was living, so I waited to write about him until after his death. I have no opinion about what other students did or did not train with Kyan Sensei - hey Siri speaks for itself and I certainly was not there. It is my opinion, however, that Sunabe Sensei trained with Kyan Sensei at his house for 12 years and on summer breaks during college. I hope that more information about him will be found in Okinawa.

I suspect that some Shotokan students may be upset about what I shared above about Sunabe Sensei's experiences at Waseda University. Some of my close friends are Shoto Kan instructors and I have great respect for the art. Please trust that I have simply repeat it what Sunabe Sensei told me and have not embellished yes. As a karate historian and researcher, I respect Funakoshi Gichin scholarship and contributions to the art. Finally, I encourage serious Karate students to explore their roots. The more we do so, the more I believe we will find common ground. Sunabe Sensei's with Kyan Chōtoku offers valuable lesson for us all.

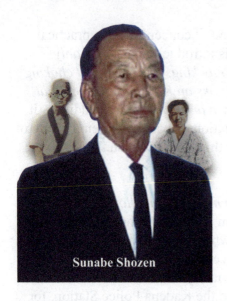

Sunabe Shozen

Notes

1. The deadliest battle of World War II, it is referred to by Okinawans as "*Kou no Kaze*," lit. "Steel Wind" [aka "Typhoon of Steel"]. The loss of life was catastrophic. There were 62,500 US casualties, of whom 12,500 died; 95,000 Japanese combatants died, and 7400 were captured; more than 100,000 Okinawans, women, children, and the elderly died, as a result of the fighting, starvation, suicide, or enforced suicide. On the granite tables at the Heiwa Kinen Koen [Peace Memorial Park] in Itoman, Okinawa, are carved the 234,183 names of confirmed the cases of all nationalities. Figures issued by the Okinawan Visitors Bureau in connection with the Japanese Imperial Navy's Underground Headquarters vary somewhat, and may be less accurate those of the Heiwa Kinen Koen for whom updating casualty records is an ongoing responsibility. The OVB figures are as follows: Japanese from other prefectures who were soldiers or otherwise employed by the military 65,908 Okinawans who were soldiers or otherwise employed by the military, 28,228; Okinawa civilians fighting in battles, 56,861; Okinawan noncombatants 37,139; US military 12,520. the population of Okinawa before the battle was 574,368 and 2,716,691 artillery shells were fired by American troops during the campaign, a ratio of 4.72 projectiles per Okinawa.

The former Japanese Navy, Underground Headquarters, updated pamphlet, published by the Okinawa convention and visitors bureau, Naha city, Okinawa.

2. I encourage readers to purchase Mario McKenna's translation, and any others by him.

Chapter 2

Through the Lens of Time
Vintage Treasures

Extremely difficult to read such remarkable handwriting I must express my deepest appreciation to Shimabukuro Zenpo Sensei's lovely wife, Michiko, who, only after considerable effort, was able to provide a transliteration of Chōfu's penmanship, and from which a subsequent Japanese-to-English translation was carried out by myself: P. McCarthy

An extremely rare piece of calligraphy masterfully hand brushed and gifted to Chōtoku by his father, Chōfu; From *Dogen Shoji* [道元禅師, 1200-1253; founder of Sōtō Zen], his profound message is from a line in *Bendowa* about attaining the state of *enlightenment*, which involves [Honsho Myoshu aka Běn Zhèng Miào Xiū] shedding the wild thoughts of body and mind, it reads…
"Release this wondrous practice and original realization fills your hands."

Scroll courtesy of Scot Mertz

Waka .... Koyo Nyosui... Intoxicated by Autumn Tints

Giwan Chōhō
宜湾 朝保
1823–1876

Waka "Koyo Nyosui"
"Intoxicated by Autumn Tints"

Giwan Chōhō was a high-ranking politician during the latter years of the Ryukyu Royal Government era. Studying under Hata Tomonori [of the Keien School], Giwan took the name Shofu Sai and became known as the foremost poet of the Ryūkyū's. This poem is believed to have been written and read in 1872 while visiting the *Fukiage Omiya Imperial Villa* [吹上御所] in Tokyo with Kyan Chōfu.

Copyright Okinawa Prefectural Government

c.1880s Shuri Gate Rickshaw

1889 Polish noble, Prince Paul John Sapieha at Shuri Castle

More than a few Shuri-based Bushi became Rickshaw drivers after the abolition of the Ryūkyū Kingdom…

c. 1880s Confucian [possible the Shiseibyō 至聖廟] Temple Kume Village; *Two Ryūkyūan gentlemen wearing "Wakasa machi-geta" [i.e. footwear popular in Kume's Wakasa district]. Note the rickshaws lined up against the temple's wall ...* * Photo courtesy of Naha City Museum of History Digital Archives

Ryūkyūan gentry deposed by the Meiji government; The gentleman in the center is Tomigusuku Uekata, a Master of Japanese battlefield horsemanship & pole arms
* 1887 Photo Wiki Commons

Late 19th century Naha street scene
* Photo courtesy of the Naha City Museum of History Digital Archives

Early Meiji Period:
Satsuma Samurai and Ryūkyu officials at a Confucian Temple in Naha
*Photo courtesy of Naha City Museum of History *Digital Archives*

Last Name, First Name:	Motonaga, Chokaku	本永, 朝鶴
Birth Year:	1898-11-15	1898年11月15日
Age:	22 yr	22歳
Sex:	M	
Relationship:	Household Head Chotoku's 朝徳 Eldest Son	戸主朝徳長男
Passport Number:	340859	三四〇八五九
Passport Date:	1920-05-25	1920年5月25日
Travel Date:		
Travel Purpose:	Language Study	語学研究
Travel Approval Authority:	Okinawa Prefecture	沖縄県
Travel Company:		
Travel Company Location:		
Home Prefecture:	Okinawa-ken	沖縄県
Home Address:	Naha-ku Kume-cho	那覇区久米町二丁目十八
House Number:	2-18	
Port of Departure:		
Ship Name:		
Destination Country:	China	中国
Destination City:	British Hong Kong	英領香港
Destination Area:	Hong Kong	香港
Reference Source Volume Page:	Okinawa Kenshi Shirohen 1912-1926 Vol: 8 Page: 777	資料編8 777

A 1920 record of Kyan Chōtoku's eldest son, Chōkaku's [DOB 1898] visa application to study [Chinese/English] language in Hong Kong ~ Source: *Okinawa Kenshi Shirohen 1912-1926 Vol #8 P777*
   * Courtesy of Thomas Feldmann

Mid-to-late 1920s or early 1930s at a celebratory party in honour of Kyan Chōtoku [seated in back 4th from the left] beside Chitose Tsuyoshi [to his right] and Motobu Chōki [beside the young lady to his left]. Yabiku Moden can be seen seated on the far left beside Kyōda Juhatsu. I had long thought this photo had been taken somewhere in Okinawa but have recently been told by my friend, James Hatch, it might very well have been in Miyakojima.   * The sign in the background reads; "*Kyan Chōtoku Support Group Inauguration Celebration.*"   * Photo courtesy of the Chitose family

Karate Kenpo
A Ryūkyuan Toudi [唐手] teacher is coming to Taiwan.

It is a unique martial art from the Ryūkyu Islands, different from Japanese jujutsu and closer to the Chinese Shaolin martial arts. At this time, everyone had heard about this well-known master, Kyan Chōtoku. One day, Yi Jiangjiang, a native of Pingcai Street, went with Yoshino Maru [to visit him]. They are currently staying at the Yoshikawa House in Ximending District in Taipei and will travel to Pingdong together with their host and stay at his home. According to reports, Kyan Chōtoku would like to travel around Asia to explain the history of Toudi and put on demonstrations that show that the techniques are all about self-defense. If this comes to pass, it would be an incredible sight to behold.

Trans. Note: *Taiwan Nichinichi Shinpo* (1898-1944) 台灣日日新報 (*Taiwan Nichinichi Shinpo*) was an official newspaper of the Taiwanese government under Japanese colonial rule. In the wake of the changing status of affairs, this daily newspaper included news about legislation and the fluctuation of the social hierarchy, in addition to chronicling current events, and cultural activities. The paper was published in Japanese from 1898-1944, and is one of the most indispensable resources for the study of Taiwanese history during the colonial period. * https://search.library.wisc.edu/database/UWI50181

* The 4 Nov 1926 newspaper clipping was graciously provided by Mr. Tobey Stansbury and the English translation was carried out by my American colleague, David Evseeff; A research and language consultant currently residing Medellin Colombia, he obtained his Master's degree at National Taiwan University.

The Yoshikawa House
The Yoshikawa House, where Kyan stayed. Located in Taipei's *Ximending* district during the Japanese occupation of Taiwan, it was a renowned ryokan or inn that provided traditional Japanese-style accommodations to visitors and travelers. Operating as a popular meeting place, it offered tatami-matted rooms, communal baths, and a taste of Japanese cuisine, attracting local Taiwanese, Japanese residents, and tourists alike. The Yoshikawa House remains a symbol of Taiwan's colonial history and the vibrant *Ximending* district continues to thrive as a bustling hub of culture, entertainment, and commerce.

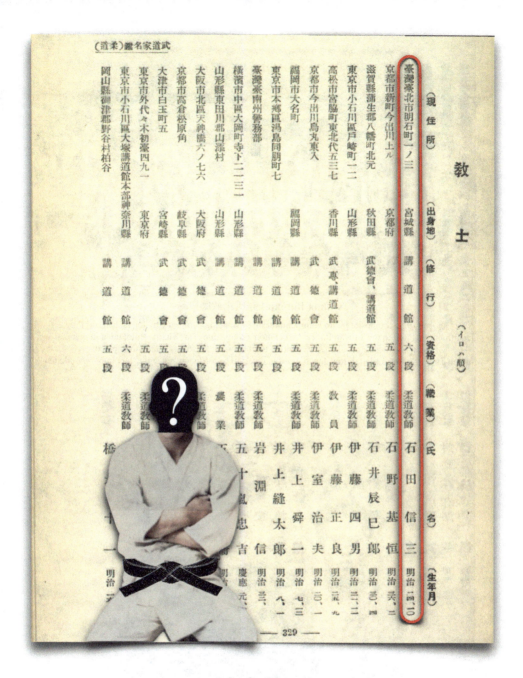

Ishida Shinzô

Continuing my research into identifying Ishida Shinzô [the person who allegedly had a "challenge match" with Kyan Chōtoku], I learned the following; Born 1881 in Miyagi Prefecture [Japan], he was an accredited DNBK Kyôshi with a Kodokan Judo 6th dan and worked as a Professional Judo instructor at the Police Academy in Taiwan during the 1920/30s. At the time this publication I have yet to locate a photo of him.

Source: *Budo Hōkan ~ Dai-Nippon Yūbenkai Kōdansha, Tokyo, 1930, p239*
Courtesy Lt. Col Lance Gatling [Ret]

Xinhua Butokuden 新化武德殿

A 10 October 1924 composite photo commemorating its opening ceremony by the [Japanese] Police Department featured in the Taiwan Police Association's Magazine. The Xinhua Butokuden in colonial Taiwan was where the alleged exhibition bout between Kyan and Ishida took place.
* More on Taiwan's Butokuden during Japan's colonial period https://www.goteamjosh.com/blog/wudedian

c. 1928 L-R: Tamashiro Teijin [玉城定仁, age 16], Arakaki Ankichi [新垣 安吉, 1899-1929, age 30], Nago Chōkō [名護 朝孝, age 17], Kyan Chōtoku [喜屋武 朝徳, age 58] & Tsuha Jinei [津波仁栄, age 16]
* Photo courtesy of Hokama Tetsuhiro

1931 Application practices as performed by two of Kyan's students, Nakazato Joen & Okuhara Bunei
* Photos courtesy of Nakazato Joen

Chōtoku & Kama

According to the folklore materials in the second volume of the "*Kadena-cho Historical Records*," related to Kyan Chōtoku and his wife, Kama…

She is mentioned as the eldest daughter of the Yara Rindō (Dendo) family; Born 24 May Meiji 5 (1872). Based on the photograph owned by Nishihira Mōriichirō, she was two years younger than her husband, Chōtoku and maiden name was Iha.
* *Photo composite by P. McCarthy*

c.1930s Kyan Chōtoku [seated] beside Chitose Tsuyoshi [to his left] and Gusukuma Shimpan beside him
* Photo courtesy of the Chitose Family

c.1930s ~ L-R: Kyan Chōtoku, Miyagi Chojun, Kyōda Juhatsu & Gusukuma Shimpan
Possibly at the 1939 opening of the Naha Butokuden
* Photo courtesy of Hokama Tetsuhiro

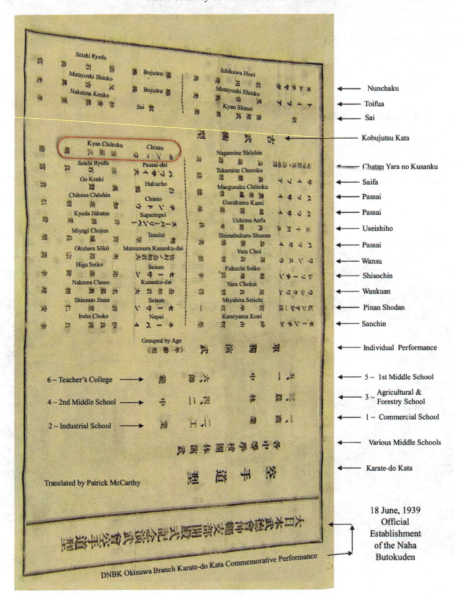

Feb 1941: Nakazato Joen, Kyan Chōtoku, Matsumoto Yoshitake, Nishihira Mōriichirō [Kyan's grandson] & Kuratō Shoichi * Photo courtesy of Nakazato Joen

June 1941; Posing for this photo on the porch outside the main guest room at Kama's [Kyan's wife] parents boarding house in the Rindo area of Yara in Chatan Village. L-R [Standing]: Higa Isamu, Taira Kazuo, former chairman of the Okinawa Prefectural Assembly) L-R [Seated]: Okuhara Bunei, Kurato Shoichi, Okuhara Numa, Kyan Chōtoku, Nakazato Joen & Iha Heitaro
  * Photo courtesy of the Naha City Museum of History Digital Archives

Dec 1941: Nakazato Joen, Kyan Chōtoku & Yonamine Shintaka
* Photo courtesy of Nakazato Joen

c.1942 L-R: Shimabukuro Zenryo, Kyan Chōtoku, Nakazato Joen
* Photo courtesy of Shimabukuro Zenpo

28 March 1965 Seibukan [*Commemorating Tamotsu Isamu's visit from Kagoshima*]
Front row L-R: Kaneshima Shinsuke [1895-1992], Shimabukuro Tatsuo [1908-1975], Shimabukuro Zenryo [1908-1969] & Nakama Chōzō [1899-1982] Back row L-R: Shimabukuro Zenji [1941-], Tamotsu Isamu [1919-2000] & Nakazato Joen [1922-2010]. Amidst this pantheon of dignitaries are three direct students of Kyan Chōtoku; Shimabukuro Zenryo, Shimabukuro Tatsuo & Nakazato Joen.

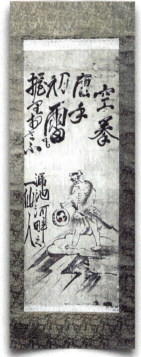

A hand-brushed *Kakejiku* by Kyan's student, *Arakaki Ankichi* [1899-1927]. Illustrating a goblin atop a mountain holding a drum, it reads, "*Kuken karate hatsukaminario toriosafu*" ["*Powerful enough to seize the first bolt of lightning, there's nothing as fierce as the grasp of karate's empty hands*"] and is signed, "*Ichisennin*" [*The Hermit*].

* Source; Nagamine Shoshin's "Tales of Okinawa's Great Masters" p112

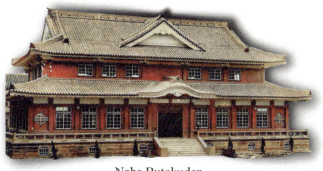

Naha Butokuden
* Photo courtesy of the Naha City Museum of History Digital Archives

Chapter 3
In the Words of Kyan

Insights & Teachings

Karate Training & What to Know About Fighting [1]
by Kyan Chōtoku
Okinawa-Prefectural School of Agriculture & Forestry
Japanese to English Translation by Patrick & Yuriko McCarthy c. 2001/2002

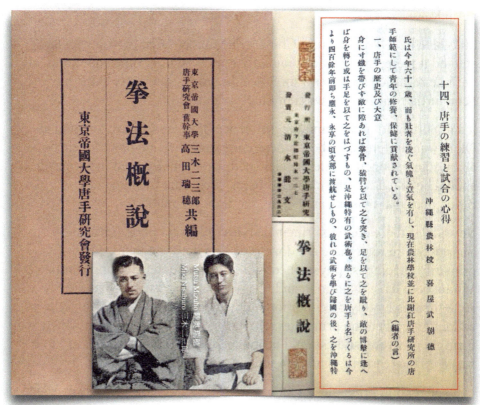

Takada [Mutsu] Mizuho & Miki Nisaburo's 1930, "Kenpo Gaisetsu"

Translators Note: Kyan Chōtoku was, according to Motobu Chosei, originally from the Motobu clan. Based on this and that he was never defeated in Kake-dameshi, I thought it worthwhile to include his important comments in this presentation. The original article (in Japanese) can be found on pp 236-241 of the second edition of Mutsu Mizuho & Miki Nisaburo's 1930 publication entitled, "Kenpo Gaisetsu." I believe it represents the information collected from him during their 1929 visit with him in Okinawa.

"At sixty-one years old this year, Mr. Kyan's face, when compared to anyone else his age, is still full of spirit and drive. Presently an instructor at the karate dojo, hosted by the School of Agriculture & Forestry, this instructor is very committed to the welfare and education of our youth."

A History & Outline of Karate [2]

In an unarmed altercation, one can take advantage of the situation any moment that the opponent is off guard by striking with the clenched fist, smashing with the elbow and or kicking with the feet. The hands and the feet can also be used to parry strikes. Moreover, one can also avoid being attacked by learning to shift the body properly. A martial art unique to Okinawa, Karate dates back about 400 years ago, to the Oei or Eikyo periods.[3]

Introduced to Okinawa from China by an unidentified person who had studied it there, the practice gradually improved over time and ultimately became regarded as Okinawan. Since that early time these skills have been further cultivated and continually improved.

It's important to understand the difference between Chinese method and Okinawan preference. The Chinese commonly use the tips of their fingers against an opponent while the clenched fist is chiefly used in Okinawa. It should be noted that the clenched fist is one of the fundamental differences that makes karate a unique fighting method.

Nowadays, there are two principal styles of karate, Shorei-ryu and Shōrin-ryu. In total there are dozens of kata between them, which primarily encompass physical conditioning and defensive application. While, both have their good and bad points, it can be said that the Shorei-style focuses largely on conditioning the body while the Shōrin-style addresses application principles. However, hasty judgments on which is the right or wrong style should be avoided, as training methods are to be based on the learners' character and physical condition.

The application principles of karate are truly kaleidoscopic, however, in the case of fighting actually only two points really count: "sei" & "ki".[4] The three ways to support the practical application of these points are a.) Observation [Go no sen] b.) Imperceptibility [Sen no sen] and c.) Transcendence [Sen]. Which of the three combative initiatives best resolves any physical confrontation depends entirely upon the individual and the circumstances.

Of course, engagement is also determined by knowing both the opponent and yourself. These are issues at the forefront of fighting and winning.

What to Know about Training

a. Teaching should take place in the following order: It is important to explain what karate is and what it is not. Then, what one should know about physical practice should follow this. Posturing, forward and backward foot movement should then come next. Gradually, evasiveness can be also introduced. Teaching how to use the clenched fists, striking with the elbows and kicking with the feet along with deflection, trapping and blocking, follow this. When these points are learned satisfactorily, kata can then be taught. When one is proficient at kata sparring can be introduced.

b. In the past, sparring was often dangerous because there was no protective equipment used. Because of this, it has, therefore, become necessary to wear protection on key parts of the body, like they do in bayonet training (*Juken-jutsu*). Using this kind of protection and rubber hand pads on the clenched fists will help reduce potential injury associated with the practice.

c. Except for what I already mentioned above, and the use of a makiwara, there's really no other special training equipment required to learn/teach karate. Moreover, training partners and spacious facilities are not required, either. These are some of the advantages of learning/teaching karate.

In short, these principles should be kept in mind during regular training as conditioning the body improves strength & flexibility for punching, kicking and mobility. Observing these principles during the course of practice over a long period of time one will naturally discover the essence of training and finally understand how it can be adequately applied to fit the circumstances.

Mental & spiritual discipline is vital to developing one's fundamental disposition. if it is neglected and training only focuses on physical technique (the body, hands & feet) the effort is worthless. This fundamental truth must be understood in order that the practice of technique develops the mind and body (hands/feet). Simultaneously, one can behave, be calm, alert and brave, etc.

1. The aim of martial arts is to prevent violence, foster humility and learn self-defence. This is why a martial artist should behave, be modest and loyal.

2. The martial arts cultivate the ability to react at just the right moment using the body and mind in unison. Those who misuse their skill, or are arrogant, poorly influence their community. Such behaviour is not appreciated by anyone and only harms one's own character. There is a wise old saying worth remembering; "A clenched fist should be like a hidden treasure up one's sleeve; it remains a secret until someone comes looking for it."

3. The purpose of karate is to condition the body, cultivate the mind and nurture the spirit.

4. Effective posturing is made possible by sinking one's "*qi/ki*" into the *dantien/tanden* being careful that it does not rise up your body. However, it is important never to be overly rooted in one's stance.

5. Kata should be practiced with the same resolve as if facing an opponent.

6. Footwork, body movement and impacting are all actions, which should always be deployed quickly. However, remember that functionally effective footwork and body movement requires one to stay on their toes (balls of the foot).

7. Understanding the application of kata establishes clarity between the upper, middle and lower target zones, otherwise one's effort is in vain.

8. Makiwara practice is essential in order to develop powerful tools of impact. Yet, powerful techniques are useless unless they are supported by rapid hand and footwork. Therefore, power and speed are like the wheels of a wagon; one cannot function efficiently without the other.

9. One's body, perception and spirit must be constantly trained.

What to Know about Fighting

1. I cannot emphasize the importance of first trying to evaluate the opponent's strengths and weaknesses in order to establish your strategy. If attacked by a more powerful opponent one should shift their attention to defensive strategy. This way the attacker is compelled to use more strength. This is the opportunity to seek out the "suki" (unguarded moment) and exploit it. This is how to best use the opponent's force.

2. Less powerful opponents can also make worthy defensive fighters as they're evasive and use many techniques. One must be careful not to attack thoughtlessly against such fighters and make good use of your hand and footwork. Letting an opponent inside is one way of setting up an immediate counter attack. However, remember that taking or giving the initiative means you that must always be prepared for the unexpected.

3. Never quickly or forcefully attack an opponent thoughtlessly. Agile fighters can often perceive the intentions of hand and foot movement and counter-attack quickly.

4. You should be careful to never telegraph your intentions or let your opponent read your body language. Irrespective of the opponent's strength or power, try never to move backwards more than three steps.

5. During a fight you must pay close attention to defending the centreline and not be caught off balance by staring at an opponent's feet or eyes. You must be especially careful not to get hit in the vital organs, grabbed or have the testicles seized when attacked. Also, it's not always wise to use too much force in defensive technique as movement tends to become slower, which also reduces the possibility for quick reaction or taking advantage of an opportunity.

6. If you seize an opponent's wrist, garment or arm, be certain to maintain a pliable strength all the time, being prepared to exploit his reaction. This way you can maintain control of the opponent's movement.

7. Naturally, quick hands are a necessary requisite for effectively attacking one's opponent. However, if you miss the intended target in the midst of an attack there's no need to fall back and try again. After achieving such close proximity to your opponent just continue freely attacking different target zones with your hands and feet. Even without using full power you can still gradually wear down an opponent this way.

8. It is not necessary to use your hands in defence of an opponent's kicks. They can be trapped, thwarted, or even swept away by your own leg while simultaneously countering with your hands. In case of the opponent falling or being knocked down, be careful not to rush in carelessly and be caught off guard.

9. Even if the opponent seizes your foot or leg, you can take advantage of it by quickly stepping down and into him, reducing the risk of injury. However, be very careful of this situation if the ground conditions are bad as you could fall down yourself.

10. Be careful not to be caught off guard by an opponent's clever deception. For example, don't be fooled by someone pretending to grab with their hand only with the intention of actually kicking with their foot. Conversely, the opposite can also be used; the kick can be used to cause a response for the purpose of being exploited by the fist. Listen and react to voice and sound, and never be caught off guard.

11. If confronted by several opponents at once be careful not to grapple with them. You must keep your distance in order to maintain the advantage. If someone attacks from the right, shift to the left. If you have to defend yourself from the front be careful not to overlook the opponent behind you. This is the only good way to deal with multiple opponents.

These are essential issues at the forefront of fighting, however, please remember that's just one example. In other words, the differences in martial arts are truly endless and mysterious. Therefore, don't solely rely on written materials. The best way to master the art is to train diligently and enthusiastically. Perhaps after lengthy study, you may achieve enlightenment.

Translator's Notes

[1] Pp 236-241 of the second edition of Mutsu Mizuho & Miki Nisaburo's 1930 publication, entitled "Kenpo Gaisetsu."

[2] It should be noted that the ideogram being used for karate throughout this work is written as China & hand: A term once commonly used in old Okinawa to describe Chinese quanfa/kenpo.

[3] In Japanese history the Oei Period was 1394-1428 & the Eikyo Period was 1429-1441.

[4] "Sei" means right, correct, fair and or pure; "Ki" means unusual, strange, unexpected and or not true. Confusing at it may seem, Kinjo Hiroshi helps us better understand them by comparing the terms to budo-related Omote (outside) & Ura (inside): The surface of things and the unseen or unexpected.

Okinawa Kenpō Karate-dō Basic Kumite
with (Explanatory) Diagrams

Preface
To the 1932 unpublished work
by Patrick McCarthy

Discovering Kyan's Book
In 2001, my wife, Yuriko, and I undertook the Japanese-to-English translation of Kyan Chōtoku's 1929 article, which had been originally published in the 1930 publication, "*Kempo Gaisetsu*" by Miki Nisaburo & Takada [aka Mutsu] Mizuho. In the book, Miki wrote that the revered karate master [Kyan Chōtoku], was on the brink of completing a transformative book on karate training, fighting, and attitude. His anticipation for the manuscript's publication mirrored the belief that it held the potential to revolutionize the art of karate. However, astonishingly, the fate of Kyan's written work has remained veiled in obscurity for nearly a century, leaving enthusiasts longing for answers and yearning to unlock the profound insights held within its pages.

Beyond the historical reference from the said 1930 work, and Kyan's "*Memories of Karate*," published in the 1942 Okinawan Times newspaper, I'd never heard anything more about Kyan's literary contributions, until 2017. On 17 March of 2017, fellow researcher, *Joe Swift*, reached out to me. Earlier that day, our mutual friend *Aihara Sinya* [Shin Karate Magazine] shared the details of Kyan's mysterious book with him. According to Mr. Aihara, *Takeishi Kazumi*, owner of *Yōju Shōrin*, our favourite old book store in Okinawa's Ginowan district, had received a copy of the unknown work. Apparently, he was also told there had actually been two separate books; One of fighting and the other on Kata. Unfortunately, he was told, the one on kata no longer exists! Over the next couple of years Joe and I casually spoke about the work on several occasions and ultimately learned that our mutual friend, Hokama Tetsuhiro Sensei, had obtained a copy.

Shortly after relocating here to Okinawa, on 17 Dec 2020, and getting settled in, I reached out to my longtime friend and noted historian, Hokama Tetsuhiro Sensei. A treasure-trove of historical knowledge, I was pleased to learn that he was more than happy to invite me over to his place and discuss the Kyan 1932 work with me. Meeting with him in person [on Friday 9 April, 2021] at his Nishihara dojo/museum, we spent the morning discussing the work, which concluded with him graciously allowing me to make a copy of the book for myself. Seemingly, a hot topic at the time, I also learned that information about Kyan's book was also being mentioned in the local newspaper. That same evening, I enjoyed having dinner with señor *Miguel Da Luz*; Miguel san is a multilingual French national who has resided here in Okinawa for three decades. In addition to having studied both karate and kobudo since his youth, and being genuinely a very modest person, he's literally a walking encyclopedia of knowledge, and one of the most respected foreign authorities here in Okinawa. During dinner I brought the Kyan-related topic up, and learned that the work was actually just being put on display at the *Okinawan Karate Kaikan* [沖縄空手会館], where he works.

Naturally, I wasted no time going up to the Okinawa Karate Kaikan, which was only 15 minutes from my home in Tomigusuku [at the time].

Sonohara Ken, Chief of the Okinawa Prefectural Karate Promotion Division, describing the Kyan book exhibition at the Karate Kaikan
Photo Okinawa Times Online 09 Apr 2021
https://www.okinawatimes.co.jp/articles/-/735203

From 8 April, 2021, through 31 March, 2022, the Okinawan Karate Kaikan had publicly displayed photocopies of the 1932 work on bulletin board panels in the hallway of building #2 outside the museum. Despite the challenging task of trying to study the work, due to the poor quality of the photocopies, I was deeply grateful for their considerate efforts. The photocopies, although frustrating in their clarity, were a kind initiative by the Karate Kaikan to make the work accessible for public viewing. From the newspaper article I was able to determine that the exhibition had been overseen by *Sonohara Ken*, the chief of the Okinawa Prefectural Karate Promotion Division; I was particularly taken with his comment, *"I want as many citizens as possible from our prefecture to come into contact with the history of Okinawa karate and use it for academic study and promotion."* Even though their office contact details were published with the article, I must admit, it was a bit disheartening that my attempts to reach out to the Okinawa Prefectural Karate Promotional Division had not yielded a reciprocal response; I was really hoping to establish a connection with them, but remain hopeful and open to future opportunities for collaboration.

Notwithstanding, I learned from Takeishi san that the work was carried out by one of Kyan's students, named *Kuramoto*-san; who also appears in the book as Kyan's partner. He told me that Kuramoto san may have also been one of the Karate students who, under the guidance of Funakoshi Gichin, performed the Karate demonstration at Shuri Castle before the visiting Crown Prince, on 6 March, 1921. From Shuri, I understand Kuramoto san worked for a sugar factory in Nago.

From what I also understand, the two unfinished works [*one of fighting and the other on kata*] had been passed down in his family and were in the possession of his grandchildren; Apparently, Kuramoto's grandson wanted to have the original [Japanese] work published through *Takeishi san* but there was some opposition from the older granddaughter! I heard rumors that the late *Nakazato Shūgorō* [仲里 周五郎, 1920-2016] might have also had the work in his possession, although I am sure of the possible connection and could not find anyone to confirm it. Later, on p166, in the English translation of the *"Shui/Tumai-di (Shuri/Tomari-te) Manual,"* [*published in 2021 by the Okinawa Karate Promotion Division and gifted to me by Shimabukuro Zenpo Sensei*] there appears three photos from the 1932 unpublished manuscript with the name, *Kanemoto Hachiro* cited as the source.

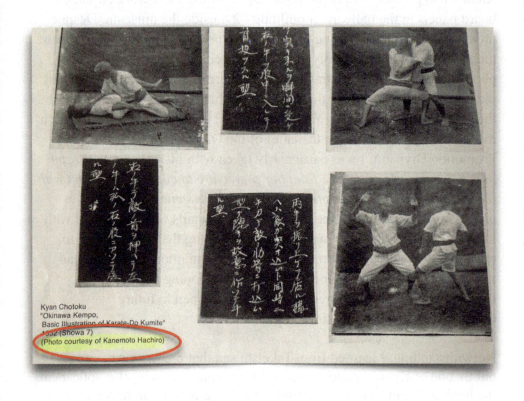

Kyan Chotoku
"Okinawa Kempo,
Basic Illustration of Karate-Do Kumite"
1932 (Showa 7)
(Photo courtesy of Kanemoto Hachiro)

 Could this be the grandson, I asked myself! However, when reaching out to my source at the *Okinawan Karate Kaikan*, I was told that he may have been the person who gave the document to *Takeishi* san, at *Yōju Shōrin,* in the first place, but he wasn't 100% sure. Reaching out to *Takeishi* san, immediately thereafter, he told me he'd never heard the name *Kanemoto* in relationship to the said work.

During my subsequent research, I located a Facebook page belonging to the, "*Okinawa Karatedo Shōrinji Ryu Promotional Association.*" On one of the pages I found the following description [I've taken the liberty of translating it into English for this work]:

"In Karate's classical literature, there are two books: "Kenpo Gaisetsu" (co-edited by Miki Nisaburo & Takada Mizuho) and "Karate-Do Daikan" (by Nakasone Genwa along with others). I [Oyakawa Hitoshi] have copies of both books as reference materials for modern Karate history, although I have never seen the original versions. This year (i.e. 2020), a book by Kyan Chōtoku, compiling Okinawa Kenpo (i.e. Karate) on fighting techniques, has been circulating on Facebook and websites, creating quite a buzz (I obtained a copy of this book c. 2016). It is being discussed with great interest by foreign Karate practitioners. Mr. H [I assumed Mr. Oyakawa is referring to my friend, Hokama Tetsuhiro] who is in charge of the Okinawa Karate Museum [in Nishihara], and T's Dojo [I also assume he is speaking about Tsukamoto Suguru... a friend on my Facebook page] of the Shōrinji-ryu in Tōkyō and the headquarters-style blog, all handle it with great interest. Recently, I [Mr. Oyakawa] visited the owner, Mr. K [again, I assume he is referring to, Kanemoto Hachiro, the name cited on p166, in the "Shui/Tumai-di Manual"], and was able to confirm this is the original version. The format of this booklet was a pocket-sized folded and bound book. I [Mr. Oyakawa] studied under my respected teacher, Nakazato Joen, for 43 years and also learned the explanations of the principles. The discovery of this book deepens my conviction in the analysis of techniques from the kata. The kata of Okinawan Karate are a specific representation of actual offensive and defensive techniques taught by my esteemed teacher.

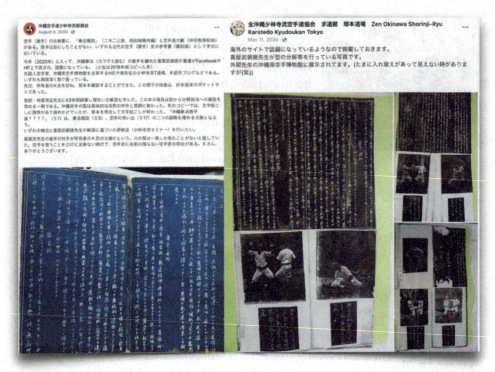

In the previous copy, there were limitations in transcribing the text, and I was on the verge of giving up. However, with the original version for reference, the transcription is now complete after comparing it with the original. "Okinawa Kenpō Karatedō Kihon Zukai Kumite," [沖縄拳法唐手道基本圖解組手] will become a document compiling of two articles; The Kenpo Gaisetsu article & [Kyan's] Memories of Karate [1942 Okinawa Times Newspaper]. I would like to hold a seminar (Shōrinji-ryu workshop) based on Kyan Chotoku's explanations at some point. The partner of Kyan [assisting him in the 1932 book] is said to be the father of Mr. K [again, I assume it's Kanemoto Hachiro]. He mentioned that he had only seen his father's [perform] Kata once. There have been Karate practitioners from the past whose names have not been passed down in the history of Karate, as it was a time when learning Karate was not made public. Thank you, Mr. K [Kanemoto Hachiro]."

Incidentally, discussing this issue with a Canadian friend of mine, Cezar Borkowski, also a respected master of Karate and equally passionate about its history, mentioned being friends with *Oyakawa Hitoshi Sensei*. I immediately asked for an introduction to which my friend happily agreed. Borkowski Sensei said, "*Oyakawa Sensei is an excellent Karate-ka, inspirational instructor and a wonderful person, who I am sure would love to meet you.*" Sadly, however, after many weeks of anxiously waiting and no reply, I reached back out to my colleague who contacted Mr. Oyakawa one more time. I learned that Oyakawa Sensei already knew who I was [*from speaking with two employees at the Okinawa Karate Kaikan*], and while appreciating my work was not interested in meeting "*another writer*" for fear of, "*secondary processing in publication.*"

For Sale Online

Imagine my surprise when, a few weeks later, on 24 June, 2021, I discovered the "never-before-published" work of Kyan Chōtoku being auctioned online through yahoo.com.jp! Hard as it was to believe, you can still find the auction details, which sold for 2000円 [i.e. approximately $20 USD] in one auction and elsewhere for more! I am citing the online references for anyone interested 1. *https://aucfree.com/items/m491631379* 2. *https://aucfree.com/items/o489678240* & 3. *https://www.ebuyjp.com/aucitem/m507009680/pro+wrestling* where it sold for 7,950円 [i.e. approximately $80 USD].

Book Description

Some additional research allowed me to discover that the 1932 work was created from a long strip of paper folded back and forth into what is known as an accordion or concertina booklet, a format that gained popularity in Japan during the 1920s. In Japan, this style of book was called *orihon* and served as a unique and portable medium for storytelling and artistic expression. These books had various uses, including sharing folk tales, depicting traditional art forms, and offering a dynamic reading experience. This particular work comprises of 26 pages, including the front page, measuring 15.5 cm in length and 9 cm in width. The content consists of an introduction to karate spanning the first 10 pages, followed by pictures and explanations of kumite postures and stances in the remaining 15 pages. The photographs feature Kyan Chōtoku, and selectively accompanied by his partner, Mr. Kuramoto, demonstrating fighting techniques while explaining technical application. Although the work concludes with the date 7 Nov 1932, it was never published.

Ruffling Feathers

On 12 April 2021, I established a special album on my Facebook page entitled the, "*Kyan Chotoku Project* 喜屋武朝徳プロジェクト." Not long after mentioning that I was undertaking this Kyan study project, I received a couple of *nasty-grams* on my social media platform; From a local style-based supporter here in Okinawa, the person criticised me for making public, this "*secret book*." The person went on to also say that, as I am NOT a Kyan lineage-based disciple, I have no right to research nor present his work!

Responding to his message [in Japanese], I politely asked if the gentleman would care to open a dialogue so we might privately discuss the matter. I also sent him all this public advertisement, openly selling the same work here in Japan on auctions.yahoo.co.jp. I never heard from him again! I think this was a case of someone either living in a bubble or simply neglecting to do their homework.

Unbiased Support
Fortunately, an unwavering passion and dedication for this work, along with my achievements as a researcher, published author, and the distinguished title of being the senior-most foreign student of Kinjo Hiroshi [1919-2013], not only captured attention but also garnered the invaluable support and collaboration of esteemed authorities in the field. Their willingness to lend their expertise and assistance greatly contributed to my endeavor to present this work in the most comprehensive and impactful manner possible. I remain deeply grateful to the pantheon of experts who graciously stepped up to lend me such overwhelming support; Joe Swift, Hokama Tetsuhiro, Takeishi Kazumi, Shimabukuro Zenpo, Irei Hiroshi, Tokumura Kensho, Konno Bin, John Sells, Graham Noble, Charles Goodin, Dan Smith, Scot Mertz, James Pankiewicz, Miguel Da Luz, Thomas Feldmann, David Evseeff, Andy Sloane, James Hatch, Neal Simpson and Brian Arthur, along with so many more.

Public Lecture
Trying as best I could to dig deeper into the history and circumstances surrounding this work, imagine my excitement when Shimabukuro Zenpo Sensei told me about the Kyan Lecture being presented by *Sonohara Ken* at the Okinawa Karate Kaikan on 17 March 2022. However, despite my enthusiasm, I was unable to attend the gathering due to the terribly limited seating capacity imposed by the pandemic restrictions. Nevertheless, I am sincerely grateful to Shimabukuro Sensei for his detailed overview. Also, thanks to both *Nakamura Yasushi* san (*Okinawa Karate Kaikan director*) and señor *Miguel Da Luz* (ODKS project manager) for providing me with details of the lecture and the actual minutes of the presentation.

Under the circumstances, I was not surprised to learn that the turnout for the lecture was understandably small. It would have been a great idea to stream or film the lecture for future reference. I was happy to hear that members of the Motonaga family had attended, as did Kyan's great-granddaughter. Not surprisingly, many other notable authorities, expected to attend, were not present. Normally, a lecture of this nature would have attracted a large crowd, however, because of the pandemic it was limited to fifty; in reality, however, only about 35 individuals attended, which included Shimabukuro Sensei (Seibukan) and Taira Yoshitaka Sensei (Matsubayashi Shōrin Ryu), along with other Kyan-lineage dignitaries and local Karate enthusiasts.

Sonohara san delivered an incredibly informative lecture, enhanced by the large monitor screen in the lecture hall that made it easy to examine detailed information, charts, diagrams, and photo images. The use of a microphone ensured that even the elderly participants seated at the back could hear his descriptions. The subject of Kyan's university attendance in Tōkyō and the absence of his name in the graduation registry remained intriguing for those familiar with his life and the 1932 publication.

The lecture raised various questions and topics of interest, such as Kyan's duration of stay in Okinawa after returning from Tōkyō in 1898, the reasons behind his decision not to pursue a noteworthy business career despite his formal education, and why he reclaimed the Kyan name. There were also inquiries about the printing of critical articles about Kyan in the Ryūkyū Shimpo in 1898 and the subsequent positive stories that portrayed him as a treasure. Further questions revolved around his relocation to Miyako-jima after taking over the Motonaga family business, his involvement in sugar cane production security, his activities during his time in Miyako-jima, and the frequency of his visits to Taiwan and Okinawa, including records of his ship travel. Additionally, there is curiosity about Kyan's other instructors in Okinawa, such as Itosu and Maeda, and his bojutsu skills prior to learning Tokumine no Kun.

Although records are scarce and unreliable hearsay abounds, I believe that further gatherings to discuss such questions could make a valuable contribution to the global traditional Okinawa Karate community.

* Sonohara's lecture, translated into English, will be presented in the following chapter.

Arriving at an Acceptable Solution

Takeishi-san graciously granted me permission to create an English translation of the aforementioned work, with the understanding that I would not replicate the original Japanese book in its entirety. To address this situation, Señor Miguel Da Luz suggested an alternative approach: *By incorporating the translated work with a substantial collection of related research I would be able to create a more comprehensive compilation for academic study. This approach effectively resolved concerns about breaking my promise not to publish the original Japanese book and provided an opportunity to highlight the significance of previously unpublished and seemingly lost work.*

Now, after nearly a century, I am delighted to present a comprehensive exploration of Kyan's unpublished work, accessible to an international audience. My sincere hope is that this endeavor will be valuable and resonate with readers worldwide and reflect favourably upon his original teachings.

I am profoundly grateful to Miguel-san for the brilliant idea and to all those who contributed to the realization of this project.

Enjoying the company of Señor Miguel Da Luz at the Hiko Unagi Restaurant in Naha's Omoromachi

沖縄拳法 唐手道基本圖解 組手

[*Okinawa Kenpō Karate-dō Kihon Zukai Kumite*]
Okinawa Kenpō Karate-dō Basic Kumite with Explanatory Diagrams

Book Cover
Explained

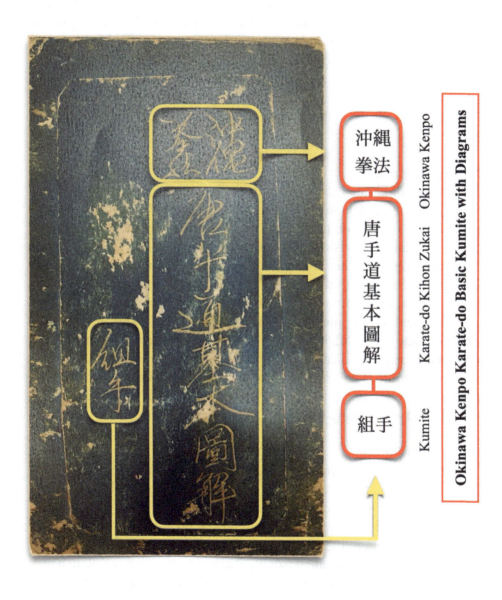

沖縄拳法 — Okinawa Kenpo
唐手道基本圖解 — Karate-do Kihon Zukai
組手 — Kumite

Okinawa Kenpo Karate-do Basic Kumite with Diagrams

The Way of Karate

Karate is not merely a technique, but a way of practicing the morals of a samurai that is based on loyalty and filial piety, as it embodies the essence of bushido. It is widely practiced by warriors and includes the way of the gentleman and the way of humanity. It is important to note that karate should not be misunderstood as simply throwing and killing people. The Russo-Japanese War was a significant event in the history of Japan, and the current success of the Japanese empire is attributed to the Bushido that was passed down by the heroes of the past, with the warrior being a key element.

Purpose of Karate

The purpose of karate is to develop the body, master the art of winning, and train the mind. Unlike ordinary gymnastics and physical education methods, the focus is on protecting oneself by working the limbs. In karate, the main focus is on physical development, and the game of how to defeat an opponent and avoid an attack is the reason for the training. The game helps to form the posture, enhance the development of the body's organs, and promote wisdom and virtue. Proper teaching methods allow for ideal development of all parts of the musculoskeletal system, and those who train with karate can easily perform physical movements with great freedom and ease, avoiding unexpected and dangerous situations. Karate is considered by some to be the superior physical training method. Even without an opponent, karate can be practiced through the kata, making it a deeply interesting art.

The Art of Winning

The art of competition aims to defend oneself and attack the enemy. To win a beautiful match, every part of the body must work in harmony with physiology, and mental actions must be in harmony with psychology. Therefore, those who practice this method should consider the principles of physical education, measure muscle development, pay attention to the effects of the mind, cultivate wisdom, practice virtue, and maintain a correct posture. These considerations are essential to increase the likelihood of success in a match.

Natural Body Method

In the past, martial arts practitioners were always mindful of their posture, not only in the dojo but also while sleeping and eating. This was done to ensure that their bodies remained free to move with ease. A proper posture was considered to be crucial to the practice of martial arts, both for improving technique and preventing injury. Thus, practitioners were careful to maintain good posture at all times to develop their bodies in a way that would be conducive to success in their martial arts practice.

The following is a Brief Explanation of Posture

The initial fear of being attacked during a fight may cause practitioners to lose their natural posture. This can lead to actions such as bending at the waist, pulling their legs backward, extending their arms forward, and unconsciously poking their arms out. This posture makes it easier for the opponent to gain an advantage.

Karate values proper posture and is not fond of the hunched over, unbalanced posture that beginners may adopt out of fear. The ideal karate posture involves standing erect, with the head not bent, the gaze forward and not fixated on any one thing, and attention focused on the next three steps. By maintaining this proper posture, practitioners can enhance their physical conditioning and endurance over time.

Trainee's Preparation

Some people begin their practice of karate without fully understanding what it entails. Some only seek self-defense techniques, some are curious about the impressive physical moves, while others pursue it for physical fitness. Some are able to pick up the basics easily and progress quickly, but others struggle and may even give up. Overexertion can lead to muscle pain and injury, while neglect of proper technique can also cause problems. Unfortunately, some enthusiastic learners may also have to stop practicing due to illness or other factors. Karate requires proper preparation, including consistent practice with a focus on technique and hygiene. It is important to avoid injury, repeat exercises regularly, and maintain patience and dedication to avoid falling into laziness or quitting halfway. Karate is a unique discipline that requires continued effort and attention to progress, and practitioners must be prepared to work diligently with a long-term focus.

Necessity
If you have a problem with karate, it can be your downfall. It's a common misconception that karate is harmful, but that's not the case. If two opponents have equal skill, the stronger one will likely win. However, relying on physical strength alone can lead to defeat against a more skillful opponent. Moreover, using karate in a way that disobeys its principles will also result in failure. Over-exertion can also hinder progress. Therefore, it's not appropriate to use karate in a haphazard way. A skilled person who can effectively utilize their strength without overworking the opponent will have a better chance of winning, even against a stronger adversary. This is the essence of "*the devil's club.*" Even if you're not as strong as you used to be, if you have mastered karate, you'll still be formidable. If you're not strong enough to overpower your opponent, you must maintain proper posture and use your technique skillfully. This is why I say that it's not appropriate to use karate carelessly.

Muscle Harmony
To effectively use karate, it's important to not only use the tips of the hands, but also maintain the correct posture and harmonize the muscles in every part of the body. If you try to use your hands without proper knowledge, you risk losing your posture and being defeated by your opponent. Even if you know how to take advantage of your opponent's broken posture, you won't achieve a beautiful victory if the way your hands, feet, hips, and body move aren't in harmony. Just like a symphony, each part of the body must work together to achieve a unified goal. In the military, every unit works in unison, and every part of the body must work in harmony to achieve success. Karate practitioners should focus on maintaining correct posture, studying how to move the legs and upper body, and how to strike when the opponent is in a certain posture to destroy them. This is essential for achieving success in karate. Using only the tips of the hands is very ineffective, and practitioners must strive for complete harmony in every part of their body to win. This is why it is crucial to study and understand the fundamentals of karate in order to execute techniques properly and achieve true mastery of the art.

Trainee Age & Physique

Karate is not limited to intense and physically strong individuals, and it is a mistake to think so. There are two teaching methods that are suitable for people of all ages and sizes. Whether one is young or old, strong or weak, anyone can learn karate. With proper teaching methods, the elderly can become stronger over the years, and even those who are young or physically weak can develop their bodies and become superior if the training is done skillfully.

If you have trained in karate from a young age, you will naturally become more skillful as you age and your body develops. During your youth, it's important to train your body and each part of it willingly and consistently, practicing in the morning and evening. In addition to physical training, it's important to acquire the necessary wisdom, fearlessness, vigilance, openness, and calmness to follow the opponent's movements, react quickly and flexibly, act with lightning speed, and be bold in defense. These qualities are essential for karate practitioners to cultivate in order to succeed.

Kyan Chōtoku
Hijabashi, Yomitan,
Nakagami County,
Okinawa
3 Nov, 1932

Illustrated Self-Defence Photos

* Translator's note: The technical section includes 15 photographs, but it should be noted that some of them lack detailed explanations. In a few cases, this lack of explanation can make it challenging to fully understand the technical application being depicted. Rather than making assumptions or guesses about the author's intentions, I have chosen to leave these photographs as they are, to ensure accuracy and avoid misinterpretation.

Illustrated Photographs

#1. Ready Posture ... Looking straight ahead in a natural state with a relaxed body and my feet apart approximately eight *sun* and my toes in the shape of the [Japanese character 八] number eight and gather your strength in your *tanden*, adjust your breathing and stay focused [or; With eyes looking straight ahead, the body is not tensed, but in a natural state; standing erect with feet apart approximately 8 sun and toes pointed out in the shape of the character (eight). Gather your strength in your *tanden*, adjust your breathing, and focus your mind.]

#2. Kicking with the toes

Trans. Note: Interestingly, the two photo inserts [not included in the original work] are from students of Kyan, which outline the same technique; The first illustration is from the 1957 book, "Kenpo Karate-do," by Chitose Tsuyoshi. The second is of Nagamine Shoshin from his 6book, "The Essence of Okinawan Karate-do."

#3. Here, I receive the attacker's right foot kick with my right hand ...

Trans. Note: The explanation appears not to match with the photo. Perhaps it was a sequence of two photos and the first with the enemy kicking is missing. Or, the photo may have been paired with the wrong explanation, as there appears to be another explanatory text under this one.

#4. Here, I seize the testicles with my left hand when grabbed from behind with both arms.

#5. Here, I receive the attackers punch and kick him with my right foot.

#6. Here, as I receive the attackers right punch he suddenly punches with his left fist and respond by kicking him.

#7. Here as the attacker punches, I receive it quickly insert my right arm between his crotch and throw him with a Seoinage [over-the-shoulder-arm-drag].

#8. This posture is with both hands raised up over the head, so that if the attacker rushes in you can strike into his ribs [body] with the sword hand; It's like creating an intentional opening

#9. Here, I receive the attackers right punch with a right sword hand and immediately strike into the attackers ribs

#10. Here, as the attacker punches from the front, I tilt my body to the side and thrust into the ribs, avoid [hitting] the hip bone.

#11. Here, as the attacker thrusts with his right fist, I seize his wrist and kick his ribs with my right foot

#12 ~ #13. In this example, I receive the enemy's thrust with their fist while kicking into them with my right foot. * *Note: The explanatory text is the same for both of these photos*

#14. Here, when facing each other, if the attacker kicks in between my legs, my left hand presses/pins down his leg and I thrust into him with my fist

#15. Here, I use my right hand to hold the attacker down by the neck while my left hand holds [the attacker's captured attacker's arm] against my right thigh.

This well known 6 March 1921 photograph with Funakoshi Gichin [seated 2nd from the left in the middle row amidst students of the Naha 1st Middle School] commemorates the Shuri Castle demonstration for the visiting Crown Prince & Commander *Kanna Kenwa*. The two photo inserts [in the upper left & right corners] are of *Wada Kihachiro* [和田喜八郎 1872-1936] Principal of the Shihan Gakko, and *Yamaguchi Sawanosuke* [山口沢之助] Principal of the Prefectural Middle School, the two main schools where Karate was being taught at the time. Additionally, there is oral testimony, particularly that of Chibana Choshin and Nakazato Joen, that suggests several others also demonstrated before the visiting dignitaries, including Kyan Chōtoku. However, the main reason I wanted to feature this important image is because *Takeishi Kazumi* told that one of the students in the photo might be the same person acting as Kyan's partner in the 1932 work. As this group photo is from 6 March 1921, and the self-defence photos in Kyan's book date from 3 Nov 1932, there is a difference of about twelve years [i.e. 11 years, 7 months & 28 days], between the said photos. Adding to the challenge of comparing likenesses is the fact that the students are all wearing *Hachimaki* [*i.e. their hairstyle and foreheads cannot be clearly seen*] in the 1921 photo, where as Kyan's 1932 partner is not. Taking into account that the quality of the 1932 images are not the best, the twelve year time difference and the *Hachimaki,* I dare not guess which might be Kuramoto san.

* Note: *The preceding translation, of Kyan's previously unpublished work, was based on the Japanese transcription, from the original hand-written Japanese, by Brian Arthur.*

1936 Round Table Discussion
[aka *"The Meeting of the Okinawan Masters"*]

Local Okinawan newspaper article from 1936 describing the October gathering …

Note: There are actually two other parts to newspaper presentation, not included with this publication; i.e. Commentary by Miyagi Chojun and Motobu Choki…

Abstract

Here in Okinawa, we celebrate Karate Day every year on 25 October. The reason we do this is because of a special gathering that was held on the same date back in 1936, historically referred to as the, "*Roundtable Discussion.*" Sponsored by the Ryūkyū Shimpo newspaper company, with Ōta Chōfu and other local dignitaries present, the gathering featured some of the most senior Karate authorities of that era, including Kyan Chōtoku. Issues which would help shape the future direction of this tradition were discussed, and even though there is no record of any commentary by Kyan, in the minutes of the meeting, I nonetheless believe it is important to include this discussion for the sake of historical accuracy and completeness in this work. By providing readers with more context, I believe it is possible to gain an even better understanding of the events that transpired during that time.

Attendees

Local Karate authorities present at the gathering included; Hanashiro Chomo (1869-1945), a former disciple of Bushi Matsumura (1809-1899), who was 67 years old at the time. Kyan Chōtoku (1870-1945), also a former disciple of Bushi Matsumura, who was then 66 years old. Motobu Choki (1871-1944), who learned the art from several sources, was regarded as "The Fighter," and known as a controversial figure during his time, was then 65 years old. Chibana Choshin (1885-1969), a former disciple of Itosu Ankoh (1832-1915), and a highly regarded master who first coined the term Shōrin-ryu, was then 51 years old. Kyōda Juhatsu (1886-1967), the senior disciple of Higashionna Kanryo (1953-1917), and a prominent Karate master who founded Tou'On Ryu, was then 50 years old. Miyagi Chojun (1888-1953), the most well known disciple of Higashionna Kanryo, and a well respected authority, who founded Goju Ryu, was 48 years old at the time. Gusukuma Shimpan (1890-1954), a former disciple of both Higashionna Kanryo, and Itosu Ankoh, and a respected school teacher, was then 46 years old; Nakasone Genwa (1895-1978), a writer, teacher and politician, who was also a Karate researcher and a Shudokan student under Toyama Kanken, he was 41 years old at the time; and Oroku Chotei.

Other dignitaries included Sato Koichi, the head of Educational Affairs; Shimabukuro Zenpatchi, the chief librarian for Okinawa Prefecture; Vice Commander Fukushima Kitsuma, regional military HQS; Kita Eizo, a section chief from the prefectural police department; Goeku Chosho, a section chief from the Prefectural Department of Security; Furukawa Gisaburo, director of the Prefectural Physical Education Board; Andoh Shigeru, a writer; Ryūkyū Shinposha President, Ōta Chōfu (1865-1938); Chief Editor Matayoshi Kouwa, and the newspaper's director, Yamaguchi Zensoku; and Mr. Tamaki, a newspaper journalist.

Translated into English for the very time [1990 *by P. & Y. McCarthy*], the 1936 "Meeting" reveals a wealth of original information through letting the reader evaluate the words and wisdom of those men most responsible for shaping pre-war modern Karate-do. Furthermore, by studying this testimony, we are able to, for the very first time, understand why the name Toudi-jutsu was changed to Karate-do, and why Okinawan's feared losing a piece of their cultural heritage.

Evaluating the minutes of this historic meeting, first published in Toyama Kanken's 1960 book entitled *"Karate-do Daihokan,"* it is also possible to gain a deeper insight into the conditions leading up to the modernisation of Karate-do, and what, if any, pre-war efforts were outlined for its unification and widespread promotion.

The principal force behind this gathering, Nakasone Genwa was born in Okinawa and graduated from the Okinawa Teachers College in 1929. After moving to Tōkyō, he became involved with Japan's Socialist movement and served as the publisher of its newspaper. In 1934, he began to support and publish several books on Karate. After the war, he continued a career in politics. In 1973, Nakasone authored *"From Okinawa to Ryūkyū,"* however, to this day, Nakasone is probably best remembered for his brilliant 1938 publication entitled *"Karate-do Taikan,"* and *"Kobo Kempo Karate Nyumon,"* the book he co-authored with Shito-ryu pioneer, Mabuni Kenwa (1889-1952).

I would like to thank my teacher, Kinjo Hiroshi [1919-2013], a direct student of Hanashiro Chomo [Gusukuma Shimpan, Tokuda Anbun & Oshiro Chojo, et al], for providing me with an original copy of Toyama's book with the minutes of this meeting, a few of the old photos, and for his assistance in helping to interpret the difficult to understand parts of this historically important work. I would like to also thank Clarence Lee for the Chibana Choshin photos, *Yabe Kenjiro* in Okinawa for the brilliant photos of his grandfather (*Yabu Kentsu*); Kanzaki Shigekazu in Beppu, for the photos of his teacher, *Kyōda Juhatsu*; The *Chitose* family in Kumamoto for the photos of *Kyan Chōtoku*; and the *Konishi* Family in Tōkyō and *Iwai Tsukuo* in Gunma Prefecture for the excellent photo[s] of *Motobu Choki*. I thank my wife, Yuriko, without whose help, and endless patience, this work would never have been possible.

Patrick McCarthy
Yokohama, Japan
1990

Toyama Kanken [遠山寛賢, 1888 -1966] & his 1963 publication, "*Karate-Do Taikan*" ~ Pp 377-392

The Meeting

Meeting commenced at 4 pm:

Matayoshi Yasukazu: Thank you for attending today. Mr. Nakasone Genwa organised this meeting. In addition to being with our company, Mr. Nakasone studies Karate at the Shudokan in Tōkyō, and is also a Karate historian.

Recently, Karate has become popular in Tōkyō; however, in the midst of this popularity, there seem to be some people who are practicing it the wrong way. We feel it is our responsibility to ensure that only an orthodox tradition that embodies the painstaking efforts of Okinawa's authentic Karate masters is the only discipline worthy of being handed down. Moreover, we are also concerned with the preservation and promotion of the research that both master and disciple have left us. I sincerely hope that everyone here today will candidly present their opinions.

We are fortunate to have with us today Hanashiro Chomo, Kyan Chōtoku, Motobu Choki, and Miyagi Chojun, etc., eminent Karate authorities. We would be truly delighted if you gentlemen could describe Karate's true nature to us all today. With that in mind, Mr. Nakasone Genwa is now going to explain this meeting's format.

Ōta Chōfu: All right, Mr. Nakasone, you have the floor.

Nakasone Genwa: Thank you. As Ota, and Matayoshi Sensei mentioned, I will speak first, even though I am just your humble kohai (junior). Since I came back from Tōkyō two months ago, I have interviewed many people in several places regarding their opinions about Karate. I was disappointed to learn that Okinawa has no society uniting its various Karate masters. However, we now have the means of establishing such an organisation through the Ryūkyū Shinposha's support.

Karate should be vigorously fostered simply because it is an appropriate and effective Budo through which to cultivate physical strength and indomitable spirit. I have been studying Karate at the Shudokan in Tōkyō for years and making every effort to disseminate the tradition there. With that in mind, I would like to invite each of our distinguished masters here today to voice their opinions about encouraging Karate throughout the entire nation.

In considering Matayoshi's suggestion, perhaps we should begin by addressing the issue surrounding the name Karate. If that is all right, then I would like to say when Karate (written as "empty hand") was first introduced in Tōkyō, it was introduced as Toudi (written as "Chinese hand"). At that time, Karate was a novel tradition that took some time before becoming popular.

Schools contended that Toudi was not a suitable term and had, when writing the first ideogram of the term, used hiragana rather than the ideogram. Some dojo are being called "*Nihon Karate Kenkyukai*" (日本から手研究会/ translated as "Japan Karate Research Society"). However, that was during the transition period. Now, just about all dojo in the Tōkyō areas, including the two principal dojo, are using the new term, Karate/空手 ("empty hand"). Most university clubs are also using the new term. How-ever, there is still some university clubs that customarily use "Toudi/唐手" ("Chinese hand; i.e., Chinese fighting art").

The reason for changing Toudi to Karate is simply because it defines a tradition in which one uses his empty hands, or Karaken/空拳 ("empty fist"). With that in mind, I would like to recommend that the current name "Karate-do" ("the way of the empty hand") become the standard in consideration of Karate's future development as a Japanese Budo. What do you think about my recommendation?

Hanashiro Chomo: In the old days, they did not say Karate ("empty hand"), only Toudi (Chinese hand), or just te/手 (meaning hand). That meant fighting with empty hands or fists.

Ōta Chōfu: We called it Toudi too.

Shimabukuro Zenpatchi: Mr. Nakasone, recently Karate has been called Karate-do. Does this mean that the cultivation of one's spirit, like that of

Judo and Kendo, will be emphasised? Is that why the "do/道" was added?

Nakasone Genwa: Yes. Its purpose seems to be the cultivation of the spirit.

Ōta Chōfu: Mr. Miyagi, do you use the term Toudi?

Miyagi Chojun: Yes, we use "Toudi" because it is in general use. However, it is a term used casually. Most people who come to my place wanting to learn usually just ask if I can teach them "te." Judging by that, I would say that "te" seems to have been used before. I believe that the term Karate is a good name because of what it represents. As Mr. Shimabukuro pointed out, Judo evolved from jujutsu. In China, they used to call Kempo, *beida* (white strike) a long time ago. Names change, like examples do, it depends upon the times.
I prefer Karate-do to just Karate. However, I believe that the name must be unanimously decided upon by public opinion.

The Dai Nippon Butokukai branch has also discussed this issue among its committee members. Following that discussion, this issue has remained a pending concern. In China, the term Toudi-do is used. Soon a promotional organisation (shinkokai) will be established, and by that time we would like to see a purposeful name used.

Oroku Chotei: Mr. Miyagi, did you purposely go to China to study Karate?

Miyagi Chojun: Although I didn't begin training in China, I went there after realizing that it was the place I had to go for more advanced Gongfu studies.

Oroku Chotei: Is there a unique style of "te" here in Okinawa?

Miyagi Chojun: Well, like Judo, Kendo, and boxing, so too has the discipline of "te" been further cultivated and improved here in Okinawa.

Kyōda Juhatsu: I agree with Mr. Nakasone. Generally speaking, people of this prefecture are still familiar with the term "Toudi." We should discuss this issue with the Karate researchers here in Okinawa, and see what their analysis discloses. It's simply too early to decide here and now.

Miyagi Chojun: I don't mean that we have to decide right here and now.

Matayoshi Yasukazu: Could we hear some other opinions?

Hanashiro Chomo: In my old book, "Karate Kumite," published in August 1905, I used the term, "Karate" ("empty hand").

Furukawa Gisaburo: From our side, we'd like to promote it in the heart of the nation. We would like to see each prefecture establish an organisation to promote Karate, a shinkokai, to get Karate into junior high schools. In this way it will be possible to disseminate Karate throughout all the prefectures. Then we can discuss ways of developing the discipline.

Nakasone Genwa: I understand Mr. Kyōda's opinion. We should consider the name and who we should question. Should we decide by majority vote? Or, should the people who enthusiastically practice Karate decide? To help promote the art, the newspaper sponsors students who often travel around the island to lecture and give Karate demonstrations. This will affect the growth and direction of Karate throughout the entire nation. These youths recognise the term "Toudi" for its historical significance. However, they believe Karate-do will develop under their own efforts. I think that numbers of these young people and their actions will influence Karate's future growth and direction.
So, "Toudi" should be changed to "Karate" as soon as possible. We must not only consider its preservation, but also its advancement.

Kyōda Juhatsu: Well, if everyone shares that opinion, then I believe that the term "Karate" will adequately serve the purpose.

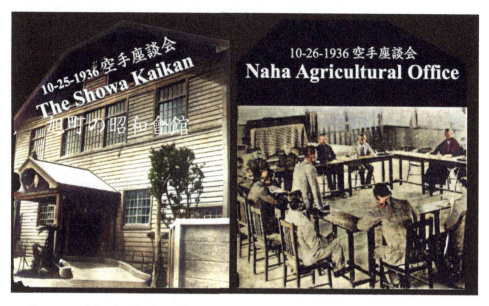

Sponsored by the Ryukyu Shinposha (Ryukyu Newspaper Co.), this historic gathering was held in Naha, Okinawa on 25/26 October 1936 at the Showa Kaikan (meeting hall) and Naha Agricultural Office. In attendance were many of the island's most prominent Karate authorities: Hanashiro Chomo, Kyan Chotoku, Motobu Choki, Chibana Choshin, Kyoda Juhatsu, Miyagi Chojun, & Gusukuma Shimpan.
English Translation by Patrick & Yuriko McCarthy

Gusukuma Shimpan: Teaching in junior high school, I have found that students were not happy with the term "Toudi" and, subsequently, I wrote the "Kempo" instead. However, I believe that supporting the term "Karate" is proper because it refers to martial ways without weapons. Therefore, on this issue, I have no objections.

Goeku Chosho: Connected with the Butokukai branch, I too would like to say something. The Butokukai recognised Karate as a martial way in 1933. At that time, Mr. Miyagi was still writing "Karate" as "Toudi." So, if the name is changed to "Karate," the Butokukai branch will rewrite and get approval. The branches will accept this change. At any rate, Butokukai honbu (HQ) approval will be required.

Ōta Chōfu: In 1905, Mr. Hanashiro was the first person to use the term Karate. Anything that is popular in the heart of the nation (Tōkyō) is customarily accepted all over the country.

For example "Anshinbira" (Anshin flat) in Naha has recently been changed to "Habu-Zaka" (Habu-slope). Also, the three-stringed instrument once called a "shamisen" is now called "jabisen."

Names used in the heart of the nation are sure to become popular as in these examples. Okinawans might not be too happy about that, but if we are the only ones left using the term Toudi, when Karate becomes a general martial way on the mainland, then I fear that people in the future will not come to know its Okinawan origins. Based on this point, I think that the term Karate is appropriate.

Nakasone Genwa: So far, we have heard from people who have lived in Okinawa for a long time. Can we hear the comments of Mr. Sato Koichi, the head of Educational Affairs, who recently came to Okinawa.

Sato Koichi: I am not that familiar with "Karate," but "Toudi" doesn't seem to have much support among the experts. I think that, "Karate" should be used.

Furukawa Gisaburo: For people from other prefectures, the term "Karate" is appealing, and has a definite ring of martial arts to it. Moreover, it appears that "Toudi" has lost its appeal.

Nakasone Genwa: May we also hear from Mr. Fukushima Kitsuma?

Fukushima Kitsuma: Well, "Karate" seems to be an appropriate designation, especially if one is to consider the relationship between the name and the discipline: an art of self-defence using the empty hands.

Nakasone Genwa: There's a story about a showman who was strong enough to pull a car. To draw attention to himself, he made a sign that read "Kojimaryu Toudi-jutsu."

Ōta Chōfu: I don't think that anybody dislikes the term "kara" however, there are those who resent the term "Tou" (China).

Miyagi Chojun: When I visited Buwa (trans. note, presumably a place in China but could also mean Hawai'i), the Chinese seemed to be familiar with the term "Toudi."

Fukushima Kitsuma: Last year, the Physical Institution changed the name "kyujutsu" to "kyudo." Like this example, a change from "Toudi" to "Karate" should not be difficult.

Kita Ezio: Before I came to Okinawa, I too believed that the pronunciation of "Kara" (the alternative pronunciation for "Tou") meant empty.

Ōta Chōfu: Originally, people in Okinawa used "Toudi."

Andoh Shigeru: I believe that China's Shōrinji Kenpo [Shaolin Quanfa] is the original source of Judo and Toudi. Therefore, it is understandable that Toudi was used. However, I agree the name should now be changed to Karate (empty hand).

Nakasone Genwa: It's incorrect to say that China's Shōrinji Kempo was the source of Judo and Karate. In Mr. Mikami Otokichi's novel, Karate is described as Toudi-jutsu: a martial art that is partly foreign. This illustrates that Karate is not generally understood that well.

Propagating Karate

Shimabukuro Zenpatchi: They simply use "te" to describe Karate in Okinawa, whereas Toudi is used to characterise self-defence methods from China.

Nakasone Genwa: Well, it appears as if we have discussed the name "Karate" enough now, so next, I would like to ask you your opinions about the best ways to promote Karate. Unfortunately, Karate in Okinawa is in a slump these days. Therefore, perhaps we should discuss ways to promote it from both the viewpoints of physical education and as a martial tradition.

Fukushima Kitsuma: There have been many Karate sects established recently, but in my opinion, we would be better off if they were all unified. Regardless of the differences between styles in Shuri and Naha, a unified Japanese Karate-do kata curriculum should be established. Kendo used to have two hundred different styles, but they were unified into the present Japanese Kendo kata. If Karate can be unified, it too would be propagated all over the nation.

For example, let's say we can 1. Develop 10 kinds of Japanese kata, 2. Use Japanese names for them, 3. Unify kata techniques and their contents to accommodate the principles of attack and pliable defences, 4. Adopt a standard uniform, 5. Study the competitive element, and 6. Plan tournaments for Karate. If we can do these things, then Karate's form and substance will be unified.

Miyagi Chojun: I quite agree with you. Concerning Karate kata, I have already submitted my explanation to the Butokukai honbu when their branch opened here. Concerning a standard uniform, we've often discussed the issue and would like to adopt one soon. Concerning technical terms, I'm confident the time will come when they will be regulated. I have been insisting upon this issue, and, actually, I have already developed some new technical terms and introduced them.

Concerning kata, perhaps it is better to develop and introduce a national kata, however, classical kata must remain. Suitable kata, with both offensive and defensive sides, for students from elementary school to university level, should be developed. The shinkokai should be responsible for developing and introducing these kata. There's the Physical Institution, and the Butokukai branch here, along with our senior practitioners (sempai) and others who are interested in Karate. We need to pool our resources and collectively research these issues.

If the experts and appropriate organisations conduct a thorough investigation, then the issues of terms, uniforms, and related problems can be concluded soon. However, classical kata must remain intact, otherwise they will be forgotten. New kata can always be developed.

Nakasone Genwa: Sometimes varying technical terms can be a problem. It is difficult to present a lecture without standardised terms that can be universally understood. A gesture only be understood if one has an audience. However, it is more difficult to make oneself understood in newspapers and other media. There-fore, the establishment of standardised technical terms is also necessary. Concerning competition, Teidai (the old name for Tōkyō University, now called Toudai) and Kansai University are presently investigating the possibility of protective equipment that may gain more popularity in the future.

The old masters have preserved the classical kata because they understand the magnitude they represent. Karate masters vigorously study techniques, however, I believe that they remain too reserved when teaching their students. Because their teaching lacks enthusiasm (not sport orientated), people generally lose interest. I think this is why Karate is not as popular as perhaps it could be.

This photo is not of the historic 1936 meeting, but rather a 1937 gathering to commemorate the establishment of Kihon-gata in Okinawa. I chose to use the image simply because it features several of the main figures from the same time frame. Front Row L-R ~ Kyan Chotoku, Yabu Kentsu, Hanashiro Chomo, Miyagi Chojun. Standing L-R ~ Gusukuma Shimpan, Maeshiro Chotoku, Chibana Choshin, Nakasone Genwa. I was also able to locate a few of the other dignitaries and made small inserts above the main photo. L-R: Shimabukuro Zenpatchi, Ota Chofu, Kyōda Juhatsu, Motobu Choki & Matayoshi Kouwa. Missing are Oroku Chotei, Furukawa Gisaburo, Goeku Chosho, Sato Koichi, Fukushima Kitsuma, Kita Ezio, Andoh Shigeru & Yamaguchi Zensoku

Therefore, I would like to recommend that a major organisation, like a *Karate Shinko Kyokai*, be established where both experts and the general public can participate together for the art's advancement. For without the kind of organisation and continued dialogue that we are sharing here today, the future efforts of individual master instructors will be inhibited. Therefore, I implore you to seriously consider establishing a *Karate Shinko Kyokai* with the cooperation of people from various walks of life.

Ōta Chōfu: We are definitely in favour of supporting that mandate. It is miraculous that Karate has become so successful in Tōkyō. We fully intend to support the movement, and I hope that communications between each group (Butokukai, etc.) will be positive in an effort to establish the organisation. How many Karate groups are there now in Okinawa?

Miyagi Chojun: Well, there is the Butokukai branch, prefectural Physical Institute, the Shuri City Physical Institute, etc.

Ōta Chōfu: Mr. Chibana, how many students do you presently have training at your dojo?

Chibana Choshin: About 40 or so.

Miyagi Chojun: *They say that Karate has two separate sects: Shōrin-ryu and Shorei-ryu. However, there is no clear evidence to support or deny this. If forced to distinguish the differences between these sects, then I would have to say that it is only teaching methods that divides them.*

Shōrin-ryu's fundamental training (kihon) and open hand techniques (kaishu) are not taught in any clearly defined way. However, the Shorei-ryu kaishu and kihon are taught according to a clearly established method. My teacher taught us according to the Shorei-ryu method.

Ōta Chōfu: We have heard that (local) masters have not studied in China.

Miyagi Chojun: I heard that (Bushi) Matsumura studied in China.

Chibana Choshin: Our teacher taught naifuanchin [aka naihanchi] for fundamental development.

Ōta Chōfu: Mr. Motobu, from who did you study?

Motobu Choki: Itosu, Sakuma, Matsumora from Tomari, etc.

Ōta Chōfu: Mr. Motobu, didn't you make up your own style of Karate?

Motobu Choki: (laughing) No, I did not.

Nakasone Genwa: The establishment of a *Karate Shinkokai* is a point of agreement by each master. As Mr. Furukawa described the necessity for a *Karate Shinko Kyokai*, we should agree upon each goal concerning this issue. The committee should start preparing for this project. (Each participant nods in agreement.)

Ōta Chōfu: What organisation is the Physical Institute?

Furukawa Gisaburo: It's a semi-governmental corporation, which the prefecture subsidises. Every kind of Budo and sport is included there.

Ōta Chōfu: Do you mean that the Physical Institute will serve as the nucleus of the *Karate Shinko Kyokai*?

Miyagi Chojun: Except for the Physical Institute, there is also the Butokukai branch. Both organisations include Karate departments. While the proposed *Shinko Kyokai* will be associated with both the Butokukai and the Physical Institute, it will also stand alone as an independent organisation of Karate, like other Budo organisations.

Sato Koichi: Unified is better than independent.

Ōta Chōfu: Will the *Karate Shinko Kyokai* be an organisation representing one part of Karate?

Miyagi Chojun: Yes. In Jukendo (bayonet discipline) they have a separate organisation called the Yudansha-kai (Association of Dan Holders), which supports the Judo and Kendo departments of both the Physical Institute and the Butokukai branch. Similar to this, the *Shinko Kyokai* will support the Karate departments of the both the Physical Institute and the Butokukai branch.

Goeku Chosho: The requirements for dan grading in Karate should be also be unified. This will also help to improve Karate's growth and direction.

Nakasone Genwa: It will be possible to do that as soon as the *Shinko Kyokai* is established and Karate groups outside the prefecture are united.

Yamaguchi Zensoku: As a sponsor, I would like to conclude the meeting with this. We have had a very productive meeting, the results of which will unquestionably affect Karate's future growth and direction. It is truly a great honour for the Okinawan people that our native Karate has become so popular in the heart of the nation. However, that popularity is not shared here in Okinawa, unfortunately. We must take steps to cope with the situation in an effort resolve the issue surrounding the name of Karate, its technical terms, the unification of kata, and the establishment of the *Karate Shinko Kyokai*. Because children have a particular interest in this discipline, I believe that our purpose would be well served by introducing Karate at the elementary school level.

Therefore, I will request the Educational Affairs Bureau look into teaching Karate in both elementary and junior high schools. If this proposal is adopted, then I believe that our aspirations will be realised.

Meeting concluded...

Translator's Notes

1 Okinawan Karate master Toyama Kanken established the Tōkyō Shudokan in 1930. Toyama Sensei had studied under such legendary masters as Itosu Ankoh, Higashionna Kanryo, Oshiro Chojo, and Chibana Choshin.

2 Two Chinese ideograms (called "kanji" in Japanese) represent the term "Karate": The first means China, or more specifically, China's Tang Dynasty (618-907), and later came to represent China itself. The second ideogram means "hand." The first ideogram can be pronounced either "tou" or "kara," and the second ideogram can be pronounced either "te" or "di."

3 The Japan of 1936 was at its peak of militarism, nationalism was widespread, and dissension with China ultimately led to the outbreak of war in July 1937.

4 Hiragana is one of two Japanese standard sound syllabi that represent the sound of Chinese ideograms but carries no inherent meaning. In other words, by looking at an ideogram, one can immediately recognise its meaning, whereby reading the hiragana, one cannot readily understand its original meaning.

5 By doing so, Karate's relationship to China became obscured.

6 The suffix "do," as in "Kendo," "Judo," and "Budo," means "way," "path," or "road," and can even mean "province." The same character is also pronounced "dao" in Mandarin and is most notably used for the Daoist philosophy of Lao Zi, reputed author of the "Dao De Jing." In the philosophical context adopted by the self-defence traditions, "do" means a "way" of life, a "path" one travels to improve oneself.

7 Gongfu (lit. ability) is a generic Chinese-Mandarin term denoting the various self-defence traditions that developed from either the Buddhist Shaolin Temple (i.e., Dragon, Leopard, Tiger, Crane, and Snake styles), or the Daoist Wudang Temples (i.e., Taijiquan, Bagua, and Xingyi); it generally means "accomplished work." There are two current, more specific Mandarin terms used, fraught with political undertones: wushu, "war arts," is the accepted term in the People's Republic of China, or Mainland China; Taiwan, or the Republic of China, uses the term Guoshu (Kuoshu in Wade-Giles Romanisation), or "National Arts." A third common term, Quanfa, "Way of the fist," is pronounced "Kempo/Kenpo" in Japanese. In general, wushu refers to the modernised, very acrobatic styles of Gongfu, whereas Gongfu, Quanfa, and Guoshu refer to the more traditional civil self-defence forms. All Mandarin Chinese terms are rendered in the Pinyin romanisation system used in the PRC.

8 Miyagi is referring to the way that the fundamental elements of Japanese Swordsmanship (Kenjutsu) and grappling (jujutsu) were brought together to establish Kendo and Judo, respectively. The principles of several Chinese-based self-defence disciplines (cultivated during the old Ryūkyū Kingdom period) were also ultimately codified in an effort to form an indigenous tradition.

With my teacher, *Kinjo Hiroshi* [1919-2013]

Memories of Karate
by Kyan Chōtoku
7 May 1942

The following translation is reproduced here with the permission of Joe Swift

Due to the fact that I was sickly and small as a child, my father Chōfu made it a daily ritual to have me practice Sumo, etc., with my elder brother Chōhitsu in order to strengthen my body.

However, on the day that I turned 15 years old and finished my hairdressing ceremony, my father brought the two of us before him and said that we could not become fully-fledged men unless we trained in martial arts. He said he would teach us real martial arts, and even if it was hard we should stick with it to the end, like real men. We began training in Karate the next day. In those days, it wasn't called Karate, but just referred to as Te, such as Passai no Te or Chintō no Te.

My father was about 168 cm in height and weighed in at about 75 kg, was stronger than the average man and he enjoyed martial arts. He worked as a steward to the Sho family, was silent and was strictly disciplined. His teaching was very rough, and when he forced us in training, I would hide in the corner of the house and cry tears of vexation. However when I woke up the next morning I forgot about yesterday, mustered my courage and threw myself fiercely into the training with my brother. This went on for a year. I will never forget that day in the spring when I was 16 years old, I went with my father to Shikina-en and first met Matsumura Sōkon Sensei, who was well known as the patriarch of Okinawan Karate. Upon my father's introduction, I was able to learn from him.

I remember that Sensei was 80 years old then, and the Karate Kata that I learned was Gojushiho, which I have never forgotten and still preserve to this day. In spite of his age of 80, Matsumura Sensei struck the Makiwara every morning, he was vigorous in his old age and surpassed the youth, had strong eyes, hard arms and was like steel or stone. He was enthusiastic in his instruction, and was in the habit of saying that the martial arts were the way of peace. I vaguely remember him saying that peace was maintained through the martial arts. Looking at the current situation, I feel those were pioneering words, and feel great respect for his foresight. I trained under the guidance of Matsumura Sensei for two years, and my passion for the martial arts grew. However, unfortunately for me, my father was ordered to go to Tōkyō as the chief retainer of Sho Tai. We brothers also followed our father to Tōkyō where we lived in a house in the premises of the Sho family's mansion. I attended the Nishogakusha in Fujimi-cho, and learned the Chinese classics under Mishima Chūshū Sensei.

On the side, I continued my Karate training with my father, but he was so strict that he would make me go out in the garden and practice Karate on cold, snowy wintry days, and unless I did, he wouldn't even let me eat breakfast. Thanks to this, my once weak body had become so strong that I never caught a cold even once in my 9 years in Tōkyō, and was able to enjoy my adolescent days.

I believe that the only people left alive who learned directly from Sensei are the venerable calligrapher and painter Yoshimura Jinsai and myself. A while after we moved to Tōkyō, Mr. Hiyagon Anko, the former chief of the Naha Police Department, came to Tōkyō with his father and stayed on the Sho family premises. We sometimes meet and talk but it is just an old dream of over 50 years ago.

I returned home at the age of 26 due to familial issues, and studied under Matsumora Kosaku Sensei and Oyadomari Peichin Sensei. The teachers in that era respected each other and only taught their own specialties to their disciples. If one were to ask them to teach, they would introduce the student to a teacher who specialized in that particular skill, and they were always humble toward each other. It was all very graceful.

However, the world had not yet opened up and looked unfavorably upon those who practiced martial arts. It was no easy feat to keep the training secret from others, including our own siblings. On top of that, there were still some barbarous customs, with many people actively trying out their skills in drinking and red-light districts. I went to the red-light district whilst always keeping this in mind.

As time went on, the martial arts went from being a solo practice to a way to be useful to the nation. The efforts of Funakoshi Gichin, who traveled by himself to Tōkyō to spread Karate, the martial art of a tiny, peaceful unarmed Kingdom, have allowed the Karate of Ryūkyū to develop into the Karate of Japan. As a citizen of Okinawa Prefecture, I am grateful to Mr. Funakoshi, while I think that the instructors and students in Okinawa should come together as one to further polish their art so as to maintain its standing as the birthplace of Karate.

Seventy-three years have passed since I devoted myself to the path of Karate. Without being ashamed of my poor writing skills I would like to put down here what I learned from my seniors during that time as well as my own beliefs, and pray for the souls of my teachers who have passed away.

The Way of Karate
The Japanese spirit is based on loyalty and filial piety, and its essence is found in the martial arts. The morality of the warrior can only be achieved through the practice of the martial arts. Therefore, Karate is not merely a technical skill, but is in a broader sense, the warrior's Way. It must not be misunderstood in the narrow sense of simply throwing or punching an opponent. Therefore, Karate-do must be practiced in the spirit of loyalty and filial piety.

The Purpose of Karate
The purpose of Karate is in the training of physical development, the way of winning confrontations and self-control. Normal gymnastics and physical education methods do not include the meaning of offense and defense without moving the limbs, so it is uninteresting and you cannot obtain the ideology of defeating an opponent. The Karate training method includes the meaning of contending with a confrontation within each of the movements of the body, in addition to the physical development of the body. That is to say, it creates the posture based on the ideals of how to defeat and opponent and how to avoid the opponent's attack, whilst maintaining a healthy body and promoting the development of the internal organs.

We do not exercise mechanically without reference to confrontation. Therefore it is interesting, allows the spirit to be actively engaged and also helps to promote wisdom. If you practice under the tutelage of the appropriate teaching method, the growth of the musculature will be balanced and one can obtain a nearly ideal physique. People who have trained in Karate are able to move the body freely and can naturally avoid unexpected danger that looms upon them.

The Method of Winning a Confrontation
This is the question of how to defeat an opponent in a confrontation. In order to beat the opponent, this simply cannot be done unless the movements of each body part are in line with the principles of mechanics and the action of the mind is not set against the truth. Therefore, those who train in the methods of winning a confrontation, must consider the senses of the body and mind, and how to fit within the nature of the universe.

The Method of Attaining Functional Spontaneity
It should be noted that the martial arts practitioners of old always studied the laws of nature, not only in the dojo but also during daily life, sleeping and eating, in order to attain freedom of technique.

The Resolution of the Practitioner
Some of those who practice karate for the first time practice merely for the purpose of self-defense without deeply studying what karate is; and some practice based on curiosity upon hearing or seeing the beauty of punching and throwing people; while even others see the physical constitution and strength of practitioners and practice only as a form of

physical education. Some of these people can, however, after hearing a couple of explanations and practicing a little bit are able to quickly understand and may be able to move their body as freely as a Tengu, and make their bodies as strong as steel.

Such people practice enthusiastically in the beginning, but if they do not make as much progress as they think they should after studying for a while, they will gradually develop a spirit of laziness and finally end up quitting. There are also people who in an effort to progress practice excessively, causing muscle ankylosis and feeling pain, so they stop training before long. Fortunately, there are some who are healthy and enthusiastic from the beginning, but there are also those who are unavoidably forced to stop from illness. This is because they do not have the purpose for their training in karate, which is very regrettable. Karate is very different from other disciplines, so it is not enough to listen to a lecture or theory. One must physically practice one's whole life to perfect the techniques, otherwise physical development will not be sufficient.

You must be prepared to practice properly and spend many years without becoming lazy. In addition, when practicing, it is necessary to follow the theory, avoid injuries and always pay attention to hygiene so that you will not fall ill.

The Necessity of Strength
It is a big mistake to say "It has been said from long ago that if one's Karate has strength that will be the cause of defeat, so strength is actually rather harmful to Karate." If the skill of two people is the same but there is a discrepancy in strength then it stands to reason that the stronger one will win.

Of course even if one is strong, that strength can be used against them by a weaker opponent with high-level technique and can be easily defeated. In addition, those with great strength may rely on that strength in a way that goes against the principles of Karate.

Such people can defeat people who are far inferior in strength, but are unable to defeat those who have greater technique or those who have about the same amount of strength. It is even more so against those who are equal or stronger. It can be said that is because such practitioners are lacking in martial power.

This martial power is not strong simply because one has a large body. Martial power is obtained only through effortful training in martial arts. Sumo has the power of Sumo, and Judo has the power of Judo. Each martial art has its own unique method of martial power, which is the person's natural body strength as enhanced by their effort in training in the Way.

Therefore, if one loses it is not because they are too strong, but because of their lack of training plus carelessness in training. If such strong people were to be fully trained and are careful of this point during training, they are not in danger of having their strength used against them, and will be able to use their strength effectively without resorting to unreasonable techniques. There is no doubt that they will become a superior practitioner due to this advantage.

There are many examples of small men throughout history who became masters, but they were able to achieve this only by training ten times harder than the normal man in order to make up for their lack of natural physical strength.

Muscular Accordance
Karate lacks efficacy if performed only with the hands. On the other hand, if one puts unnecessary strength (into the movements), their posture will be broken and will end up losing to the opponent. One must harmonize the entire musculoskeletal structure in order to topple the opponent while maintaining the proper posture.

Even if you know that you can surely win if you perform a certain technique because the opponent is off balance and has an opening, unless you harmonize the extension and contraction of the arms, the working of the feet and the movement of the waist or torso, for example in the way of punching with the hand or kicking with the foot, you cannot win if the techniques are not performed in accordance with the technical principles.

This is exactly the same as the military regulations of the Imperial Japanese Army, where once the order is given, the artillery, the engineers, the infantry and the cavalry all take on their respective duties, and their movements are united as they push forward and attack to great success. Karate practitioners must pay utmost attention to muscular accordance.

The (Ideal) Age and Physique of the Practitioner
There is a tendency amongst the public to think that Karate practitioners are a bit too ferocious and that its practice is not suitable for the weak, the elderly or children, but nothing could be further from the truth.

There exists in Karate teaching methods that are suitable for the physiques and ages of such people. It does matter if one is old or young, strong or weak, it can be practiced by one and all. If one practices for a considerable amount of time in accordance with an appropriate teaching method, the older practitioners will become healthier, and the young boys and weaker practitioners will see the promotion of physical development. As they become more skillful this will help to make up for shortcomings in those who are small in stature or weak in strength. If practitioners start as young boys and are well trained, their body will grow and their skills will naturally become more sophisticated as they mature.

If one trains the body from the time they are a boy and is able to move the various parts of the body freely, practices morning and evening and realizes the Way of the martial arts, then he will not fear the strong nor despise the weak. He will be able to remain open minded, composed and heartfelt. He will be able to react in accordance with changes in the opponent's movements with lightning speed, acting with agility and boldness.

The Chishi and the Makiwara
There are those who think that the Chishi and Sashi are absolute requirements for Karate training, but this is a gross misunderstanding. The Chishi and Sashi are used to strengthen the muscles of the arms and legs, as well as the grip.

One does not necessarily need to use the Chishi and Sashi in order to train their physical body and grip. In order to cultivate the muscles, one can use dumbbells, gripping jars, rubber bands, the high bar and other methods. However, merely strengthening the body will not allow one to achieve the striking power required by Karate, so therefore one must also strike the Makiwara in order to create this striking power.

I firmly believe that the Makiwara is what sets the Karate of Okinawa apart from all other martial arts. Both Matsumura Sensei and Itosu Sensei both struck the Makiwara even into their eighties. The Makiwara should be afforded the same importance as Kata for the Karate practitioner.

Conclusion

The reason that I, who have lived 73 years without contributing anything of use to society, have decided to publish by poor writings about my recollections of Karate-do, is that as the Second Sino-Japanese War devolved into the Greater East Asia War, the officers and men of the Imperial Japanese Army appeared unexpectedly in the sea and the sky and scattered our physically huge Caucasians.

The fruits of battle are based on the glorious virtues of our Emperor, and when I think of how our officers and men have heightened the essence of Bushido, it is unbearable for me, an old man like a withered tree, to sit comfortably by the charcoal brazier and live out the rest of my life.

Endnotes

1. Kyan Chōfu (喜屋武朝扶, 1839-unknown) was politician and martial artist. It is said that his teacher was Matsumura Sōkon.
2. The age of 15 was considered when one became an adult in the Ryūkyū Kingdom, when the traditional topknot (for men), known as the Katakashira (欹髻) in Okinawa.
3. 手 a.k.a. Ti, was the old Ryūkyūan word for martial skills.
4. In this context Te (手, Ti) seems to refer to what we now call Kata. It is also interesting that Kyan uses the modern Ateji for the Kata names, i.e. 抜塞 for Passai and 鎮闘 for Chintō, rather than the more common Katakana renderings.
5. Matsumura Sōkon (松村宗棍, 1809-1899, other theories exist as to dates of birth and death) was one of the most famous martial artists of the Ryūkyū Kingdom. He served as a bodyguard to three kings. He is often called the patriarch of Okinawan Karate for his unique blend of Chinese and Japanese martial principles into a uniquely Okinawan practice.
6 The forerunner of Nishogakusha University, its formal name was Kangaku-juku Nishogakusha (漢学塾二松学舎).
7 Mishima Chūshū (三島中洲, 1831-1919) was a scholar of the Chinese classics and the founder of the Kangaku-juku Nishogakusha.
8 This is a Confucian ideal. In Japanese it is written 忠孝両全.
9 Yoshimura Chogi (義村朝義, 1866-1945) used the name Jinsai 仁斎 for his artworks. He was the second son of Yoshimura Chomei, a staunch Ryūkyūan nationalist who is said to have gained passage for Higaonna Kanryo to the Ryūkyūkan in Fuzhou, to deliver a letter of protest against the Japanese political takeover Ryūkyū. Yoshimura Chogi's mar7al arts autobiographical article is presented in English in The Essence of Naha-te by Joe Swift.
10 Hiyagon Anko (比屋根安昂, 1880-date of death not yet found).
11 Matsumora Kosaku (松茂良興作, 1829-1898) was a famous Karate teacher from Tomari. A famous folk story is told about him disarming a Satsuma warrior with nothing but a towel.
12 Oyadomari Kokan (親泊興寛, 1827–1905) was a famous Karate teacher from Tomari.
13 Here Kyan used the term Bushido (武士道) but the context makes it clear he was discussing the practice of martial arts, not the Samurai "code of conduct."
14 Funakoshi Gichin (富名腰義珍, 1868-1957) is considered the Father of Japanese Karate. He was born in Shuri, Okinawa and learned mar7al arts mainly under Asato Anko and Itosu Anko. He moved to Tōkyō to teach Karate in 1922.
15 Defined by Kyan as Jutsu or 術.
16 Defined by Kyan as Do/Michi or 道.

17 The Japanese term 勝負 (shoubu) is open used to represent a competitive match, however considering the context of this document, I have opted to translate it as "confrontation," which can represent both competitive matches as well as other instances of violence.
18 The translator believes this term, coined by Patrick McCarthy, best represents the spirit of the Japanese phrase 攻防自在 (Koubou Jizai, indicating the image free-flowing defense and offense).
19 Tengu (天狗) are mythological Japanese mountain goblins who were said to be skillful in martial arts.
20 Defined by Kyan as Buryoku or 武力. Motobu Choki is said to have used the same Kanji but pronounced it as Bujikara.
21 Described by Kyan using a typical Japanese phrase 鬼に金棒 which describes giving an iron rod to a demon, i.e. giving the advantage of a weapon to an already formidable entity.
22 Known in Japanese as Shina Jihen (支那事変), this conflict lasted from 1937-1945.
23 This is the English rendering Japanese term 大東亜戦争 for the Pacific theater of WWII, and lasted from 1941-1945.

The Bubishi, featured on the left side, stands as Okinawa's original compendium of knowledge. It goes beyond mere striking, showcasing highly functional fighting skills. Intriguingly, both Motobu and Kyan employ techniques identical to those depicted in the Bubishi. The images, arranged from left to right and top to bottom, include two of the forty-eight Bubishi illustrations. Centre top are Nakazato Joen & Okuhara Bunei, and below them are Kyan Chotoku and Kuramoto of Nago. Top right are Shimakukuro Tatsuo with John Bartusevics, and a small insert featuring Shimabukuro Tatsuo with Steve Armstrong. Bottom right is Motobu Choki portrayed with Yamada Tatsuo. This visual representation highlights the interconnectedness of these martial artists and their shared techniques, drawing a compelling link to the timeless wisdom encapsulated in the Bubishi.

Chapter 4

Beyond Boundaries
Challenging the Legacy of Kyan Chotoku

Rising from The Ashes
by Charles Joseph Swift

All rights reserved. No part of this work [previously published under the name, "*The Downfall of a Ryūkyūan Samurai,*" may be reproduced without the express permission of the copyright holder. This work is reproduced with the expressed permission of the copyright holder; Charles Joseph Swift.

Introduction

This is a bit different from my other forays into writing and translating, in that it is not really an expose on *Karate* or *Kobudo, per se*, but more of a glimpse into the lives of the Okinawan gentry as they were being deposed and the new Meiji government was coming into power. It focuses on one man, whose name will become self-evident to *Karate* practitioners. It is about a scandal he *allegedly* became embroiled in after returning to Okinawa from Tōkyō, at the very end of the 19th century.

All in all, this is not really about *Karate* per se, but it is my hope that the *Karate* community at large reads it for its obvious historical significance in understanding the cultural landscape in which modern *Karate* was shaped.

Joe Swift
October 2018
Tōkyō, Japan

Part 1

Historical Context

The Fall of a Kingdom

When the Tokugawa Shogunate fell and the rule of government was passed back to the Emperor of Japan, the Ryūkyū Kingdom was also thrown into great upheaval. This entire process was known as the Meiji Restoration, and the policies that brought Ryūkyū officially under Japanese jurisdiction were known as *Ryūkyū Shobun* (琉球処分), commonly translated into English as the Disposition of Ryūkyū. The actual background to this issue centers on territorial disputes between Japan and China over the ownership of Ryūkyū and Taiwan. In order to get a feel for the process without getting too bogged down into details that have little bearing on the main part of this publication, let us look at a timeline of some of the major events of the *Ryūkyū Shobun*

1868: The Tokugawa Shogunate fell and the Meiji Era began, marking the start of the modernization (i.e. the westernization) of Japan.

1871: The feudal Provinces of Japan were abolished and the modern Prefectures were established.

1872: Narahara Shigeru, who would later become Okinawan Prefectural Governor, led an Imperial mission to Shuri to discuss the future of Ryūkyū; Ryūkyūan mission to Tōkyō to congratulate the new Emperor (Kyan Chōfu was part of this mission); the Kingdom of Ryūkyū (琉球王国) was made Ryūkyū Province (琉球藩), placing the former king, Sho Tai (尚泰), as the titular head of this new political entity.

1873: The Ryūkyū Province was transferred from the auspices of the Foreign Ministry to the Ministry of the Interior.

1874: Japan launched a punitive military campaign against Taiwan in retaliation for an incident in 1871 in which several Miyako Islanders were killed in Taiwan; China signed a treaty that recognized the Ryūkyūans as Japanese subjects.

1875: Ryūkyū Province sent a tributary delegation to Beijing, one development that led Okubo Toshimichi to push for a total annexation of the Ryūkyū Islands into Japan; Sho Tai is rebuked for not severing independent tributary ties to China upon the establishment of Ryūkyū Province; Matsuda Michiyuki is appointed as the government agent in charge of deposing Ryūkyū and bringing it into the Japanese fold.

1876: The resident Japanese Diplomatic Minister in Beijing attempts to meet with the Ryūkyū delegation, but is refused; Ministry of Interior begins police and law enforcement operations in Ryūkyū; the first Japanese military barracks is established in Ryūkyū; Minister of the Interior suggests a complete abolishment of the Ryūkyū Province and total annexation into Japan in an enquiry to the Prime Minister.

1877: Several Ryūkyūan officials, who had snuck out on a ship the previous December, arrived in Fuzhou.

1878: Chinese officials met with Japanese officials to protest the meddling of Tōkyō in the relations between China and Ryūkyū; the Ryūkyū satellite office in Tōkyō was closed and the Ryūkyūan officials expelled; the chief secretary of the Ministry of the Interior presents his proposal for the deposal of Ryūkyū.

1879: Matsuda Toshimichi delivered a missive rebuking the actions of Ryūkyū for sending a diplomatic mission to China; China urged Japan not to absorb Ryūkyū as a prefecture; On official appointment from the Prime Minister, Matsuda traveled again to Naha with government officials, military police and soldiers; Matsuda delivers the message that Ryūkyū is dissolved and the Prefecture of Okinawa was established; King Sho Tai was granted the title of Marquis, assimilated into the new Japanese peerage and ordered to move to Tōkyō; After Sho Tai left Shuri Castle, it was immediately commandeered by the military; Sho Tai was granted an audience with the Meiji Emperor; Sho Tai informed Beijing of the situation and requested Chinese intervention; China proposed that representatives be appointed to negotiate over the sovereignty of Ryūkyū; There was a possibility of US mediation but this never materialized.

1880: Tōkyō agreed to negotiations with China over Ryūkyū; Japan offered to repay any debts to foreign governments owed by Ryūkyū that were incurred after 1843; Chinese and Japanese officials met in Beijing for the aforementioned negotiations; An agreement was reached including Japan recognizing Chinese sovereignty of southwestern islands including Miyako and Yaeyama; China finally refused to ratify the agreement in December.

1881: Japanese ambassador to China informs the Beijing government that he considers the Ryūkyū dispute to have been settled.

As regards the spread of *Karate* in mainland Japan, we can perhaps speculate as follows. Okinawa was the newest prefecture, and was geographically quite far removed from the mainland. Indeed, until recently, the Okinawans were, technically, foreigners. Add to that the new-fangled martial arts of *Kendo* and *Judo* were gaining in popularity throughout the land, as the remnants of the "noble" *Samurai* arts, and a kind of source of national pride. Where in this picture was there room for a strange looking dance (*Kata*) practiced by a backward country bumpkin in the national martial fervor?

China wanted Okinawa, but strategically, Japan needed Okinawa to stay on her side. To that end, after the deposition of the Ryūkyū Province and the establishment of Okinawa Prefecture, the last King, Sho Tai, was granted the title of Marquis and "invited" (read: coerced) to live in Tōkyō along with a retinue of his trusted advisors. The Meiji Government seems to have gone out of its way to provide Sho Tai special privileges, to keep him on "their side."

Along with advisors such as Asato Anko and Kyan Chōfu (*Karate* masters in their own right), it is safe to assume that Sho Tai also brought with him his closest, most trusted personal guards as well. Naturally these men would have had extensive martial arts training.

At that time, regardless of the political background behind some of the decisions behind leadership at the *Dai Nippon Butokukai*, it is no exaggeration to state that Yamaoka Tesshu was "the man" with regards to *Budo* in Japan. Having the ear of the Emperor, if there was indeed a powerful political force at work, Yamaoka would have indeed had the influence over such luminaries as Jigoro (*Judo*) and Nakayama Hakudo (*Kendo*) to "persuade" them to support the spread of the Okinawan pugilistic methods. Though further, formal research is needed to determine the truth, this author hopes this speculation will fuel further studies into this potentiality.

To round out this section we will end with a list of the major changes to the Ryūkyū Kingdom as it transformed into Okinawa Prefecture is as follows.

- ✓ In the place of the Royal government, Okinawa was ruled by a Governor who was dispatched by the central government
- ✓ The class system was abolished in favor of the *Shimin Byodo* (details in the next section), and the rights of the commoners and the gentry were made equal.
- ✓ The Royal Government's bureaucratic, court and criminal justice systems were revoked and the same laws as the rest of the nation were applied.
- ✓ The Royal Government's military and police forces were disbanded and military and police forces from the central government were stationed in Okinawa.
- ✓ Okinawa Prefecture came under the unified currency issued by the Meiji Government.
- ✓ The tax on estate wards in the Yaeyama Islands was abolished.
- ✓ Compulsory education was put in place. Education had hitherto been the providence of the gentry but now everyone, regardless of their class under the old system, received elementary school level education.

The Decline of the Class System

At the end of the Ryūkyū Kingdom, 5% of the population belonged to the gentry (*Keimochi, Shizoku, Samuree*), whilst the remaining 95% consisted of farmers, fishermen, merchants and other "commoners" (*Hyakusho*). Out of the total number of aristocrats, only 5% were considered upper class gentry. This is somewhat different from the social structure of mainland Japan. As such a comparison is beyond the scope of this small presentation, interested readers are urged to do some research of their own for details.

The gentry classes are described variously as *Keimochi* (those with familial lineages, 系持ち), *Yukatchu* (ユカッチュ、良か人), *Samuree* (さむれー、侍, after the Japanese *Samurai*), or *Shizoku* (士族). This last term was applied to the aristocrats by the Meiji Government at the time the Ryūkyū Kingdom was designated Ryūkyū Province in 1872, much like the same term was applied to the ex-*Samurai* class in mainland Japan a few years earlier. It has since become the standard term in both Japanese and western sources about the Okinawan class system.

As the Meiji Restoration started, the hitherto class system was abolished across Japan. As outlined in the previous section, this happened several years later in Okinawa than in mainland Japan.

By 1866, the Samurai class in mainland Japan numbered 5% of the entire population, roughly 2 million people in total. Various social and economic factors contributed to dissatisfaction amongst not only the peasant classes, but also the various ranks of *Samurai*. The new military conscription, universal education and outlawing of the public wearing of swords by those of the former warrior class all contributed to its gradual abandonment.

As the Meiji government phased out the old *Shi-No-Ko-Sho* (士農工商)[2] system, its slogan was *Shimin Byodo* (四民平等). By 1870, the use of family names was allowed amongst the non-*Samurai* descendants; by 1871, intermarriage amongst the gentry and the commoners; in 1872 universal education came into existence, and the government guaranteed that individuals had the freedom to chose their own profession. The government mandated that discrimination based on social class would be abolished.

However, in reality, even though the traditional caste system had been abolished, the government also installed a new system of naming of groups of people based on their social status. They were: *Kazoku* (華族, hereditary peerage, based on that of Britain but using ancient Chinese based titles), *Shizoku* (士族, the former *Samurai* class) and *Heimin* (平民, the "common" people), which allowed the social-class based discrimination to remain in place to a certain extent.

In Ryūkyū, princes and other direct members of the Royal family were made into *Kazoku* whilst those of *Chikudun Pēchin* or higher rank were designated as *Shizoku*, much in the same way as their mainland counterparts.

---

[2] The traditional class system of feudal Japan broke society into four distinct groups: the warriors, the farmers, the merchants and the artisans. Of course, there were other professions, but the main four are represented by this term. Indeed some of the other classes are not mentioned in this general term precisely because they were considered to be literally "sub-human." These include people from professions such as executioners, tanners, butchers and other professions that were considered to be "sinful" in the Shinto and Buddhist paradigms. Even in modern Japan, discrimination rears its ugly head toward people descended from such outdated social classes.

Simplified Table of Social Classes of the Ryūkyū Kingdom

Main Class	Sub Class	Number of Households	Percent of Population
Upper Gentry	*Oji*	2	0.002%
	Aji	26	0.032%
Middle Gentry	*Uekata*	38	0.047%
	Pēchin	296	0.367%
Lower Gentry	*Satunushi, Chikudun*	20,759	25.79%
Commoners (*Heimin*)		59,326	73.71%

The above table is a breakdown of the population of Ryūkyū during the old Kingdom. It is known that only the top classes were able to live in luxury due to rather rich stipends. This accounts for less than 0.5% of the entire population. 98% of the gentry lived near the poverty line, dreaming of gaining an appointment to the administration. There is evidence that the majority of those who opposed the *Ryūkyū Shobun* were from that elite 0.5% whereas the rest of the population generally welcomed the change, including the lower level gentry.

It seems that the majority of disenfranchised gentry in both Ryūkyū and mainland Japan ended up joining the new conscript military, becoming police officers or even trying their hands at politics. Even more turned to other honest means of making a living[3], such as agriculture, fishing, performing arts or in some cases even selling their skills as fighters to open martial arts schools and taught all who came[4]. However, this does not always seem to be the case. There are cases where these men turned to a life of crime.

---

[3] Until the Meiji Restoration, with some exceptions such as the rural warriors in Satsuma, members of the *Samurai* were actually often forbidden by law from taking on other professions.

[4] This can be considered the start of the spread of warrior arts such as *Kenjutsu, Jujutsu* and *Toudi*, amongst the hitherto "commoner" classes. It can likely also be seen as the start of the downfall of true martial arts and the formulation of modern *Kendo, Judo* and *Karate-do*, to name a few.

For example, gangs of organized criminals were known to hire ex-*Samurai* as bodyguards and enforcers. This phenomenon existed during as far back as the Edo/Tokugawa era, or even further, with masterless warriors (*Ronin*, 牢人, often romantically written as 浪人, or "wave man" signifying a wandering loner[5]) sometimes undertaking criminal enterprises.

The most common warrior-turned-criminals were bandits and highwaymen, or organized crime gangs in the cities. Others were thieves and muggers. With the abolition of the class system and the downfall of the feudal hierarchy, it is no surprise that some former *Samurai* would have turned to crime, either to survive or to keep up a formerly lavish lifestyle.

The Practice of *Yaadui*

During the Ryūkyū Kingdom, an estimated 26% of the total population belonged to the gentry. However, the number of government jobs was limited, which meant that many could not really make a life in the urban centers of Shuri and Naha. This prompted many of them moved to the rural areas, clear out a plot of land and to try and eke out a living in the field of agriculture. These down and out aristocrats actually formed new villages of their own, through a practice known in the Shuri dialect as *Yaadui* (Jp. *Yadori*, 屋取). It is estimated that about 130 villages across Ryūkyū were formed though this practice. Indeed, many of the government positions also seem to have been non-salaried positions. A look into the life of an Edo Era *Yukatchu* can be seen in the excellent presentation entitled *Okinawan Samurai: The Instructions of a Royal Official to His Only Son*[6].

---

[5] In modern Japanese, this term is still used to describe young people who failed their university entrance exams and are studying to take them again the next year, thus marking them as "unaffiliated." The average western ideal of the loner as a quasi-positive image is not necessarily shared in Japan.

[6] By Andreas Quast with Motobu Naoki, ISBN 1985331039. This author considers this translation to be required reading for all non-Japanese readers looking into *Karate* history, second only to the works of Patrick McCarthy.

Yaadui is one of the ways that the culture of Shuri was spread to the outlying villages, and in the view of this author, can likely be considered as one of the main sources of the so-called "village styles" of martial arts and even some of the festival dances that revolve around the use of the quarterstaff and other "weapons" (such as *Mura-bo*, 村棒). One modern *Karate* system to have been based on the influx of Shuri culture into the rural areas is *Okinawa Kenpo*, whose founder, Nakamura Shigeru, was from the northern city of Nago.

Nakamura Shigeru 中村 茂, [1893–1969] 沖縄拳法

As can be imagined, this practice intensified as the Kingdom fell and even most of the upper level members of the gentry lost their position, status and government stipends. At the time of the establishment of Okinawa Prefecture, most members of the gentry lost their privileges, causing a great change in their labor habits. There was no real economic support from the Meiji government, and the gentry with no stipends were left socially "naked" and became like refugees.

With no money to start a business or land to cultivate, and the doors to government work closed to them, they barely kept alive while searching for work. An old adage from that era compared these gentry to draft horses, as they engaged in labor that was hitherto beneath their station, as they hid their faces (in shame) with their hats.

One area where Shuri *Samuree* settled and spread the warrior culture was the northern town of Motobu, the birthplace of *Uechi-ryu Karate-do* founder Uechi Kanbun. In fact, even now, the phrase *Bu-Motobu* or 武本部 (implying the martial spirit of the people from Motobu) is prominently displayed in the Town Hall.

Indeed, so important is this legacy to Motobu that in 2018, a monument to their hometown hero Uechi Kanbun (born in the Izumi neighborhood of Motobu, studied martial arts in China and was the founder of *Uechi-ryu Karate*, 1877-1948, 上地完文) was erected to forever commemorate his indelible contributions to the global *Karate* phenomenon.

The Uechi Kanbun monument at Sakura no Mori Park on Yaedake in Nago, Okinawa
* Photo by P. McCarthy

Part 2

A Scandal!

The Matsuura Brothel in Fukuhara, Kobe as it looked in the late 1800s. Scanned from an old postcard the author [Joe Swift] obtained in 1994 in Osaka, the image was repaired and colorized by P. McCarthy for this publication

Kyan Chōtoku's story is a fascinating part of Okinawa's Karate history. There was an allegation that Kyan was involved in some misadventures, and he was ostracized, but no concrete evidence ever came to light. The 1898 articles that share his supposed misadventures lack verifiable evidence and rely solely on uncorroborated hearsay. It's difficult to know what to believe given the dirty politics of the era and the tendency to smear others' character.

However, despite the lack of evidence, these stories offer a unique and endearing window into a bygone era and provide texture to the cultural heritage of old Okinawa. It's essential to approach them with a critical eye and a willingness to question the veracity of their claims.

Unfortunately, hearsay evidence often builds reputations rather than documented proof, making it challenging to separate fact from fiction in Kyan's story. Nevertheless, it's worth remembering that Kyan was a product of his time, and the cultural and political landscape of Okinawa was complex and challenging.

In conclusion, while the lack of evidence may undermine the credibility of the stories, they offer an intriguing and sympathetic perspective on Okinawan history and culture. It's crucial to approach them with sensitivity and an understanding of the complex historical context in which they were created.

Presenting translations of period-based newspaper articles

The 1898 Articles
1. *The Downfall of a Privileged Man,*
Ryūkyū Shimpo, April 25, 1898, page 2.　有禄者子弟の堕落
2. *The Downfall of a Privileged Man 2,*
Ryūkyū Shimpo, April 27, 1898, page 2.　有禄者子弟の堕落云々
3. *The Prostitution Broker,*
Ryūkyū Shimpo, June 7, 1898, page 3.　酷業婦仲買人
4. *The Prefectural Governor Saves the Prostitutes,*
Ryūkyū Shimpo, August 7, 1898, page 3.　酷業婦知事の救恤に逢
5. *The Terrible Actions of Kyan and the Kagoshima Newspaper,*
Ryūkyū Shimpo, August 11, 1898, page 3.　喜屋武某の非行と鹿児島新聞

The Actual 1898 Articles
Courtesy of the National Archives

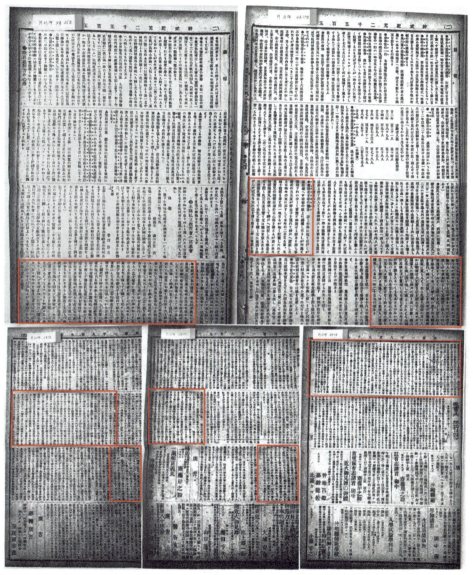

Left to right and top to bottom, in chronological order, the Kyan-related articles are surrounded by red borders.

The Downfall of a Privileged Man

The third son of the stipend-holding[7] aristocrat, Kyan, of Gibo, Shuri, traveled by boat to Kobe in Hyogo Prefecture with four or five young women under the guise of working in the textiles business at the end of last year [1897]. In addition, at the beginning of this month[8], the eldest son of the clan boarded the *Satsuma-maru*[9] ferry to Kobe where he joined his younger brother as an accomplice. As a result [*of their dastardly deeds, tr.*], among the girls who were taken are Ushi (born 1878), the daughter of a commoner named Higa who lives at 147 Kubagawa in Shuri Ward; and Kamado (born 1878), the daughter of an aristocrat[10] named Arakaki who lives at 9 Mawashi in Shuri Ward, are being held at the residence of Sakai Tatsuzo of Fukuhara[11] in Kobe City. There are rumors being spread about this setup. That is to say that the Kyan brothers took the girls to Kobe in order to sell them to a brothel. It is also whispered that the reason may also be that they plan on running such an establishment of ill repute themselves.

We do not know if these rumors are true or not, but the truth is that the Kyan brothers have taken other people's daughters and forced them to stay in Kobe. In addition, it is also an undisputed fact that they have already completed the formalities for the temporary residence of two of the girls. Fukuhara is the red-light district of Kobe, and is clearly not an area where people of good repute live. If one is involved in the field of prostitution, then the place of temporary residence is within the red-light district. The fact that the Kyan brothers brought someone else's daughters to Kobe, and that they had applied to have them live in the red-light district, the logical conclusion one should be able to draw from these two points is that the previously mentioned rumors must be true; or at least that it is no surprise that such rumors have been spread.

---

[7] For simplicity's sake, I have translated the title of this article and the following article as "a privileged man," but the actual term is "the son of an aristocrat who (still) receives a government stipend." See the first chapter of this article for a breakdown of what this meant in Meiji Era Ryūkyū.

[8] The original article has an error and says at the beginning of today. However, from the following article it becomes clear that it was meant to say the beginning of this month.

[9] *Satsuma-maru* was a steam-powered ferry owned and operated by the now defunct Kagoshima Kisen Kaisha. Such steamships were the main way of travel to and from Okinawa in this period.

[10] The term *Shizoku* (士族) is used here.

[11] Fukuhara (福原) was the old red-light district of Kobe. It was established in 1868, the time that Kobe opened as an international port. In addition to brothels it also had several restaurants, cafes, etc. It is comparable to Yoshiwara (吉原) in Tōkyō and Tsuji (辻) in Naha.

The fact that the Kyan brothers forced these girls to live in the red-light district, where a proper business should not be headquartered, allows us to conclude that their true intentions were to use these girls and obtain ill-gotten gains. It seems inconceivable that a stipend-holding aristocrat would be so vague about their reasoning for being involved with a brothel, which is exactly what the Kyan brothers have done. Even though it is said to be an age of decadence, this is indeed the true ending of the fall of a once privileged man.

The Downfall of a Privileged Man [2]

Regarding the article in our previous edition, it was hastily written without obtaining the proper verifications, and deeper research revealed that there were statements therein that were not factual. The third son of Kyan took the girls to Kobe not at the end of last year, but in February of this year [1898]. In addition, it was written that his elder brother Chōho was in cahoots with him, but in actuality Chōho traveled to Kobe on the *Satsuma-maru* at the beginning of this month in order to correct his younger brother's wrongdoings. Rumor has it that when this third son lived in Tōkyō with his father in the past, he would spend his days pursuing fleshly pleasures and being a great nuisance to his father, who in the end had enough of his son's philandering and sent him packing away from Tōkyō. Even after his return to his homeland, Kyan's third son was afflicted with a pathological addition to sex, and in the end this led him down a path of crime. His older brother did not notice what a dastardly fellow he had become. Convincing his older brother that he was going to get into the textiles business, he conned his brother into forking over some money, which he used to buy passage. At that time, he brought the aforementioned girls to Kobe's red-light district Fukuhara, and tried to sell them to a local pimp. When word got back to Chōho, he was utterly shocked and rushed to Kobe on the *Satsuma-maru* at the beginning of this month to try and correct his brother's actions. He met with his younger brother, scolded him about his evil ways, shed tears and tried to stop the whole affair. However, his younger brother said he had already sold the women and would not listen to his older brother's admonitions. Indeed, he started to roundly curse his elder brother out, not showing the slightest inkling of correcting his behavior. Chōho became angry, and not having any other recourse, ended up disowning his brother, and left him in Kobe, shedding tears of vexation as he got back on the *Satsuma-maru* and returned to this Prefecture on the 25th of this month.

The Prostitution Broker

At any rate, the world these days is all about the money, and that any pursuits that do not lead to monetary gain are looked down on as foolish. Depending on how one makes their money they could easily head down the road to evil deeds. In past editions of this periodical, we have written about the actions of a certain Kyan and a certain Tamagusuku who took girls to Kobe to sell them into prostitution. Our sources say that when they took the girls to Kobe, they went through a local broker and tried to sell them as *Geiko*[12], but they of course had no formal training in any of the entertainment arts so they finally decided to sell them as prostitutes. The girls were taken to the residence of a certain Sakai Tatsuzo, who ran a *Kashi-zashiki*[13] in Fukuhara. They negotiated a contract to sell the girls for the sum of 120 *yen*[14] for three years of servitude, but he [*Kyan, tr.*] was told that without the girls' certificates of family registry that no advance payment could be made. Kyan immediately contacted his brother and Tamagusuku, advised them of the situation and instructed them to assist in obtaining the proper documentation. The contracts they passed to the families of the girls had words to the effect of the families needing to provide a family registration certificate, or some other application form sealed[15] by both parties; if the families agree to entrust their seal to the contractor, then they had the option of extending the contract from three to four years. However, no matter how long they waited the money never came, so all parties became suspicious.

Kyan himself left the girls in Kobe and returned to Okinawa by himself. The families of the prostitutes tried to collect their money from Kyan but he never replied and so the families were thrown into a state of discomfiture. An old woman accompanied Kyan from Kobe, saying that she was a broker and that she had already negotiated the purchase of a girl named Higa Ushi from 147 Kubagawa, Shuri and already concluded a contract with her family. She said that there was another girl named Ishikawa Ushi from 233 Tomari, Naha, who was also in Kobe, and was

---

[12] Better known in the west as *Geisha*, these were professional entertainers versed in many arts such as song and dance. They were also sometimes known, depending on the era, area and circumstances, to also engage in prostitution, though as licensed entertainers, were not legally allowed to market sexual services.

[13] Written 貸座敷. Literally a "room for rent," Although the literal translation is seemingly innocuous, it actually comes from an edict passed in 1872 that voided indenture contracts for prostitutes, but not outright outlawing prostitution. Under this scheme, which started in Osaka and quickly spread to other cities, the prostitute was considered as a "licensed private contractor" and the brothel acted as a "room rental service."

[14] In modern currency, this would be about 1.8 million *yen*, or approximately 16,000 US dollars, based on exchange rates issued on of October 23, 2018.

[15] In Japan, personal seals/stamps are used in lieu of signatures in many instances.

here to meet this girl's family and negotiate a contract with them. Her family said that they knew nothing about such dirty deeds, and became incensed at the woman, who could only leave their house. If it was Kyan who took the girl to Kobe then it is Kyan who must bring her back home. If he would just leave here there, then this girl Ishikawa Ushi would have no other recourse than to become a beggar. This indeed is a dastardly thing to have done.

The Prefectural Governor Saves the Prostitutes

As we have written about several times in the past few issues of this paper, Kyan had taken Higa Ushi of Kubagawa 147, Shuri and Ishikawa Ushi of Tomari, Naha to Kobe and tried to sell them as indentured prostitutes. However, they were not popular with the patrons, and having no skills in the performance arts or other abilities, no one would take them on as either *Geiko* or prostitutes. Kyan, foreseeing he could not make any profit from such a situation, cold-heartedly left the girls in Kobe and ran back to his family manor (in Okinawa).

The two prostitutes' hardships only increased, as did their ability to afford food, but they were picked up by the *Hokoku Gikai*[16] of Kobe, which was the only thing that saved their lives, which were by then as fragile as morning dew. The organization contacted their parents to arrange for them to pick up their daughters. However, these families were so desperately impoverished as to have to sell their daughters, so of course they did not reply. Without any other recourse, the organization contacted the Prefectural Governor, who was in Tōkyō at the time, explained the situation and requested his assistance in rescuing the girls. In response, the Governor stopped by Kobe on his way back to this Prefecture, confirmed the identity of the girls and confirmed the facts of the case as true. He became very incensed about this situation. Thanking the organization for their intervention, he then provided travel money to the girls and brought them back to this Prefecture on the same ship. Even the ignorant prostitutes shed tears of joy, as if they had met the Buddha in Hell. It goes without saying how merciless and cruel the acts of Kyan were, conning girls for profit without even thinking about the unhappiness he would cause. When we think of the girls and their parents we cannot help but feel sorry for them. However, from an outsider's

---

[16] Written in *Kanji* as 報国義会, this was a group that focused on protecting the socially weak, especially children. It was founded in 1890, and by 1892 had built an orphanage and a medical clinic. The organization still exists under the name *Kobe Koyukai* (神戸光有会), and runs several social welfare programs including retirement homes, etc.

perspective, it can also be said to be their own fault for being seduced by the promise of profit, and thus others should also condemn their actions.

The Evil Actions of Kyan & the Kagoshima Newspaper
On the third of this month, the Kagoshima Newspaper also picked up the story of Kyan that we have been running in recent editions with an article entitled *"Okinawa Prefecture Governor Narahara[17] and the Two Women."*

According to this article, Okinawa Prefecture Governor Narahara stopped by Kagoshima on his way back to Okinawa from Tōkyō, accompanied by two young women of about 18 or 19 years of age. When asked what was going on they explained that the girls had been kidnapped by a certain man named Kyan from Shuri who had secretly taken them to Kobe in the spring of this year and left them there. When pressed about the details, it turns out that the parents of these girls (Ushi and Kami) owed this Kyan a bit of money. He took advantage of this situation with a plan to make some easy cash. Kyan told the parents of Ushi and Kame that if they were to go to Kobe, then no matter how weak the girls were, there were many high paying jobs for them and that such jobs were easy to come by, so they should send their daughters up. He regaled them with tales of the wonderful sights that Ushi and Kame have never seen. He saw that they were falling under the spell of his words, and in his heart he was laughing.

In the end, he took these two girls to Kobe, but after two months, their funds ran out. Using the fact that they had no real skills as an excuse, and in spite of the fact that they could have probably found other means of employment, he boldly applied to the police to register the girls as legal prostitutes. However, the police immediately contacted the girls' parents, who replied that they never had any intentions of sending their daughters to Kobe to become prostitutes. Just like that, Kyan's long-awaited plans went up in smoke. When the girls heard that Kyan had applied to register them as prostitutes, they cried and screamed about their misfortune without being wary of the prying eyes of people who heard their voices from outside their doors.

---

[17] The eighth Governor of Okinawa Prefecture was a former Satsuma warrior named Narahara Shigeru (奈良原茂, 1834-1918). He served in this role from 1892 to 1908. As an aside he was also an adept in *Nodachi (Yakumaru) Jigen-ryu* swordsmanship, and the head of the Okinawan Branch of the Dai Nippon Butokukai. For more information on this organization please see *Legend of the Fist* or *Ancient Okinawan Martial Arts Volume 2*, both by Patrick McCarthy.

Finally, the story reached the ears of the chairman of the *Hokokusha*[18] (a charitable, merciful group), who decided to take the girls under his care. Perhaps Kyan may have heard about this, went into hiding, his whereabouts unknown. When Governor Narahara landed in Kobe, the chairman of the *Hokokusha* told him the entire story. Governor Narahara thanked the chairman deeply for his kindness, and used his own money to bring the girls home.

The son of Kyan, the honorable steward of the Sho Family, took part in dastardly, inhumane deeds. The fact that his name is now sullied even in other Prefectures is nothing more than his own fault, and he should just deal with it himself. However, that he has also sullied his father's own good name, and by extension, that of the Sho Family, is not something that can be taken lightly.

---

[18] Here, the name of the charity who took the girls in is called by a different name than in part four of the series. The *Kanji* used is 報告社, rather than the correct name, which is 報国義会. The latter is a real organization but a cursory search does not reveal any hits for the former in the context of these articles.

Part 3

Prince Shō Jun with Ota Chōfu [insert]

Analysis

About the *Ryūkyū Shimpo*

The *Ryūkyū Shimpo* (琉球新報) newspaper was founded by Prince Shō Jun (1873-1945), the fourth son of the last King of Ryūkyū, Sho Tai (1843-1901). Although the actual Romanization of the title could also be spelled *Ryūkyū Shinpo*, for the purposes of this publication I have opted to use the company's own official English nomenclature.

The periodical's stated intended purpose was to assist in the modernization of Okinawa, or in other words assimilation into the mainstream of mainland Japan. Its first editor was a man named Ōta Chōfu[19] (1865-1938), who was a Shuri aristocrat himself.

Its first edition was printed on September 15, 1893 and was run every other day. Its dimensions were 35.6cm by 28.5cm, and was originally four pages. On April 1, 1906, it became a daily publication.

The stated purpose of its founding was to promote the assimilation of Okinawan citizens into Japanese society. The founders determined that the only way for Okinawa to take back control of the prefecture's businesses, which were mainly run by the so-called *Kiryu Shonin*[20], was for Okinawa to assimilate.

One of the ways to promote the modernization (read: assimilation) of Okinawa was to turn the tide of popular opinion against the old ways and the status quo. They needed to get the population on board, and to that end many earlier articles seem to be thinly-veiled hack jobs against the hitherto ruling class and those pro-China stalwarts who maintained their desire to remain independent and protected by the Qing Dynasty. For example, there are examples of articles from the late 1890s describing proponents of the fighting arts as uncouth, renegade ruffians, or even outright criminals.

---

[19] Ōta Chōfu's name will be recognizable by *Karate* history enthusiasts as one of the participants in the 1936 "Meeting of the Masters" at Naha's *Showa Kaikan* building, where a consensus was reached by the participants to formally change the *Kanji* for *Karate* from 唐手 to 空手. A complete translation of the meeting minutes can be found in this work by Patrick McCarthy and his *"Ancient Okinawan Martial Arts" Vol. 2*.

[20] Written in *Kanji* as 寄留商人 this term represents merchants from other prefectures who moved to Okinawa to open up shop. The majority of them were from Kagoshima and Osaka. Some of them went on to serve in the Prefectural Assembly and some of the governors of the prefecture (dispatched from Kagoshima) protected them, causing many Okinawans to resist.

However, by the early Taisho Era (1911-1924), the newspaper articles that revolve around the local fighting traditions and the past martial heroes of Ryūkyū took on a more positive tone. See, for example, the 1914 Asato Anko articles (as transcribed by his student Shoto/Funakoshi Gichin), the series of articles from 1915 commemorating the life of Itosu Anko, etc.

All in all, the political leanings of the newspaper in its early days are obvious to the careful reader. This background can sometimes be overlooked, leading to wishful thinking about the contents of the articles by enthusiastic, well-meaning researchers when using them as primary source material. Just like today's super-charged political-media environment, the contents of the articles should be taken with a grain of salt, as well as a healthy dose of critical thinking and common sense.

Indentured Prostitution during the Meiji Era

The history of the most destitute of times can, across almost all parts of the world, be inexorably tied to the history of forced prostitution and sexual slavery. Meiji Era Japan was no exception. Indeed, the practice of selling daughters into indentured prostitution seems to have been practiced in poorer, rural areas in the Tokugawa (Edo) Era and most likely even further back in time. This brief section will deal with the same time frame as the articles herein, to give the reader an idea of what actually was going on in our story.

In Pre-WWII Japan, prostitution was actually a regulated industry. Indentured prostitution was in fact a contractual agreement between the brothel and the woman (or her family) and was, as such, legally binding. In our story, it seems the families of the girls were conned and the girls themselves likely taken against their will, but in many instances, women entered the profession of their own volition.

In order to understand this background, we need to start in 1872 when a Peruvian ship, the *Maria Luz*, came into Yokohama Port for repairs. Commodore Perry pried open Japanese ports to the world in 1853, so this incident came less than two decades later.

At any rate, there were reported to be 231 Chinese "coolies[21]" hired under eight-year indenture contracts, aboard the *Maria Luz*. One of these men, apparently fed up with this arrangement, jumped ship and swam to an English gunship nearby. Long story short, he was eventually turned over to the local authorities, and the Japanese, seeing this as an opportunity to instate themselves as a modern civilization, and a local judge declared that the coolie trade violated international public law.

However, a savvy lawyer for the Peruvian side declared that Japan had its own slaves, indentured in the brothels across the land. Embarrassed, the Japanese government took corrective action and in October of the same year liberated all indentured prostitutes and declared that the courts would entertain no suits against the women regarding debts they may have owed to the brothels.

This decree did not outright ban prostitution, it merely made null and void the indentured contracts. Brothels cooked up so-called "room rental" schemes, by which they would rent out the room, and the prostitute, as an independent contractor, would then provide the service.

However, by 1875, indentured contracts for prostitution were made legal again by the federal government. Though the new law made it clear that the outright sale and mortgage of human beings was illegal, indentured contracts could be made in cases where a debtor could repay the debt by entering into a fixed-period labor contract.

Without getting too bogged down in the details, the normal term of indenture for a trained *Geisha* (licensed entertainer, of whom some are said to have engaged in sexual services) was for three years, whereas the contracts for prostitutes stipulated a maximum number of years of servitude, but were able to keep track of their earnings and take early retirement if successful. In our story above, the contract seems to have originally been for three years, with the option to extend to four years (allowing for more earnings).

---

[21] A coolie is an outdated word, considered pejorative, that represents native unskilled indentured laborers from South Asia, Southeast Asia and China.

Fake News! So Sad! Unbelievable!

The articles presented in the previous chapter, if taken at face value, seem to point to the individual in question as a dastardly criminal involved in human trafficking. Even in today's day and age, although many of us understand the concept of innocent until proven guilty, such a series of articles would be enough to incite a lynch mob.

But, when we stop and really read the articles, and think about them, we might be able to come to a different conclusion.

The first article states clearly that it is based on a mere rumor and offers nothing in the way of evidence. However, based on this initial article, the remaining articles jump off as if this unconfirmed rumor was the gospel truth. There are enough inconsistencies in the articles to call into question the journalistic integrity of the writer, if not the entire periodical. One example is how the names of the girls in question keep changing from article to article.

Although the title of this section is not the conclusion of this author as regards the contents of the article (I am still in the process of coming to that conclusion myself), it will provide a potential narrative as to how this series of articles could be interpreted as, "fake news."

Armed with a rudimentary knowledge of the historical background of the times, the state of human trafficking during that era, and the stated intention of the *Ryūkyū Shimpo* to spring Okinawa into modernity, the reader is invited to consider the following.

In order to bring a new paradigm of modernization into Okinawa, Shō Jun and his cohorts had to sow seeds of discontent amongst the general populace. They seem to be doing that by turning the tide of public opinion against the established upper classes[22] and the status quo.

Indeed, in later editions of the newspaper, into the Taisho Era, the martial arts and local warriors were presented in a positive light. However, in the early days of the newspaper, a couple of articles referred to the martial arts practitioners as nothing more than violent ruffians.

---

[22] Shō Jun, Ōta Chōfu and others on the staff of the newspaper were also from well-off upper-class families, with Shō Jun literally being royalty. In this case they can probably be considered true revolutionaries.

That being said, it can also be said that where there is smoke, there is fire. There is mention of the Prefectural Governor making a stop by Kobe on his way back to Okinawa from Tōkyō, via Kagoshima. There is mention of a woman from Kobe visiting the families of the girls in question. Through exhaustive research, these types of things can likely be verified through travel records, etc. Perhaps we can say that there is some truth in the kidnapping of the girls and the forceful selling of them into sexual slavery.

Speculation hat on, what if the antagonist of our story was duped by the simultaneously mentioned Tamagusuku into traveling with the girls to Kobe, but our hero was not aware of the full extent of the endeavor? He could have been recruited by Tamagusuku as a kind of "bodyguard" for the girls' travels to Kobe, but lied to by Tamagusuku as to the actual reason he was taking them to the mainland.

If this turns out to be the case, then we can perhaps conclude that this series of articles was nothing more than a hatchet job on the son of a famous family, based on flimsy evidence and hearsay. What better way to sow the seeds of discontent against those who still harbored the old ways than to invoke a public moral anger? More diligent research into this story would likely reveal a kernel of truth, but is beyond the scope of this modest presentation.

Appendix

Haiban nu Bushi [Samuree]

* Photo: Shuri Bushi Higa Kanematsu [aka Machu Higa] is said to have worked pulling a rickshaw following the abolition of the Ryūkyu Kingdom

The Background

The plight of the disenfranchised gentry has even made it into traditional Okinawan pop-culture. A folk song for the *Sanshin*[23] called *Haiban nu Samuree* (廃藩ぬ武士) regales the listener with the sense of melancholy at the end of the Ryūkyū Kingdom during the *Ryūkyū Shobun* period. The lyrics were written by Kadekaru Ushi, the mother of famed *Sanshin* artist Kadekaru Rinsho[24]. The tune is said to have been written by both of them when Rinsho was eight years old.

Haiban is an Okinawan pronunciation of the Japanese term *Haihan* 廃藩, which itself is an abbreviation of *Haihan Chiken* 廃藩置県, the abolishment of feudal provinces and the establishment of modern prefectures. As already seen, the way this was done in Okinawa was different from that of mainland Japan. The word *Samuree* is, obviously, from the Japanese term *Samurai*, and was used in the latter part of the Ryūkyū Kingdom to describe the gentry.

There is a saying in Okinawa that the Chinese aristocrats hang calligraphic scrolls in their alcoves, Japanese warriors place their swords in their alcoves and the Bushi [aka *Samuree*] of Ryūkyū placed their *Sanshin* in their alcoves. As the Ryūkyū Kingdom came to and end, many of these *Samuree* lost their jobs and their authority, so they turned to other sources of income such as agriculture, business and entertainment. In this light, their skills in the *Sanshin* and Ryūkyū dances came in quite handy. All in all, the song provides a humorous yet warm glimpse at an elderly ex-aristocrat who had lost all he had. It seems to be a general caricature rather than a description of one specific individual.

---

[23] *Sanshin* (三線) is a three stringed instrument popular in Okinawa. Its origins are said to lie in China, and the *Sanshin* was also introduced into mainland Japan where it was transformed into the Japanese *Shamisen* (三味線).

[24] Kadekaru Rinsho (嘉手苅林昌, 1920-1999) was one of the restorers of Ryūkyūan folk music in the post WWII era, and was one of the founding members of the Ryūkyū Folk Music Association (琉球民謡協会), one of the largest and most influential groups of *Sanshin* enthusiasts.

The Song

The following represents a translation of the lyrics of one version of this song, to allow the reader a sense of the feelings in Okinawa in the late 1800s. There are a few variations of this tune, but these lyrics are those provided by the author's friend, the lovely Ms. Ao Reika, an up-and-coming *Sanshin* artist.

Verse One
- 拝でぃ懐かさや 廃藩ぬ武士 背骨小や曲ぎてぃ うすんかがん
- *Ugadi nachikasa ya haiban nu samuree Koogugwāa ya magati usunkagan*
- It makes me sad to see you like this, a warrior at the end of an era, with your back all stooped over.

Chorus (Repeats after each verse)
- 唐や平組 大和断髪 我した沖縄片結
- *Too ya hiragun, yamatoo danpachi washita uchinaa ya katakashira*
- The Chinese wear their hair in a queue, the Japanese have cut their hair and we Okinawans (still) wear our topknots.

Verse Two
- 思みば 懐かさや 青傘や片手. 木フージョウ小腰に アダニ葉サバ小
- *Umiba nachikasa ya oogasaagwāa ya katadi Kiihuujoogwāa kushi ni adaniba sabagwāa*
- It makes me sad to think of you with a blue umbrella in one hand, a wooden tobacco case on your hip and wearing straw sandals.

Verse Three
- しばし国頭ぬ 奥に身ゆ忍でぃ 共に立ち上がる 時節待たな
- *Shibashi kunjan nu uku ni mi yu shinudi Tumu ni tachi agaru jishichi matana*
- I will hide in Kunigami[25] for a while waiting for the time to rise up.

---

[25] Even after the Meiji Restoration, some members of the Bushi [*Samuree*] still held out hope that they could rise up against the government. This group was known variously as *Ganko-to* (Stubborn Party, 頑固党), *Kuru* (Black, 黒) or *Fusanshii* (Those who disagree, 不賛成). They had grand plans to maintain the old status quo, against the Meiji government. Even well into the modern era they refused to shave off their topknots, and swore allegiance to the King. Some of these men had contact with Qing China and hid in Kunigami awaiting their chance to counterattack. Their opponents were those who supported modernization and the Meiji government and were known variously as the *Kaika-to* (Enlightenment Party, 開化党), *Shiru* (White, 白) and *Sanshii* (Those in agreement, 賛成).

Verse Four

- タンメー片結 あん美らさあたし　廃藩になたれ 断髪けなてぃ
- *Tanmee katakashira anchurasa atashi　Haiban ni nataree danpachi kenati*
- The beautifully braided topknot of the old aristocrat was (unceremoniously) shorn off at the end of the Kingdom era.

Verse Five

- 大和世になたれ 大和口タンメー　うっちぇーひっちぇー 何にんくぃーにん あんしてくださいね
- *Yamatuyuu ni nataree yamatuguchi tanmee　Uccheehicchee nuuninkwiinin Anshite kudasai ne*
- Here in the Japan-controlled era, even the old man speaks standard Japanese. Everything has been turned on its head, so go ahead and do so.

Trans. Note: While the Japanese kanji [武士] unequivocally portrays the term '*Bushi*,' in this lyrical verse, harking back to Okinawa's old Ryūkyū Kingdom era, the term resonates as '*Samuree*' [sic, i.e. Samurai]. A deeper exploration into the rationale behind this divergence unveils a poignant intention - to grant Ryūkyū Bushi a rightful place alongside their more renowned Japanese counterpart.

Selected Bibliography

1. Arakaki K. (2011) <u>Okinawa Karate no Rekishi</u>. Tōkyō: Hara Shobo.　新垣清著『沖縄空手の歴史』
2. Bishop, M. (1999) <u>Okinawan Karate: Teachers, Styles and Secret Techniques, 2nd Ed</u>. Boston: Charles E. Tuttle Co., Ltd.
3. Funakoshi G. (1956) <u>Karate-do Ichiro</u>. Tōkyō: Sankei Shinbun.富名腰義珍著『空手道一路』
4. Gima S. and Fujiwara R. (1986) <u>Taidan Kindai Karate-do no Rekishi wo Kataru</u>. Tōkyō: Baseball Magazine. 儀間眞謹・藤原稜三共著『対談近代空手道の歴史を語る』
5. Hokama T. (1999) <u>Okinawa Karate-do Kobudo no Shinzui</u>. Naha: Naha Shuppansha.　外間哲弘著『沖縄空手道古武道の真髄』
6. Hokama T. (2001b) <u>Okinawa Karate Retsuden Hyakunin.</u> Nishihara: Self Published.　外間哲弘著『沖縄空手列伝百人』
7. Hokama T. (2010) <u>Ryūkyū no Rekishi</u>. Self-Published. 外間哲弘著『琉球の歴史』
8. Iwai K. (2000) <u>Motobu Choki to Ryūkyū Karate</u>. Tōkyō: Airyudo.　岩井虎伯著『本部朝基と琉球カラテ』
9. Kinjo H. (2011) <u>Karate kara Karate e</u>. Tōkyō: Nihon Budokan. 金城裕著『唐手から空手へ』

10. *Matsuo K. (1990)* <u>Ryūkyū Oke Hiden Bujutsu</u>. *Tōkyō: Baseball Magazine.* 松尾兼徳左近『琉球王家秘伝武術』
11. *McCarthy, P. (1995)* <u>Bubishi: The Bible of Karate</u>. *Tōkyō: Charles E. Tuttle Co., Inc.*
12. *McCarthy, P. (1999)* <u>Ancient Okinawan Martial Arts: Koryu Uchinadi (Volume 1-2)</u>. *Boston: Charles E. Tuttle Co., Inc.*
13. *McCarthy, P. (2002)* <u>Motobu Choki's 1932 Watashi no Karate-jutsu</u>. *Brisbane: IRKRS.*
14. *McCarthy, P. (2018)* <u>Legend of the Fist</u>. *Brisbane: IRKRS.*
15. *Miki, J. and Takada, M. (1930)* <u>Kenpo Gaisetsu</u>. *Tōkyō: Tōkyō Imperial University Karate Research Society.*
16. *Miyagi T. (1987)* <u>Karate no Rekishi</u>. *Naha: Hirugisha.* 宮城篤正著『空手の歴史』
17. *Nagamine S. (1986)* <u>Shijitsu to Kuden ni Yoru Okinawa no Karate Sumo Meijin Den</u>. *Tōkyō: Shin Jinbutsu Oraisha.* 長嶺将真著『史実と口伝による沖縄の空手角力名人伝』
18. Ramseyer, J.M. (1991) "Indentured Prostitution in Imperial Japan: Credible Commitments in the Commercial Sex Industry." *The Journal of Law, Economics, and Organization*, V7 N1, pp. 89-116.
19. *Ryūkyū Shimpo, 1898, 04/25, 04/27, 06/07, 08/07, 08/11 editions.*
20. Stanley, A. (2012) *Selling Women: Prostitution, Markets, and the Household in Early Modern Japan.* University of California Press.
21. *Takamiyagi S., Nakamoto M., Shinzato K. (2008)* <u>Okinawa Karate Kobudo Jiten</u>. *Tōkyō: Kashiwa Shobo.* 高宮城繁、仲本政博、新里勝彦共著『沖縄空手古武道事典』

Chapter 5

Unraveling the Legacy
Delving Deeper into the World of Kyan Chotoku

Kyan's 1932 Book Lecture
by Sonohara Ken
Curator ~ Okinawa Prefectural Karate Promotion Division

On 17 March, 2022, a lecture on Kyan Chōtoku's 1932 book was conducted by Sonohara Ken san at the Okinawan's Karate Kaikan. Due to Covid Pandemic restrictions, I was unable to attend in person, but I am grateful to Nakamura Yasushi [Okinawa Karate Kaikan Kanchō] and Mr. Miguel Da Luz [ODKS Project Manager] for providing me with both its outline and the original lecture. The edited translation presented here is the result of the combined efforts of Mr. Brian Arthur and myself [Patrick McCarthy].

Date, Time & Venue
17 March 2022
Thursday: 2-4pm
Okinawa Karate Kaikan
Sponsor: The Okinawa Prefecture Culture, Tourism and Sports Department; Karate Promotion Division.

Abstract

The Okinawa Karate Academy is organizing a series of six meetings to facilitate academic research on Okinawan karate. Presented by Sonohara Ken, the curator of the Okinawa Karate Promotion Section, [this] the 6th meeting will focus on the image of Okinawan karate as portrayed by karate master Kyan Chōtoku in various documents, with a particular emphasis on, "*Illustrated Kumite,*" by Kyan Chōtoku [1870-1945]. Kyan Chōtoku studied various kinds of *"Te"* [手] under teachers such as Matsumura Sōkon (松村 宗棍) of Shuri, Matsumora Kosaku [松茂良興作], and Oyadomari Kokan [親泊 興寛], both from Tomari, and was considered to be one of the eminent prewar figures of Okinawan karate.

He went to Tōkyō with his father at a crucial moment in the history of the dissolution of the Ryūkyū Kingdom and later [upon his return] settled near Hijabashi in Yomitan, where he taught younger generations, including students at the Agriculture College. The discussion will focus on Kyan Chōtoku's [*article as it appears in the 1930*] "*Outline of Kempo,*" his 1932 "*Okinawa-kenpo Karate Kumite,*" and his newspaper contributions that shed light on his image of Okinawan karate.

1. Profile

Name: Kyan Chōtoku
DOB/D: 1870-1945 (died at the age of 75)
Hometown: Gibo-cho, Shuri
Education: Studied Chinese literature at Nishōgakusha under Mishima Chūshū. * His enrollment status needs to be verified for the year 1878.
Career: Worked at the *Shō* Family Residence [while] in Tōkyō. After returning home [to Okinawa], he oversaw the Makihara [Machibaru] Farm, owned by the Shō Family in Yomitan.
Karate Career: Each time Kyan returned home, he trained under his father's teacher, Matsumura Sōkon and also with Matsumora Kosaku. Learned Kūsankū (aka "Chatan Yara no Kūsankū") from Yara Pēchin. He possessed such formidable skills that he was nicknamed "*Chanmī-gwā*" [Small-eyed Kyan].

Disciples: Kyan taught karate at the request of the Kadena Police Station, Prefectural Agricultural School, aspiring teachers at the Teacher Training Institute, and the neighborhood youth.

Style: None noted but Kyan's disciples went on to establish the Shōrin-ryū (少林流) and Shōrinji-ryū (少林寺流) schools.

Family: Kyan was the third son among his siblings, comprising six boys and six girls, making a total of twelve children in his family. He received instruction in karate from his father, Kyan Chōfu, as well as his father's teacher, Matsumura Sōkon of Shuri-te. Additionally, he learned from Matsumora Kōsaku and Oyadomari Pēchin of Tomari-te.

Writings: Affiliated with the Okinawa Prefectural Agricultural & Forestry School, Kyan Chōtoku wrote "*Karate Training and Understanding Fighting*," which was published in the revised edition of Kenpō Gaisetsu on 1 June, 1930. Additionally, he authored, "*Okinawa Kenpō Karatedō Basic Kumite with Explanatory Diagrams*" as a folding booklet (dated 3 Nov, 1932, which included kumite photos. It is uncertain whether a volume on kata was also written. Furthermore, Kyan contributed a 4-part article to an unknown newspaper, entitled "*Memories of Karate*," dated 7 May, 1942.

Accomplishments: In the Karatedō Kata demonstrations, to Commemorate the Establishment of the Okinawa Branch of the Dai Nippon Butokukai, held under the authority of the Okinawa Branch of the Dai Nippon Butokukai, a 69-year-old Chōtoku performed Chintō as a representative of Karate in the Prefecture, in the final performance of the day; The event was held on 18 June, 1939.

During the memorial demonstrations for the construction of the Yomitan airfield (North Airfield), at the age of 75, Chōtoku made a profound impact on men and women of all ages with his demonstrations of Chintō, bōjutsu (using the Tokumine no kun), and tameshiwari (breaking techniques).

2. *Shizoku* ("old Samurai class") mentality, as seen in the Kyan Family:

Considerations from Kyan's 1942, 'Memories of Karate,' at 72 years old.
 • From a young age, Kyan was physically weak and small in stature.
 • He was forced to wrestle [*sumō*] with his older brother [Chōhitsu], on a daily basis, which helped to build his physical strength."
 • When Kyan was 15 years old [14 by the Western calendar], on the day of his hair-tying ceremony, his father [Kyan Chōfu] persuaded his sons to practice martial arts, believing that without an interest in it, they could not become true men."
 • *"The training was extremely rigorous and demanding. There were occasions when I would hide in the corner of the house and cry like a child. But the next morning, I would muster up my courage, forget what happened the day before, and train intensely with my brother."*
 • *After arriving in Tōkyō, during cold and snowy winters, we were purposely sent out into the garden and not given breakfast unless we practiced karate."*
 • When Kyan was 16 years old [15 by the Western calendar], in 1885[26], he accompanied his father to Shikina Gardens, where he first met Matsumura Sōkon; a master of Okinawa karate during its renaissance. Through his father's connection, Kyan was able to receive training from Matsumura Sōkon.
 • *"At that time, Matsumura was around 80 years old, and I learned the Gojushiho kata from him, which I still remembered even now. Despite his advanced age, Matsumura would hit the makiwara every morning."*

---

[26] Changed from 1886 to 1885 by the translator, as the source (Karate no Omoide) consistently uses kazoedoshi. Irei Hiroshi also agrees in his book on 1885.

- *"[Matsumura] Sensei's physical condition exceeded that of young people, he had a penetrating gaze, and his wankotsu (upper arms or hand bones/wrists) were tough and felt like iron and stone."*
- *"Almost like a habitual phrase, he [Matsumura] was very fond of saying, "Martial Arts [武] are the path to peace," and that peace is maintained by the Martial Arts [武]."*
- Kyan's interest in martial arts gradually increased during his 2-year training under Matsumura Sōkon sensei, but unfortunately, when he was around 18 years old [17 by the Western calendar], his father, who was the chief retainer to the Marquess Shō Tai, was sent with him and his brothers to Tōkyō, which cut short his training.
- During his fifth year in Tōkyō, when Kyan was approximately "29[27]" years old, Matsumura Sōkon sensei passed away at the advanced age of 88.
- **Kyan Chōtoku's View of Karate: From His Writings & Contributions**

1. Kyan's View of Karate in, "*Kenpō Gaisetsu* [1930 revised edition] as viewed by students of Tōkyō University.
- As students from Tōkyō University, co-authors *Miki Nisaburō* and Takada (Mutsu) Mizuho conducted interviews of karate masters in Okinawa in 1929, and compiled them into a classic karate book.
- Kyan's Contribution; "*Karate Training & Understanding Fighting*" [The Okinawa Prefectural Agriculture and Forestry School]
- In the book, other karate masters residing in Okinawa were also featured. Kyan Chōtoku was introduced with his address at the Karate Research Institute located at Hija bridge street, Mt. Yomitan (Yuntanza), Nakagami district in Okinawa prefecture.
- Kyan instructs karate at Kadena-chō Agricultural School and Mt. Yomitan [Yuntanza] Karate Research Institute.
- Sensei practices karate without a shirt.
- *"Sensei's practice of performing karate shirtless intrigued me, so I asked him about it. He explained that it was a custom he had followed since childhood and that he also encouraged his students to practice in this way."*
- *"The purpose is to strengthen the skin and become clearly conscious of the distribution of power. Wearing clothes or other items can make it*

---

[27] Changed from "25" years old by the translator. The lecturer apparently calculates the age of 25 based on Matsumura's accepted year of death (1899). As Kyan writes it, one would assume he went to Tōkyō in 1887 at 18 (*kazoedoshi*) (after 2 years of training with Matsumura sensei). Kyan also states in *Karate no Omoide* that he returned to Okinawa at 26 (Western age: 25) and studied under Matsumora Kōsaku sensei, Oyadomari Pēchin sensei, and others of Tomari. As the former king Shō Tai was granted the title of Marquess in 1885 after having already being forced to move to Tōkyō in 1879, the Kyan men accompanying the Marquess 10 years later (1894 or 1895) when Kyan was 25 years old, as the lecturer suggests, seems unlikely and quite late for his father, the chief retainer, to do so.

harder to detect if someone is being deceptive in their power distribution, which is why shirtless training is preferred."
- *"Chan no migwā"* (small eye'd Kyan) is a famous phrase and I have heard that even a child of 3 shaku (90 cm / 3 feet) will stop crying at hearing it.
- Guidance on how to improve makiwara training.

- Contributions from the book, "*Karate Training & Understanding Fighting*," include:

- 1. A history and outline of Tūdī [Tōde/Karate].
- 2. Training guidelines.
- 3. Guidelines for actual fighting.

- **2. Kyan Chōtoku's perspective on karate as reflected in his book, "Okinawa Kenpō Karatedō Kihon Zukai Kumite," 3 Nov, 1932**

- A folded book, possibly private, from a personal collection.
- Book dimensions are 15.5 cm in height and 9 cm in width, with a total of 26 pages.
- The book provides a summary of karate and includes blueprint photos with explanations of kumite.

- **3. Memories of Karate**
- In a series of 4 or 5 articles, entitled "*Karate no Omoide*" [Memories of Karate], published 7 May 1942, in an unknown newspaper, Kyan Chōtoku shared his views on karate in his later years. The articles were cut out from the newspaper and also provided insights into the social conditions during the war.
- [*The State of Karate Instruction*]
- At the time, different karate masters respected each other's expertise and only taught students the techniques they were proficient in.
- The process of seeking instruction from a skilled sensei was a respectful and harmonious experience, as they would connect you with a knowledgeable teacher upon request.
- [The general perception of karate during that period]
- "Martial arts practitioners were regarded as nonconformists in a less open world during that time."

- "Karate practice was kept secret even from our own siblings, and we had to train in private to avoid public attention, making it quite challenging."
- Additionally, given the persistence of savage practices, and having personally tested myself [Kyan] in bars and the entertainment district, I was always cautious and alert when visiting such places.
- [Regarding the nationwide spread of Karate]
- Karate was publicly introduced by Funakoshi Gichin in April 1922 at the first Sports and Physical Education Exhibition sponsored by the Ministry of Education. Funakoshi also wrote, "Ryūkyū Kenpō Karate" in the same year.
- The concept of Bushido evolved over time, transforming from a personal code of conduct to a beneficial aspect for the nation as a whole.
- "Karate originated from the small, unarmed, peaceful and weaponless Ryūkyū Kingdom."
- [Kyan Chōtoku] witnessed the development of this small, weaponless fighting art evolve into Japanese Karate, through the efforts of his junior, Funakoshi Gichin, who introduced it in Tōkyō.
- "While I [Kyan] am grateful to Funakoshi-kun as a citizen of Okinawa, it is important to preserve the dignity of our birthplace in the development of karate."
- "To refine karate further, both instructors and non-instructors must unite in their devotion, here in its birthplace."

Please refer to the related material for further information

3. Learning Kyan's Karate-dō from a student of the Agricultural & Forestry School.
- "To refine karate further, both instructors and non-instructors must unite in their devotion, here in its birthplace."
- "Chan mīgwā," aka Kyan Chōtoku sensei, along with the Okinawa Prefectural Agriculture and Forestry School, was featured in the "Okinawa Prefectural Agriculture and Forestry School Alumni Association Bulletin" No. 3 (1998), provided by Nakamura Akira. Taira Kazuo, former chairman of the prefectural assembly (1926-2017), was also mentioned. While he was studying at the Agricultural & Forestry School, he received instructions in karate from Kyan Chōtoku, who was the head of the school's karate program.
- The 40th class of the Agricultural Department had 196 students who graduated in December 1943 (Shōwa 18), out of which 102 lost their

lives during the Battle of Okinawa. Taira Kazuo, who joined the 40th class in 1941 and graduated in 1943 (Shōwa 16-18), served as the student manager of the karate club at the school. As the person closest to Kyan sensei at that time, he shares his experiences.
- Kyan Chōtoku had ceased to be an instructor at the school by the time the 42nd class enrolled.

- **"Residence of Kyan Chōtoku"**
- If you approach from the Yomitan side, you can find Kyan Chōtoku's home on the right side near the base of the Hija bridge.
- Near the riverbank, there was a small garden that was not very spacious and a large plum tree.
- The house was surrounded by a bamboo fence and had a roof made of thatched bamboo.
- Inside the yard, there was a makiwara.
- Kyan Chōtoku's wife operated a dyeing shop and utilized the garden for this purpose.
- Kyan Chōtoku did not collect any tuition fees
- Taira was asked to wear the karate uniform of his senior, Kuratō, who was a student of Kyan Chōtoku from Katsuren.
- Training sessions were held on Mondays, Wednesdays, and Fridays, and the initial six months were solely devoted to *arukikata* [which refers to walking, stepping, and footwork].
- The phrase "*Tīya narāsan (Don't teach karate)*" meant to focus only on *arukikata*!
- His [Taira] opinion/impression [feelings] of/about Kyan sensei.
- Kyan Chōtoku had a remarkably modest and humble personality.
- I (Taira) felt that Kyan Chōtoku was like the ear/panicle of rice that bears fruit and bows its head in humility. Despite his mastery and position, he remained remarkably modest and humble, embodying the spirit of "*Mīnuīnāka, kubi ūriri.*" This metaphor perfectly describes Kyan sensei's personality and left a lasting impression on me.
- One time, a karate student, from the South Seas islands, visited and began striking the makiwara with full force, producing a loud "whack!" He called it the "tiger posture," (*toragamae*), and boasted about his ability to move and bend the makiwara. However, whenever Kyan sensei observed this kind of manner/behaviour, he would immediately expel them.
- Kyan emphasized, that the principle was to train the body with karate while always showing respect and courtesy (*rei*) at the beginning and end of each session.

- Kyan sensei always advised us to urinate before leaving home because even the most skilled individuals can be caught off guard if/when they need to use the restroom.
- What is the origin behind the story of "Chan mīgwā's triangle jump?"
- After receiving the hand of a daughter from the Rindō residence in Yara village, it was customary before the war to pay the village youth group 100 yen or 50 yen for *umadema/umadima* (literally, horse labor) when taking a bride from another village.[28]
- It appears that Kyan left the payment unsettled and he and his wife were chased by the young men of Yara. As they ran toward Yomitan and crossed the Hija bridge, Kyan reportedly jumped down from the railing. Although they saw him jump off, he mysteriously disappeared, leading to the legend of the triangle jump.
- He actually jumped down to the bridge girder and hid, which was the truth of the matter.
- The young men of Yara were amazed that such a small man was able to carry his wife under his arm.
- Kyan sensei was known for his powerful shutō and tsuki (knife hand and punching techniques). He was able to generate so much force with his knife hand (which is commonly known as nukite, or spear hand) that he could thrust it all the way down to the bottom of a 1.8 liter bottle pot filled with sand.
- Once a year, there was a karate demonstration held at the Rindō residence in Yara village, where Kyan sensei would be seated at the head position and observe his students perform, whether it was at the Rindō residence or other houses.
- Okuhara Bunei from Chibana village, who had even trained karate in China, also studied under Kyan sensei.

- **One More Recollection of Kyan Sensei**
- Another account of Kyan sensei comes from the 1941 graduating class of the Okinawa Prefectural Agricultural & Forestry School's 37th Agriculture Course & 18th Forestry Course [Published in 1989 by the Okinawa Prefectural Agricultural & Forestry School Editorial Board].

- At the Agricultural & Forestry School, the karate club played a vital role, and students who wanted to participate would practice two to three times per month after school.

---

[28] Intermarriage between villages was rare, so when it did happen, it was customary for the groom to pay *umadema* to the youth group of the bride's village. *Umadema* was a donation of money for sake or sake itself. (Source: 世界大百科事典 第2版 (株式会社平凡社))

- Standing at the center of the upper position in the auditorium/lecture hall, Kyan sensei appeared to be a thin, small elderly man (*tanmē gwā*) from the countryside, no more than 5 shaku tall and around 70 years old. One might think that if they pushed him from behind, he would just fall over.
- The first kata [Kyan] taught, was Ānankū.
- When that elderly man, who appeared frail and thin, demonstrated a kata, there would occasionally be a sudden change in his movements. His once precise and deliberate movements would become quick and forceful, akin to a gale or lightning strike, with an impact that could knock down even a large tree. The power and spirit of his movements were so great that they could bring the viewer to a state of self-effacement.
- Sensei's karate was a result of studying under the titans of karate at that time - Matsumura Sōkon of Shuri, Matsumora Kōsaku, and Oyadomari Kōkan of Tomari. He inherited the goodness of coming from an old established family and the lessons of his teachers, resulting in a martial art that was the epitome of a gentleman's art, characterized by a blend of spirit and technique (*shingi*).
- Sensei, like many members of the shizoku, lost his job due to the abolishment of feudal domains and the establishment of prefectures. He became a so-called "samurai of the abolished domain" (*samurē*) and faced financial strain in his livelihood.
- The first place Kyan sensei moved to was the Shō family residence in Machibaru, Mt. Yomitan (*Yuntanza*). There, he supported himself by pulling wagons and raising silkworms, all while continuing to train in martial arts without neglecting his practice.
- After building a house near the Hija bridge by Mt. Yomitan, Kyan sensei moved there to continue his instruction. He taught not only the youth of Mt. Yomitan and Chatan village, but also Agricultural & Forestry School students, the Kadena police station, and students of the Youth Normal School.
- To accommodate his small stature, Kyan sensei had to put in extra effort to "acquire techniques contained within the kata of karate that suited his own body." This meant enduring repeated penance and bleeding twice as much as others during his training.
- He emphasized the importance of effort over physical ability, saying "the body is always 30% and effort (*nanji*) is 70%." He also believed that success or failure depended on one's unrelenting effort, regardless

of body size, stating "Being able to execute this or not is the crossroads of success or failure. Having a large or small body is not a problem.[29]"
- When he reached his 30s, he gained a reputation and was referred to as "*Chan mīgwā*."
- During the peak of his career, sensei traveled extensively not only within Okinawa, but also to Osaka, Kyushu, and Taiwan, where he performed demonstrations and worked towards promoting and popularizing karate-do.
- During the Meiji era, when sensei was in his prime, the youth were hot-tempered, confident in their abilities and driven by pride. Such young men often liked to test the skills they'd acquired in actual practice. Such a thing often lead to the common and so-called, "challenge matches!" Beginning from a crossed-hands position" (aka *kakedameshi/kakidamishi*), teachers had little choice but to accept such challenges. Sensei must have been challenged many times, but there are no rumors of him being defeated found in the history of Okinawan martial arts. Many stories of his bravery, however, have been left behind.
- Given that it had long been believed that karate practitioners had a shorter lifespan and that the average life expectancy was around 50 years old, it is remarkable that sensei lived until the age of 76 (75 by Western reckoning). He passed away shortly after the end of the war on 20 September, 1945, at the Ishikawa Civilian Internment Camp, indicating that he had lived a long and fulfilling life.

4. Key Questions for Moving Forward
- "Can we verify when he [Kyan] moved to Tōkyō and obtain more information on his studies of the Chinese classics at the *Nishōgakusha*, particularly under Mishima Chūshū?"
- I wonder why Kyan, who came from an old family with a long history, left Shuri and moved to Mt. Yomitan, unlike Yabu or Hanashiro.
- Amidst the turmoil of wartime, the grief experienced by a karate practitioner highlights the teachings of his sensei, Matsumura, who emphasized that martial arts serve as a path to peace.

---

[29] *"Judge me by my size, do you?"*

- Related Material

- **Kyan Chōtoku's Profile: "Through the Ages & His Training."**
- Journal: In the "Okinawa Prefectural Agricultural & Forestry School Alumni Association Journal" No. 3 (1998), there is a discussion among three sources regarding Kyan Chōtoku's karate training.
- Encyclopedia Entry: *Okinawa Karate Kobujutsu Jiten*, pub 2008.
- Memoir: "*Karate no Omoide*" (1942).
- Kyan Chōtoku was born in 1870 and passed away shortly after the Battle of Okinawa in 1945, at the age of 75.

[Kyan's] Childhood [1870-1879]
Age 6: Kyan Chōtoku was introduced to karate by his father, Chōfu. This is according to Kyan's own recollection in "*Karate no Omoide*" (1942).

[Kyan's] Teens [1880-1889]
At the age of 12, he went with his father, Chōfu, to Tōkyō to accompany the Marquess Shō Tai during his visit there [according to the encyclopedia].

At 16 years old, in 1886, he visited the Shikina gardens with his father [Chōfu] and had his first encounter with Matsumura Sōkon, a prominent figure in the revival of Okinawa karate. As a result of his father's connections, he received training from Matsumura Sōkon [according to the encyclopedia].

He studied the Chinese classics at Nishōgakusha, an educational institution established by Mishima Chūshū (1830~1919); an educational institution founded by Mishima Chūshū (1830~1919) in 1877 [according to the encyclopedia].

[Kyan's] Twenties [1890-1899]
When he was 24 years old, and in his fifth year of living in Tōkyō, Matsumura Sōkon sensei, his karate teacher, passed away at the age of 88 [as recorded in Omoide].

[*Lecturer's observation*] Matsumura Sōkon is thought to have lived from 1809 to 1899, so it seems that Kyan would have gone to Tōkyō in 1894.

[*Translator's observation*] I do not concur with the lecturer's observation, as it implies that Kyan remained in that place after Shō Tai's demise in 1901, which contradicts his [Kyan's] account that he came back to Okinawa at the age of 26 after being away for 9 years!

———

At the age of 25, he had an incident at the Shō family's Tōkyō residence where he subdued a thief who had discharged several shots [according to the encyclopedia].

Every time he returned to his hometown, he received guidance from Itosu Ankō of Shuri-te, his father's teacher Matsumura Sokon, and Oyadomari Kokan of Tomari-te [as recorded in Omoide].

He lived in the residence of the Shō family in Tōkyō and studied Confucianism at the Nishōgakusha School in Fujimi-chō under Professor Mishima [recorded in Omoide].

During his nine years in Tōkyō (1894-1903), he never fell ill, and his weak body became robust, spending a delightful youth without any setbacks.

[Kyan's] Thirties [1900-1909]
In 1902, the year after Shō Tai passed away [in 1901], Kyan Chōfu returned back to the home to Okinawa with his family. Chōfu retired to seclusion in Kume village and pursued the craft of making Sanshin [3stringed guitars] [according to the encyclopedia].

At the age of 33, he returned to his hometown with his father and devoted himself to the training of Shuri-te and Tomari-te. He possessed such formidable skills that he was nicknamed "Chan mīgwā," meaning "small-eyed Kyan" [as recorded in Omoide].

"Chan mīgwā" is interpreted as "small-eyed Kyan" [according to the encyclopedia].

His father [Chōfu] retired in seclusion to Kume village and spent his remaining years crafting Sanshin. At an "appraisal meeting" held at a museum, a Sanshin known as "Chan mī" was shown. Was it a work of Kyan Chōfu's? Why did he live a reclusive life crafting Sanshin?

Related Material
* At the age of 38, he became the manager of the Machibaru grazing land at the Shō family's ranch in Yomitan.
* He was taught "Kūsankū [Kata] by a local official named, Yara Pēchin. Later, it became known as "ChatanYara Kūsankū" [according to the encyclopedia].

[Kyan's] Forties [1910-1919]
* He was taught "Kūsankū [Kata] by a local official named, Yara Pēchin. Later, it became known as "ChatanYara Kūsankū" [according to the encyclopedia].
* At the age of 40, Kyan relocated his residence just near the Hija bridge.
* At the request of the Kadena Police Station, the Prefectural Agricultural and Forestry School, along with aspiring teachers, and local young people, Kyan was invited to teach karate (recollection).

[Kyan's] Fifties [1920-1929]
* By his 50s, Kyan was, in addition to practicing and teaching, also giving lessons to the general public..
* Did the pioneers of the various branches of Shuri-te receive instruction from Chōtoku after he was in his 60s?
* Newspaper Article: [At age 56] "Instructor [師範/Shihan] of Karate-jutsu [唐手術] visits Taiwan" [3 Nov, 1926, "*Taiwan Nichinichi;*" Provided by Nakamura Akira.
* Kyan Chōtoku, the Karate-jutsu instructor from Okinawa, arrived in Taiwan aboard the ship "Yoshimaru" and stayed with Dr. Ie in *Kaohsiung* and *Pingtung-cho*. He is currently, lodging at Yoshikawa House on Ximen Street, in Taipei City.
* He [Kyan] is staying with Dr. Ie in Pingtung and will give a demonstration of karate-jutsu. In the afternoon of the second day, Dr. Ie gave a talk on the origin and career of the instructor, the history and development of karate-jutsu, and explained its various types [styles], before the [Kyan's] demonstration. Watching the demonstration, it seemed to be defensive from start to finish without a single offensive technique. I thought there were many takeaways for practitioners from other martial arts styles, and it also appears to be very good exercise for physical education.

* "*I believe it is an ideal form of self-defense, but since many people in Taiwan are not familiar with karate-jutsu, it would be good for them to witness it being performed,*" he [Kyan?] said. After going to Pingtung, they plan to gradually give talks [and demonstrations] in various places to promote and spread knowledge about the art of karate-jutsu.

[Kyan's] Sixties [1930-1939]
* In 1930, Kyan Chōtoku, then 61 years old, contributed to the cultivation and health of the youth as a karate instructor at the Okinawa Prefectural Agricultural & Forestry School and the Hijabashi Karate Kenkyukai. His article, "*Karate Training and Understanding Fighting,*" was published in [the revised edition of] "*Kenpō Gaisetsu,*" on 1 June, 1930. In the article, he discussed the history and outline of Karate, training, and guidelines for actual fighting.
* By 1932 he continued on imparting his knowledge as a karate instructor.
* Age 63 (62 by Western reckoning): 3 Nov – "*Okinawa Kenpō Karatedō Basic Kumite with Explanatory Diagrams*" (privately owned) and a volume on kata is said to have existed but was apparently lost. The book is A6 size with more than 10 photographs and commentary in blueprint. *The kumite is with a 62-year-old Chōtoku and his student, with explanations of the kumite shown in the images. It is unknown how many copies of the book were produced.*

Related Material
* The attached material is extremely valuable as practical documentation of fighting application [kumite] and kata left by Kyan Chōtoku, who studied under masters like Itosu, Matsumura, and Tokumine. The illustrated photographs are particularly noteworthy as they even document ground techniques, making it a precious resource for understanding the diversity of karate techniques that were inherited before World War II.
* On 18 June 1939, the age of 69, Kyan Chōtoku performed a demonstration of karate at the opening ceremony of the Okinawa Butokuden; The first martial arts hall [established] in Okinawa. It was organized by the Okinawa Branch of the Dai Nippon Butokukai. He demonstrated the Chintō kata, and was the elder representative of the Okinawan karate community at the event [*according to the "Program of the Opening Ceremony of the Okinawa Butokuden by the Okinawa Branch of the Dai Nippon Butokukai." From personal collection*).

* In 1940, at the age of 70, and according to the testimony of Taira Kazuo, who was born in Yonabaru and graduated from the School of Agriculture & Forestry [Class of 1943], Kyan had already retired from his position as an instructor at the time of his enrollment entrance. . .

Kyan Chōtoku's Residence
- Kyan Chōtoku's residence was located at the foot/edge of the Hija bridge on the right side, approached from the Yomitan side.
- The house had a thatched bamboo roof and was surrounded by a bamboo fence.
- There was a small garden with a large plum tree near the river bank and a makiwara in the yard.
- His wife ran a dyeing shop and used the garden for it.
- Kyan sensei did not charge tuition for his karate lessons.
- Mr. Taira was made to wear the karate uniform of his senior Kuratō, a student of Kyan sensei's from Katsuren.
- Six months were spent on just arukikata (walking/stepping/ footwork) training on Monday, Wednesday, and Friday.
- Kyan sensei was known for his emphasis on *arukikata* and famously said, "*Tīya narāsan* (Don't teach karate), *only arukikata!*" [Trans. Note: *Arukikata*, means the focus footwork, and not other karate techniques].
- Kyan sensei was highly respected and admired by those who knew him.

[Kyan's] Seventies [1940-1945]
* "An article about "*Memories of Karate*" was published in four parts in an unknown newspaper, with the author [Kyan] assumed to be 73 years old. The date of publication is believed to be 7 May [1942] . However, the source of the article cannot be confirmed by a newspaper clipping."

* Discussion 1: Began practicing karate as a child with his father's guidance. Met the Okinawan karate master who was credited with revitalizing the art, Matsumura Sokon sensei, at Shikinaen and received training from him through his father's connection. Learned Gojushiho from Matsumura Sokon during this time. Despite his age of 80, Matsumura Sokon practiced striking the makiwara every morning. He often said, "*Martial arts is the path to peace,*" and that peace is preserved through it. After two years of training with Matsumura, he

[Kyan] went to Tōkyō and studied Chinese classics at Nisho Gakusha." [as recorded in Omoide]
* Discussion 2: When Kyan returned to Okinawa, at around 26 years old, he studied under the leading figures of Tomari-te, including Matsumora Kōsaku and Oyadomari Pēchin. During this time, instructors who only taught their own specialties to students out of respect for other teachers, they held in high esteem. Kyan saw the development of karate on Japan's mainland, through the efforts of his junior, Funakoshi Gichin, who departed Okinawa to introduce/spread it in Tōkyō. "*As a native of Okinawa, of course, I am grateful to Funakoshi-kun* [Trans. Note: "Kun" is a way of politely addressing one's junior], *for leaving his home to travel to Tōkyō, in the name of establishing Ryūkyū karate on Japan's mainland." However, we must preserve our own [i.e. Okinawa's] dignity as the birthplace of karate by having instructors and non-instructors join together here in its birthplace to further refine it."*
* Kyan spread karate according to his own beliefs and convictions; "Memories of Karate" is divided into the following sections:
* 1. The Way of Karate
* 2. The Purpose of Karate...
* 3: Fighting; The Art of Winning
* 4: Natural Body Method
* 5: Trainee's Preparation
* 6: Necessity [Value of strength]
* 7. Muscle Harmony
* 8. Trainee Age & Physique
* 9. Use of Chīshi and Makiwara
* 10. Conclusion

* "As I reminisce about the Way of Karate, my mind drifts to the brave soldiers of the Imperial Army, soaring through the skies and sailing the seas in battles that spanned from the Second Sino-Japanese War to the Greater East Asia War. They were like fierce deities, scattering the colossal Caucasians with ease. The outcome of these battles rested solely on the grandeur of the Emperor, and I cannot help but picture our officers reveling in the clandestine teachings of Bushidō. For this elderly gentleman [Kyan], I cannot bear the thought of withering away like a tree; Sitting comfortably next to a warm charcoal stove seems like a betrayal of the warrior spirit.
* In 1944, at the age of 74, he [Kyan] showcased his physical prowess when demonstrating Chintō kata, Tokumine bōjutsu and board-breaking at a martial arts memorial event held during the construction of the

Yomitan Airfield (North Aerodrome). His performance left a lasting impression on both young and old, male and female, who were working on the construction project.
* On 20 September 1945, at the age of 75, Kyan Chōtoku passed away at the Ishikawa Civilian Internment Camp. [Source: "Okinawa Karate and Kobudo Encyclopedia," 2008; Personal archives including his 1932, "*Okinawa Kenpō Karate-dō Zukai: Kumite*" [*Okinawa Kenpō Karatedō Basic Kumite with Explanatory Diagrams*] and his 1942, "*Memories of Karate,*" along with newspaper clippings.

Chapter 6

Tradition Continues
Lighting the Pathway for Future Generations

Zen Influence in Karate

Balancing Tradition, Critical Thinking & Adaptability continues
In the world of classical fighting arts, the transmission of knowledge and wisdom is a fundamental aspect of preserving tradition and ensuring the art's relevance for future generations. Drawing inspiration from Zen philosophy, the metaphor of pouring the contents of one vessel into another without spilling a drop symbolizes the seamless transmission of teachings and principles from master to disciple. Despite their apparent differences, Zen and Karate converge in teaching us to confront fear, act instinctively, and gain clarity in the face of adversity. Understanding the delicate balance between preserving tradition and fostering critical thinking helps us helps ensure the continued growth and adaptability of the humble art we love so much.

The Zen Connection
The inward journey advocated by Zen philosophy might seem at odds with the aggressive nature of karate training. However, these seemingly disparate paths complement one another, enabling karate practitioners to confront fear and accept the uncontrollable aspects of hostile conflict. By acknowledging and embracing what lies beyond our control, we attain mental clarity, allowing us to respond effectively and decisively in challenging situations.

Acknowledging Critical Thinking
While the metaphor of unchanging transmission holds importance for Zen's principles, it is essential to recognize the need for critical thinking in the technical and tactical aspects of karate. The danger lies in transforming teachings into rigid doctrines that stifle innovation and hinder adaptability. To ensure the continued evolution of karate, a delicate balance must be struck between preserving tradition and encouraging practitioners to think critically, explore possibilities, and adapt techniques to various contexts. By embracing both tradition and open-mindedness, karate remains a vibrant and living fighting art.

Embracing Evolution

In spite of our unwavering resistance to it, change is the only inevitability in life, and whether we accept it or not, the fighting arts are inherently a part of this process. Each generation brings forth individuals who reinterpret traditional practices, breathing new life into the art while maintaining its essence. This dynamic process facilitates the emergence of innovative approaches that address the evolving needs and challenges of the present. True mastery of karate lies not solely in replicating movements but in practical application, where the art is adapted to meet the demands of contemporary circumstances. By embracing application and evolution, karate remains relevant, effective, and an adaptable martial discipline.

Recognizing Individuality and Variation

Dispelling the misconception of a universal approach, it is crucial to acknowledge that each karate practitioner possesses unique abilities and limitations. Not everyone can execute the same actions in identical ways to achieve identical results. Hence, recognizing the existence of variables and variations within a shared foundation is vital. Differentiating between the act of performing and the act of teaching allows for flexibility and adaptation while preserving the core principles that underpin karate's rich heritage.

The Legacy of Kyan Chōtoku

Among the esteemed students of Kyan Chōtoku, a distinguished master of karate, a consistent theme emerged. His exceptional technical skill, fearlessness, tactical brilliance, and ability to adapt swiftly to rapidly changing circumstances earned him widespread reverence. Kyan's approach epitomized the essence of karate as an art form that evolves, adapts, and remains effective across diverse situations. His legacy serves as a testament to the enduring influence of Zen principles in karate.

Conclusion
The indelible influence of Zen philosophy on karate is evident in the seamless transmission of knowledge, the ability to confront fear, and the pursuit of clarity amid adversity. While the preservation of tradition holds undeniable importance, it is equally crucial to embrace critical thinking, adaptability, and innovation. By recognizing the individuality of practitioners and the need for variation, karate can evolve harmoniously while remaining true to its roots. The legacy of masters like Kyan Chōtoku serves as a poignant reminder that the true essence of karate lies not only in its historical significance but in its practical application and continuous pursuit of excellence within a dynamically changing world.

The Torchbearer's Code

The information presented in this chapter comes to me through many direct conversations, in both English and Japanese, over the past three years with Shimabukuro Zenpo Sensei, at various places here in Okinawa. As with any conversation or interview, especially in a second language, there is always a possibility of misunderstandings or errors in interpretation. Any errors in the following transcript are solely mine. As such, I believe this presentation provides valuable insight into the life, philosophy, and teachings of one of the most respected Karate masters of our time.

Profile

Shimabukuro Zenpo is the 2nd generation inheritor of Kyan-style Karate learned from his father Shimabukuro Zenryō [島袋 善良,1908-1969], who was a direct disciple of Kyan Chōtoku. Zenpo was born the fourth of five children, to Zenryō and Tsuru on 11 October, 1943 in Chatan, Okinawa. He's married to Michiko-san and together they have [three girls and two boys] with twelve grandchildren. Having served as the Chairman of the Okinawa Prefectural Karate-do/Kobudo League [Rengokai], until his retirement in 2022, he is currently a Karate-do Hanshi 10th Dan the chief instructor of the Seibukan. Residing in the USA for three years, during the early to mid-1960s, he is fluently bilingual and taught karate all over the world for more than a half century; In addition to studying under his father he's also gained valuable direction while studying for five years under the watchful eye of *Nakama Chōzō* [名嘉真 朝増, 1899-1982], until his passing in 1974; Nakama had also been a close friend of his fathers. Zenpo Sensei currently oversees branch schools here in Okinawa, and on Japan's mainland, with more than 300 branches all over the world.

He's been the subject of local, national and international recognition for much of his life; Been featured on the cover of magazines, TV news, programs and documentary films. He's an incredible martial artist, husband, father, grandfather, instructor and friend, with an insatiable training and work ethic. He's received every kind of award one can think of and yet, as hard as it may be to believe, Shimabukuro Zenpo remains remarkably modest.

Introduction
Karate, an ancient martial art form originating from Okinawa, captivates practitioners and enthusiasts worldwide. Within the realm of Karate, few names hold as much reverence and respect as Shimabukuro Zenpo Sensei. In this article, we delve into the profound wisdom shared by the senior-most Kyan lineage inheritor, Shimabukuro Zenpo, as we explore the intricate tapestry of his life, philosophy, and teachings. Through a synthesis of firsthand conversations and personal insights, we aim to shed light on the profound impact Zenpo Sensei makes as a Karate master, both in preserving tradition and embracing contemporary perspectives.

A Legacy Carved in Tradition
Shimabukuro Zenpo Sensei's journey in Karate traces its roots back to his father, who has the extraordinary privilege of being a direct student of the legendary Karate master Kyan Chōtoku. With deep respect for his father's training, Zenpo Sensei absorbs the teachings of Kyan, which emphasize technical excellence and the significance of kata. This foundation instills in him a profound understanding of the traditional methods and principles of Okinawan Karate.

The Cultural Tapestry of Okinawan Karate
Beyond the technical aspects of Karate, Shimabukuro Zenpo recognizes the importance of immersing oneself in the rich history and cultural heritage of Okinawa. Under his father's guidance, he develops a deep appreciation for the evolution of Karate from a local self-defense system to a global martial art. This knowledge allows Zenpo Sensei to comprehend the wider implications and values associated with Karate as a practice, extending beyond mere physicality.

Preserving Tradition, Embracing Evolution
In a conversation with Zenpo Sensei, he shares his perspective on the delicate balance between preserving tradition and embracing the evolution of Karate in contemporary times. While emphasizing the significance of preserving traditional techniques and values, he recognizes the need to adapt to the interests and needs of new generations of practitioners. Zenpo Sensei believes that Karate should not be solely about competition and winning but should encompass personal growth, development, and the harmonization of mind and body.

The Evolution of Okinawan Karate

Zenpo Sensei acknowledges that Okinawan Karate evolves over time, with various masters contributing their unique styles and approaches to the art. Nevertheless, he emphasizes that the core principles and techniques of Karate remain timeless. As he envisions the future, Zenpo Sensei sees Karate continuing to evolve, adapt, and resonate with the new generations of practitioners while retaining the essence that makes it a truly unparalleled martial art.

Character Development & Self-Improvement; The Essence of the Art

Throughout his teachings, Shimabukuro Zenpo consistently highlights the intrinsic values of respect, discipline, humility, and character development. He believes that the pursuit of rank or status should never overshadow the pursuit of perfection in one's character. For Zenpo Sensei, Karate is a never-ending journey of growth and self-improvement, transcending physical boundaries and encompassing the entire spectrum of one's being.

Unveiling the Art of Karate

Master Shimabukuro Zenpo's remarkable Karate journey and profound insights emphasize the significance of approaching Karate as a way of life, rather than a mere physical exercise. He emphasizes the importance of understanding the history, philosophy, and practical applications of Karate.

Zenpo Sensei's dedication to preserving the original purpose of Karate, as taught by Kyan Chōtoku, while embracing new perspectives, ensures the timeless relevance of this ancient art form. He carries forward the values and teachings passed down from his father, Shimabukuro Zenryō, who also studied under Kyan Chōtoku.

Zenpo Sensei's teachings go beyond physical techniques, delving into the essence of character development, self-discipline, and personal growth. By emphasizing the values of respect, humility, and perseverance, he inspires his students to cultivate not only their physical abilities but also their inner selves.

The art of Karate, as unveiled by Shimabukuro Zenpo, is a transformative journey. It instills self-confidence, mental fortitude, and an unwavering spirit. Through rigorous training and dedicated practice, practitioners gain a deep understanding of the connection between mind, body, and spirit.

In a world driven by instant gratification and fleeting trends, Zenpo Sensei's unwavering dedication to the traditional teachings of Karate serves as a reminder of the value of patience, discipline, and perseverance. His guidance encourages practitioners to delve into the rich history and philosophy of Karate, fostering a deeper appreciation for the art and its cultural significance.

Zenpo Sensei envisions a future where Okinawan Karate continues to thrive and evolve, adapting to the needs of each new generation while staying rooted in its timeless principles. He advocates for a balanced approach that honors tradition while embracing innovation, ensuring that Karate remains relevant and impactful for years to come.

Zenpo Sensei's legacy as a Karate master extends far beyond his technical prowess and accomplishments. His contributions to the preservation and evolution of Okinawan Karate have left an indelible mark on the art form. Through his teachings, he imparts not only the physical techniques but also the invaluable life lessons that Karate offers. As we continue to explore the depths of Karate, let us draw inspiration from the wisdom and guidance of this esteemed master, carrying his legacy forward with reverence and dedication. The founder to disciple, to father and son, the legacy of Kyan Chōtoku lives on through Zenpo Sensei, ensuring that the essence of Okinawan Karate continues to thrive and inspire generations to come.

Lighting the Pathway for Future Generations
Consummating the torchbearers' code, Shimabukuro Zenpo, like his father before him, has dedicated his entire life to keeping the pathway lit for future generations to journey. A timeless concept learned from the pantheon of dignitaries who mentored Kyan Chōtoku, and passed down to Zenpo Sensei from his father, Shimabukuro Zenryō. The essence of such timeless teachings, he maintains, should serve to inspire each new generation not impede it. Teachings that convey the idea of responsibility and leadership in carrying forward wisdom and knowledge. This is the

unwritten code of a torchbearer in illuminating the way for future generations, as a sense of purpose and direction, has long been the coveted wisdom handed down from one generation to the next. Kyan style karate represents the perfect fusion of science and art coming together to create a transformative magic. This time-honoured process is the pathway upon which a journey of self-discovery offers the opportunity to enjoy a happy and meaningful life; A highly challenging, and deeply pensive, method of conditioning the body, cultivating the mind and nurturing the spirit; Karate-do, according to Shimabukuro Zenpo, is Okinawa's gift to world peace.

Postscript
by Scot Mertz

It has been an absolute joy to assist McCarthy Sensei on this project. There are numerous revelations in this book that even the most knowledgeable historians may find new and unfamiliar. Undertaking a project of this magnitude was no easy task, but he was most certainly the perfect person to take on the challenge.

It warms my soul to see items like Kyan Chofu's scroll being brought into the public sphere and translated for the first time. His previously undiscovered work and even the controversial newspaper articles shed more light on Kyan Chotoku's story, revealing not only his deep insights but also how he was treated by his peers during his lifetime along with the negative press he overcame to continue teaching the next generation of enthusiasts

McCarthy Sensei executed a brilliant translation of Kyan Chotoku's original kumite book by employing a cross-reference method. He combined translations from various individuals, including his own, to arrive at the most accurate interpretation possible. This pioneering mindset distinguishes him from other Karate historians and translators. Throughout this entire work, I witnessed an unbiased person constantly striving to provide the most accurate and comprehensive view of Kyan Sensei to date. Moreover, I believe this work is a must-have book for anyone who takes karate history seriously, and hope it graces the bookshelves of many martial artists for decades to come; Possibly even becoming source material for future writers on this subject.

I genuinely cannot express enough how well this book has come together and how much impact I believe it will have on the Okinawan Karate community now, and in the future. Kudos to Patrick for his unwavering commitment and meticulous efforts in safeguarding and imparting authentic historical knowledge, a valuable resource that will undoubtedly enrich both present and future generations of martial artists.

Final Word
By Patrick McCarthy

The Benefit of Perspective: Harnessing Diverse Contributions
Throughout the course of this project's research, I encountered numerous instances where I was questioned about my decision to seek contributions from others. One of the primary reasons I sought the input of esteemed colleagues in the development of this work was to embrace the power of perspective. Recognizing that no individual possesses all-encompassing knowledge and that different individuals perceive the world through their unique lenses, I firmly believe that collective contributions are instrumental in enhancing our perspectives and understanding.

By involving respected colleagues with varying backgrounds, experiences, and expertise, we open ourselves to a multitude of viewpoints. Each person brings their own set of knowledge, insights, and interpretations, which can shed light on aspects that might otherwise remain unnoticed. Embracing this diversity of perspectives enriches our work and enables a more comprehensive exploration of the subject matter.

When we collaborate with individuals who see the world differently from us, we are presented with the opportunity to challenge our own assumptions and broaden our horizons. Engaging in discussions and exchanging ideas with colleagues who hold diverse viewpoints encourages us to examine our own biases, explore alternative interpretations, and uncover new layers of understanding. This iterative process allows for personal growth and the refinement of our own perspective.

It is crucial to acknowledge that individual perspectives can be shaped by factors such as education and impeded by rivalry. Education plays a significant role in shaping viewpoints, providing access to knowledge, critical thinking skills, and analytical frameworks. While those with higher levels of education may contribute valuable insights, it is important to include perspectives from individuals with different educational [i.e. learning] backgrounds to challenge assumptions and bridge gaps in knowledge.

Additionally, rivalry and competition can sometimes hinder the sharing of perspectives. Recognizing and addressing these challenges is essential for fostering a collaborative and inclusive environment. By actively seeking contributions from respected colleagues and creating a space that prioritizes mutual growth and shared understanding, we can overcome rivalry and benefit from diverse perspectives.

Inviting multiple perspectives not only enhances the quality of our work but also fosters an inclusive and open-minded environment. By valuing and respecting the contributions of others, we create a space where diverse ideas can be freely shared and discussed. Such an environment encourages creativity, collaboration, and innovation, leading to a more comprehensive exploration of the subject matter and the potential for groundbreaking insights.

Collective contributions pave the way for a deeper and more nuanced comprehension of the subject matter at hand. By amalgamating the diverse insights and knowledge offered by our learned colleagues, we create a tapestry of understanding that surpasses what any one individual could achieve alone. This collaborative effort not only benefits our own growth but also enriches the field as a whole, promoting the advancement of knowledge and the development of innovative solutions.

Incorporating the perspectives of respected colleagues in our work yields invaluable benefits. The collective wisdom gained from diverse contributions enhances our understanding, challenges our preconceptions, and promotes inclusive collaboration. By harnessing the power of perspective while acknowledging the influences of education and navigating rivalry, we embark on a journey of continuous improvement, collectively striving for a deeper, more comprehensive understanding of the subject matter.

Valuable Lesson
One important lesson that I have learned is that we should never simply accept oral testimony as fact, nor should we allow confirmation bias to cloud our judgment. Kyan's own words help us understand the type of man he was and his message, which I believe extends beyond the realm of karate and into life itself. I am grateful for the many sources of reference that have contributed to this work.

History books focus largely on describing the issues which have helped shape culture, society, and life. One thing, however, that such books don't often tell us, paraphrasing my friend Joe Swift, are the stories of those individuals whose lives were drastically affected by catastrophic changes in history! This book makes it perfectly clear that Kyan, not unlike other young men born into aristocracy of his generation, grew up enjoying life to the fullest. Despite a promising start, his life took a turn for the worse when his island kingdom was hit by a catastrophic social upheaval and a tumultuous political aftermath, leading to long-lasting difficulties. Yet, despite these life-altering challenges, he managed to live a productive and relatively long life, along with making important contributions which continue to inspire people around the world.

I believe Kyan's life serves as a testament to the enduring power of character and resilience, even in the face of attacks on one's reputation. As he navigated through challenges and adversity, he left a valuable and indelible footprint in the history of Okinawa's martial arts heritage. In the pursuit of his passion, he remained unwavering in his commitment to the principles of his fighting art. Despite the temporary storms that tried to overshadow his legacy, he persevered, holding true to his values and demonstrating the strength of his character. His unwavering dedication and the invaluable contributions he made to the fighting arts community are a testament to the Japanese saying, '*Ningen wa ichidai ni shite mugen no gotoshi*' [人間は一代にして夢幻の如し] - '*Human life is like a fleeting dream.*' Chōtoku's story reminds us that the substance of a person's character and the impact they leave behind are what truly matter.

By honoring Kyan Chōtoku's memory and recognizing the depth of his accomplishments, we pay homage to his unwavering spirit and dedication to the pursuit of martial arts excellence. His story serves as a powerful reminder of the enduring power of character and resilience, inspiring us to draw strength from his journey and strive for greatness in our own lives. In remembering Chōtoku, we not only celebrate his invaluable contributions to Okinawa's martial arts heritage but also acknowledge the indomitable human spirit to overcome adversity and leave a lasting impact. His memory becomes a guiding light, illuminating the path for us to embrace the values he embodied and pursue our dreams with unwavering determination and character.

Let us be inspired by Chōtoku's unwavering commitment, drawing from his resilience to forge our own paths of success. As we honor his legacy, may his memory continue to inspire us to overcome challenges, embody the principles of martial arts, and leave a profound and lasting impact on the world around us.

In seeking to comprehend the private motivation behind a person's actions, we can gain valuable insight by closely examining the consequences of their behavior. Actions are often purposeful, driven by underlying goals and intentions. When faced with the challenge of better understanding such actions, looking at the outcomes they produce can offer a window into their deeper motives. By recognizing that actions have meaning and consequences, we equip ourselves with a powerful tool to decipher the invisible threads that tie behavior to intention. This approach not only fosters empathy but also enables us to build stronger connections and navigate the complexities of human behavior with greater understanding.

As we come to the end of this book on Kyan Chōtoku, I can't help but feel a sense of gratitude for the incredible learning experience this challenge has bestowed. Through my investigation I have unexpectedly encountered cultural roadblocks, which led me to meet wonderfully interesting people and resulted in gaining a much deeper understanding of Kyan's life and work. The research process has been a journey that has taught me the value of persistence, even in the face of adversity. When reflecting on Kyan, the third son among twelve siblings, it becomes abundantly clear that his aristocratic education in one of Tokyo's premier colleges and his frequent journeys between the mainland and Okinawa aboard the Sho Family's private ship, the Kyūyo Maru, played a pivotal role in shaping his distinctive fighting art. In stark contrast to dismissive detractors who labeled it as "*Inaka-de*," a mere simple country practice, Kyan's martial prowess exudes a profound depth and sophistication, emphasizing the genuine value of his skill. Furthermore, his association with some of Japan's greatest luminaries during his college years adds an extra layer of distinction to his journey, as he gleaned inspiration and guidance from a circle of exceptional minds and extraordinary talents.

I would like to express my deepest appreciation to everyone who has assisted in my efforts to bring this work to light. Even though I am unable to thank each and every one of them personally, I sincerely hope that this book reflects favorably upon them and serves to achieve several things: First and foremost, I hope that it is interesting, informative, and inspiring. I also hope that those who already know the Kyan story are satisfied that his work and life has been well presented in this compilation. For those who knew little or nothing about him, I hope that this book has provided new insights and information. As there was such an overwhelming amount of research for this project, and I'd already surpassed 300 pages, I was not able to find the space necessary to properly accommodate the story of Tokumine Pēchin and his bojutsu lineage brought back to Okinawa by Kyan after his visit to Yaeyama. In Vol #2 of this work, and thanks to the assistance of *Tokumura Kensho*, I will discuss Kyan learning Tokumine's bojutsu in Miyara-mura on Ishigaki-jima from *Kedabana Gisa* [aka Gisuke, 慶田花 宜佐, 1843~1943].

I believe that Karate represents the perfect fusion of art and science coming together to create transformative magic. This time-honored process offers a pathway to self-discovery and a meaningful life. Karate-do can be a bridge between self-acceptance and self-protection, a unique method of conditioning the body, cultivating the mind, and nurturing the spirit. It is Okinawa's gift to world peace.

Thank you for taking this journey with me.

Patrick McCarthy
Uruma, Okinawa
2023

Pictorial Lineage

Thanks to the meticulous and artistic assistance of friend, Neal Simpson, a creative approach to working with both genuine profile photos and AI-generated images was undertaken. My goal was to craft a pictorial lineage chart that portrayed the diverse and profound influences, which had helped shaped Kyan's learning experiences and subsequent field of influence.

The undertaking comprised two pivotal challenges: Firstly, harnessing artificial intelligence to generate images of influential figures in Kyan's life, even in the absence of actual photos, and secondly, skillfully arranging these AI-generated images into a comprehensive pictorial lineage chart. I think the lineage chart serves as a vibrant narrative, illuminating the connections and impact of historical figures, family members, mentors, and cultural icons on Kyan's remarkable journey. In the face of the seemingly impossible, we are merging technology and artistry to wholeheartedly celebrate his unique life story.

While a countless myriad enjoyed learning from Chanmi-gwā, during his time as an instructor, this chart focuses exclusively upon the principal disciples who studied directly under his tutelage; It does not include the broader range and large groups of regular school students he taught. Nor does it underscore the select few notable individuals who enjoyed a brief, irrespective however impactful, period of mentorship under his guidance. Beyond other accounts of such individuals, a perfect example can be found on p183 of Nakamoto Masahiro's 2006 book,"*Okinawa Kobudo;*" "*Kyan went over to the residence of Oshiro Chojo in Tabaru Village ... to teach karate* <snip> *among the youngsters that learned under Chanmi-gwā at Oshiro's place in Shuri were Oshiro himself, Gusukuma Shimpan, Maeshiro Chotoku, the Goya brothers, Nakama Chozo and Izumikawa Kantoku.*"

Pictorial Lineage Chart

Informal Chronology
Moments in Time

- **1870:** Kyan Chōtoku is born on December 5th in Gibō-mura, Shuri.
- **1872:** Ryūkyū Domain is officially established.
- **1876:** Kyan starts learning sumo from his father at the age of six.
- **1879:** Collapse of Ryūkyū Kingdom, Shuri Castle surrendered. Kyan begins karate training under Matsumura Sokon at age 9.
- **1882:** Kyan travels to Tōkyō with his father.
- **1884:** Kyan begins studying with Matsumura Sokon. He also learns Naihanchi from his father.
- **1885:** Kyan learns gojushiho from Matsumura.
- **1887:** Kyan moves to Tōkyō with his father. Enrolls in Nishogakusha University. Begins learning Karate from his father again
- **1892:** Matsumura Sokon [allegedly] passes away at the age of 88.
- **1894:** Sino-Japanese war starts.
- **1896:** Kyan returns to Okinawa after 9 years. Learns Chintō from Matsumora Kosaku and Passai from Oyadomari Kohan.
- **1898:** Matsumora Kosaku passes away at the age of 69. Kyan is adopted into the Motonaga family. Enforcement of Conscription law causes a scandal.
- **1901:** Shō Tai, last Ryūkyū king, passes away
- **1902:** Kyan's father, Chofu, returns to Okinawa.
- **1904:** Russo-Japanese War begins.
- **1905:** Karate begins in the school system. Oyadomari Kohan 78 years old passes away. Kyan moves to Makihara (Machibaru), Yomitan Village.
- **1910:** Kyan moves to Yomitan-son, Hijabashi, and starts teaching Karate to young men of Chatan-son, Agriculture & Forestry School, Kadena Police office, and Shihan Gakko.
- **1911:** Kyan's first daughter, Yasuko, is born.
- **1913:** Chofu, Kyan's father, passes away at the age of 74.
- **1915:** Itosu Anko passes away at the age of 86.
- **1916:** Kyan goes to Miyakojima.
- **1918:** Kyan and Motobu Choki demonstrate Karate.

- **1919:** Kudaka Kori becomes a student.
- **1920:** Kyan relocates from Makishi-cho Okinawa to Miyakojima.
- **1921:** Crown Prince [Hirohito] visits Shuri Castle to watch a Karate demonstration while visiting Okinawa with esteemed battleship [Katori & Kashima] commander, Kanna Kenwa, originally from Okinawa.
- **1923:** Tameshiwari at Fufu-Makura at Shuri Castle Minami-Den Demonstration.
- **1924:** Demonstration with Motobu Choyu and Mabuni Kenwa at Karate dai Enbu Taikai.
- **1925:** Aragaki Aikichi becomes a student.
- **1926:** Okinawa Karate Club is established. Kyan, Motobu Choyu, Miyagi Chojun, Kyōda Juhatsu, Mabuni Kenwa, and Uehara Seikichi participate.
- **1927:** Kanō Jigorō arrives in Okinawa and watches local Karate-jutsu experts, including Kyan Chōtoku.
- **1929:** Kyan helps found the Okinawa Kenpo Karate-do Association.
- **1930:** Kyan's 1929 interview/article is published in Miki & Takada's [aka Mutsu] book, "Kenpo Gaisetsu."
- **1931:** Kyan visits Yaeyama again to promote Karate. The Yaeyama Shinpo puts a headline about Kyan. Nagamine Shoshin becomes a student.
- **1932:** A public demonstration is held for the Japanese Empire Navy combined fleet. Kyan successfully performs tameshiwari. Kyan's student, Kudaka Kori, goes to Manchuria.
- **1936:** Ryūkyu Shimpo hosts "Round Table Discussion" on 25 Oct
- **1939:** Opening ceremony of the Naha Butokuden; Kyan performs "Chintō" kata.
- **1941:** Outbreak of the Pacific War; Pearl Harbor.
- **1942:** Kyan performs Karate before Admiral Kanna Kenwa at the age of 73.
- **1943/44:** Kyan participates in demonstrations despite being in his seventies.
- **1945:** Kyan Chōtoku passes away 20 September at the US Ishikawa Civilian Internment Camp, Uruma City, reportedly due to malnutrition.

The many wonderful people [past & present] who helped unravel the timeless threads of history and reveal the delicately woven fabric of Kyan Chōtoku's enigmatic legacy: L-R: 1st row – Nakazato Joen, Uehara Seikichi, Nagamine Shoshin, Shimabuku Eizo & Miyahira Katsuya. 2nd row – Kinjo Hiroshi, Irei Hiroshi, Shimabukuro Zenpo, Konno [Bin] Satoshi & Hokama Tetsuhiro. 3rd row – Matsuda Yoshimasa, Tokumura Kensho, Takeishi Kazumi, The Kyan Monument [next to the Hija River in Kadena] & Kyan's Haka [his final resting place in Shuri's Ishimine district]. 4th row – Scot Mertz, Dan Smith, Miguel da Luz, Brian Arthur & Joe Swift.

Three of the many source from which I gained deep insights into Kyan's life; "*Shōrin Ryu Seibukan,*" by Shimabukuro Zenpo & Dan Smith; "*Okinawan Karate, A Man Called Chanmie,*" by Irei Hiroshi; & "*Chanmiguwa,*" by prolific novelist & award-winning author & Konno Bin

Kyan Chōtoku passed away here in the Ishikawa camp on 20 September 1945

Kyan Chōtoku's final resting place in Shuri's Ishimine-cho, Naha-shi, Okinawa

Kedabana Gisa
1843-1934

Kedabana Hobuta
1882-1974

Tokumura Kensho with **Kedabana Sadayoshi** at the Kedabana family Haka on Ishigakijima

* Photos courtesy of the Kedabana Family via Tokumura Kensho

Kyan Chōtoku's personal *rokushaku bo*/六尺棒 [6' staff] & Yumi/弓 [archer's bow] made from Kuba wood
Photo by Patrick McCarthy taken at the home of Irei Hiroshi

Selected Bibliography

1. Bishop, M. (1999). **Okinawan Karate: Teachers, Styles and Secret Techniques**. Tuttle Publication.
2. Cook, H. (2001). Shotokan Karate, A Precise History. **Classical Fighting Arts**.
3. Funakoshi, G. (2005). **Karate-Do Kyohan**. Neptune Publications.
4. Funakoshi, G. (2012). **Karate-Do: My Way of Life**. Kodansha International.
5. Funakoshi, G. (1956). **Karate-Do, Ichiro**. Sankei Shimbun.
6. Fujiwara, R., & Gima, S. (1986). Taidan Kindai Karate-do no Rikishi wo Kataru. **Baseball Magazine**.
7. **Gekkan Karate-do**, Tokuda, Anshu (1 June 1956). "Busaganashi," Vol. 1 Issue 2, Pp 44-45.
8. **Gekkan Karate-do**, Nakazato, Joen (Aug 2006). "Kensei Kyan Chōtoku & Shōrinji Ryu," Vol. 432, Parts 1-6, Pp 5-34.
9. **Haihan toji no jinbutsu** (1915).
10. Haines, B. (1995). **Karate's History and Traditions**. Tuttle Publishing.
11. Harrison, E. J. (1913). **The Fighting Spirit of Japan**. T. Fisher Unwin.
12. Hokama, T. (2005). **100 Masters of Okinawa Karate**. Ozato Print Co.
13. Hokama, T. (2007). **Timeline of Karate History.** Ozato Print Co.
14. Hyams, J. (1979). **Zen in the Martial Arts**. Bantam.
15. Ikeda, H. **Karate Do Shugi**.
16. Irei, H. (2011). **Okinawan Karate, A Man Called Chanmie**. C-Sky Project.
17. Iwai, T. (2000). **Motobu Chōki & Ryūkyu Karate**. Airyudo.
18. Kerr, G. H. (1958). **Okinawa: History of an Island People.** Tuttle Publishing.
19. Kinjo, A. (2005). **Karate Denshinroku (Vol 1), Unraveling the Mysteries of the Origin & Transmission**.
20. Kinjo, A. (2008). **Karate Denshinroku (Vol 2): Unraveling the Mysteries of the Origin & Transmission.**
21. Kinjo, H. (2011). **From Todi to Karate**. Nippon Budokan.
22. Kinjo, H. (1997). **Gekkan Karate-do** [Magazine Compilation Reprint]. Yoju Shōrin.
23. Konno, S. (2017). **Chamīgwā.** Shueisha Bunko.

24. Kyan, C. (1932). **Okinawa Kenpō Karatedō Kihon Zukai Kumite,** 3 Nov 1932.
25. McCarthy, P. (1987). **Classical Kata of Okinawan Karate.** Ohara.
26. McCarthy, P. (1995). **Bubishi.** Tuttle Publishing.
27. McCarthy, P. (1999). **Ancient Okinawan Martial Arts, Vol 1.** Tuttle Publishing.
28. McCarthy, P. (2001). **Tanpenshu.** Brisbane, IRKRS.
29. McCarthy, P. (2002). **Motobu Chōki, My Art of Karate.** Brisbane, IRKRS.
30. McCarthy, P. (2018). **Legend of the Fist.** Brisbane, IRKRS.
31. Motobu, C. (1977). **Okinawa Kempo: Karate-jutsu on Kumite.** Kanas, Ryūkyu Imports.
32. Nagamine, S. (2000). **Tales of Okinawa's Great Masters.** Tuttle Publication.
33. Nagamine, S. (1976). **The Essence of Okinawan Karate-Do.** Tuttle Publication.
34. Naganori, K. (2008). **Nufani, Kumiodori & Okinawan Poetry.** Okinawa Book Service.
35. Nakamoto, M. (2006). **Okinawa Traditional Old Martial Arts/ Kobudo.** Bunbukan.
36. Nakasone, G. (1938). **Karate-do Taikan.** Tokyo Tosho Co.
37. Nakazato, J. (2021). **Kyudo.** (S. Mertz, Trans.).
38. Matsumura, K. (1970). **Karate (Tomari-te) Chūkō no So** – Matsumora Kōsaku Ryakuden.
39. Miki, N., & Takada (1930). **Kenpo Gaisetsu.** Yojusha.
40. Miyagi, T. (1987). **Karate no Reishiki.** Hirugi Sha.
41. Murakami, K. (1975). **Karate-do to Ryūkyu Kobudo.** Seibido.
42. Sells, J. (2000). **Unante, Secrets of Karate** (2nd edition). W.M. Hawley Library.
43. Shimabukuro, Z., & Smith, D. (2012). **Shōrin Ryu Seibukan, Kyan's Karate.** Shōrin Ryu Seibukan.
44. Shimabukuro, E. (1964). **Okinawa Karate-do Narabini Ōto-ki.** Rendokan.
45. **Shui/Tumai-di Manual** (2021). Okinawa Karate Promotion Division.
46. Smith, D. (2003). **The Uechi-Ryu Karate-Do Master Text: A Historical Perspective During the Reign of Uechi-Ryu** (Unofficial Translation).
47. Swift, J.,. (2018). **The Downfall of a Ryūkyūan Samurai.** Lulu Press.

48. Takamiyagi, S., Shinzato, K., & Nakamoto, M. (2008). **Okinawa Karate Kobudo Jiten**. Kashiwa Shobo.
49. Tamae, H. (1973). **Karate-Do.**
50. Toyama, K. (1960). **Karate-do Daihokan**. Tusru Shoo.

Academia
51. Barske, V. (2009). **Performing Embodied Histories: Colonialism, Gender, and Okinawa in Modern Japan**. PhD diss., University of Illinois Urbana-Champaign.
52. Barske, V. (2013). **Visualizing Priestesses or Performing Prostitutes?, Ifa Fuyū's Depictions of Okinawan Women, [1913-1943]**. Interdisciplinary Journal of Asian Studies, Series IV, 3(1), 65–108.
53. Bennett, A. (2013). **A Reconsideration of the Dai-Nippon Butokukai in the Purge of Ultra-nationalism and Militarism in Post-war Japan.** 國士舘大學　武德紀要　第29号 **(Kansai University).**
54. Caroli, R. (2013). **Travels of a National Treasure: The Records of the Ryūkyuan Royal Family Shō** (Ryūkyū Kokuō Shō Ke Kankei Shiryō).
55. Hara, T. (2011). **On the Internal Diversity and Complexity of Okinawan Identity.** Asian Studies, Shizuoka University.
56. Hokama, T., & Kinjo, M. (2014). **Okinawan Karate as a Lifelong Sport (Part 1) - Dynamics of Karate Practitioner Population**. University of the Ryūkyus Academic Repository.
57. Iwa, S. (2011). 1872年における日本政府の琉球政策 — 清国使節と維新慶賀使の邂逅をてがかりにして — ("The Japanese Government's Policy Toward Ryūkyu in 1872 - Using the Encounter Between the Qing Dynasty Envoy and the Meiji Restoration Celebration Envoy as a Clue"). Waseda University, Graduate School of Social Sciences, Journal of Social Science Research, Vol. 18, September.
58. Johnson, N. C. G. (2012). **The Japanization of Karate?: Placing an Intangible Cultural Practice.** Journal of Contemporary Anthropology.
59. Kadekaru, T. (2017). **The Creation and Development of Okinawan Karate - Using the Evolution of Terminology as a Clue**. Waseda University Graduate School of Sports Science.
60. Kuroda, G. (1921). **Karate & Intoxication** (English translation by Mario McKenna). The Journal of Statistics, 36 (428), 446-452.

61. Maeda, Y. (2018). **Political and Social Historical Study on Early Okinawan Prefectural Administration: Focusing on Aristocratic Prefectural Governors and the 'Customary Practices' Policy**. University of the Ryūkyū's.

62. May, S. K. (2015). **Uchinaaguchi Language Reclamation in the Martial Arts Community in Okinawa and Abroad**. PhD Diss., University of the Ryūkyū's Academic Repository.

63. Meyer, S. (2007). **Citizenship, Culture and Identity in Prewar Okinawa**. Doctoral Thesis, University of Hong Kong.

64. Nakamura, A. (2023). **Exploring the Evolution of Karate: A Comprehensive Journey through Modern History, Unveiling the Global Impact of Karate** [lecture]. Okinawa Prefecture Karate Promotion Division and Okinawa Prefectural University of Arts Institute of Arts and Culture.

65. Nikolai Nevsky's Life and Legacy - Collection of Articles. (2013). The Institute of Oriental Manuscripts of the Russian Academy of Sciences (Institute of Cultural Studies), St. Petersburg.

66. Osterkamp, S. (2015). **A Sketch History of Pre-Chamberlainian Western Studies of Ryūkyuan.** In Heinrich, P., Miyara, S., Shimoji, M. (Eds.), Handbook of the Ryūkyuan Languages: History, Structure, and Use. De Gruyter Mouton.

67. Zacharski, A. J. (2019). **Current Status & Challenges of Modern Okinawan Karate: The Spiritual Essence of Karate Pursued by Karate Practitioners.** University of the Ryūkyus Academic Repository.

Newspapers

68. *Ryūkyu Shimpo* (25 April 1898)
69. *Ryūkyu Shimpo* (27 April 1898)
70. *Ryūkyu Shimpo* (7 June 1898)
71. Ryūkyu Shimpo (7 Aug 1898)
72. Kagoshima Shimpo (11 Aug 1898)

Online Sources

73. Ishigaki City Office https://www.city.ishigaki.okinawa.jp/soshiki/shishihenshu/1_1/3187.html
74. Ryūkyu Bugei https://Ryūkyu-bugei.com
75. Motobu-ryu Karate https://ameblo.jp/motoburyu/

IRKRS Profile

The International Ryūkyu Karate-jutsu Research Society, also known as Ryūkyu Karate-jutsu Kokusai Kenkyukai (琉球唐手術国際研究会), is a collective of likeminded individuals committed to exploring the origins, evolution, and tactical applications of traditional karate and kobudo. Founded by Patrick McCarthy in Japan in 1988, the Society initially catered to a select group of foreign enthusiasts fascinated by his research and publications. However, in January 1996, recognizing the growing interest and diverse needs of an evolving community of learners, the Society opened its doors to the general public.

Renowned for our High Percentage Application (HAPV) theory, two-person drills, quarterly journal, Karate Study List (KSL), instructional DVDs, and thorough English translations, we take pride in making key original works and historical documents accessible. These include but are not limited to "The Bubishi," Matsumura's 1882 "Seven Precepts of Bu," and his 1885 "Zaiyunomei"; Itosu's 1908 "Ten Lessons"; Miyagi Chojun's 1934 "Outline of Karatedo"; the minutes of the historic 1936 "Round Table Discussion" with Okinawan Masters; Motobu Choki's "Watashi no Karate-jutsu"; Taira Shinken's 1964 "Encyclopedia of Kobudo"; Funakoshi Gichin's early [1914 thru 1934] writings; "Nagamine Shoshin's Tales of Okinawa's Great Masters"; "Ancient Okinawan Martial Arts Vol #1 & #2"; and "Legend of the Fist," among others.

Services

Our services encompass an online network fostering intellectual exchange among members. Our primary focus lies in mentoring both learners and teachers of Japanese/Okinawan Karate/Kobudo, spanning classical and contemporary practices. This mentoring occurs through various means, including dialogue, lectures, journals, instructional DVDs, and special-interest activities. For over three decades, we have successfully built bridges across styles, uniting like-minded learners worldwide through these exchanges.

Visit the International Ryūkyu Karate-jutsu Research Society at http://www.koryu-uchinadi.com for more information.

IRKRS Recommended Reading

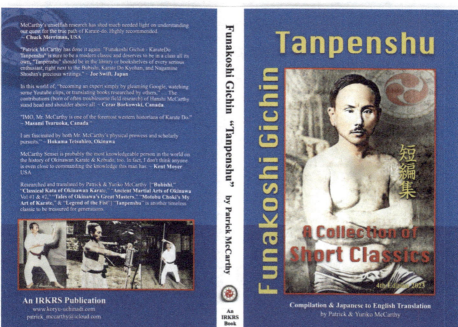

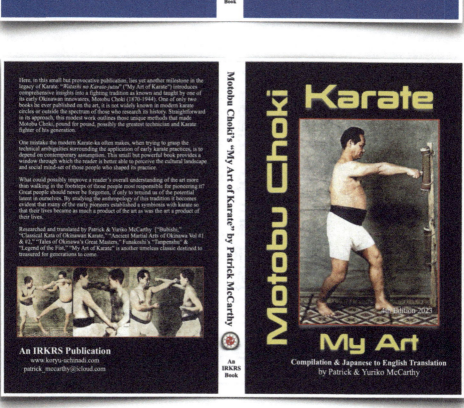

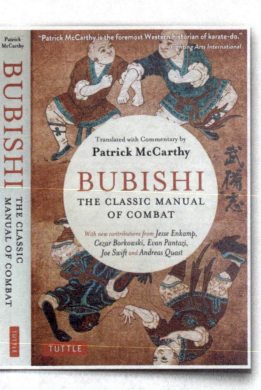
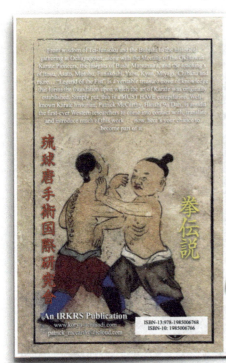
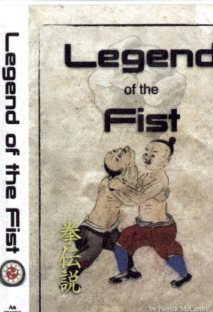

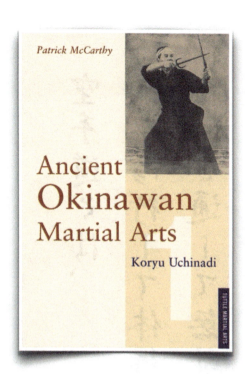
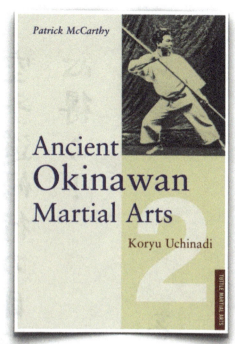

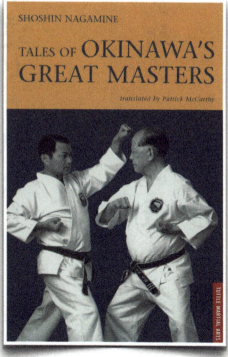

空手道とは、長年修行して体得した空手の技が、生涯を通して無駄になれば、空手道修行の目的が達せられたと心得よ！

喜屋武朝徳（チャンミー）　口伝

Oral Tradition [of] Kyan Chōtoku [*Chanmi*]

What is Karate-do? "*If you train extensively in karate, but never have to use it, you have achieved the essence of its practice.*"

Kensei
Kyan Chōtoku
The Man & His Art
15 Oct 2023

Copyright 2023 IRKRS
Uruma, Okinawa, Japan